Cyrus Hamlin

Among the Turks

Cyrus Hamlin

Among the Turks

ISBN/EAN: 9783337319878

Printed in Europe, USA, Canada, Australia, Japan

Cover: Foto ©ninafisch / pixelio.de

More available books at **www.hansebooks.com**

AMONG THE TURKS.

BY

CYRUS HAMLIN.

NEW YORK:
ROBERT CARTER AND BROTHERS,
530 BROADWAY.
1878.

PREFACE.

It is the privilege and solace of age to go back upon the past and recount what has been, as the future closes up and little remains to be achieved or attempted.

The writer of the following pages has availed himself of this privilege in giving so large a place to narratives of personal experience.

No one can live thirty-five years in so strange a country as the Turkish empire is, and come into contact with its government, institutions, religions, peoples, and industries without having many experiences which illustrate the peculiarities of the land. These personal narratives are of interest to the reader only so far as they are thus illustrative. It must not be supposed that they are intended to indicate the ordinary course of duty. They are selected out of many years of a quiet life. They are the aluminium extracted from a large mass of common clay. No other one has had so long a residence in Turkey without a more varied experience — but also without the time to record it. It is life coming in contact with life, it is new forces coming into contact with the old, that bring out the real nature of existing things and enable us to judge of them.

The origin, character, growth, and extent of the Ottoman empire are briefly delineated. The social life, educational institutions, laws, religion, evangelistic efforts, reforms, military character, and many other topics, are referred to or illustrated incidentally. The prescribed size and design of the book allowed these subjects to be merely sketched, not treated of in full.

BANGOR THEOL. SEM., Oct. 3d, 1877.

CONTENTS.

CHAPTER I.

Origin and Extent of the Turkish Empire—Institutions of the Empire the Cause of its steady Growth—Standing Army—Uniforms—Bashi-bozooks—Village Governments Simple and Democratic—Laws of War—Preservation—Blade of Grass that doesn't Grow—Captives—Property—Standing Army then a new Institution—Janizaries—Fall of Nice—Alladin the true Founder of the Empire—Seljukian Turks and Byzantine Greeks—Demoralization and Poverty 13

CHAPTER II.

Growth of the Empire gradual and steady—Brusa, 1326—Lodgment in Europe, 1357; Constantinople, 1453—Influence of the Fall of Constantinople upon the East—Christianity on the Defensive—Legal Position of Christianity—Freedom from Military Service—Growth of Population—Decrease of Moslem Population by Military Service—Female Infanticide—Fatalism—War—Famine—Epidemics—Position of the Clergy—Benefits accruing—"Capitulations"—The West.................................... 20

CHAPTER III.

State of the Turkish Empire—Navy and Army—Evangelistic Movement—Armenian Teacher—Evangelical Union and its Secretary—Concealment of Papers—Banishment—Second Teacher—Mr. Mesrobe Taliatiné—Seizure by Order of the Russian Ambassador—M. de Boutineff—Banishment to Siberia—Escape—Becomes Editor—The Dying Sailor.. 28

CHAPTER IV.

Accession of Abdul Medjid—European Interference in the Eastern Question—Hatti Scheriff of Gûl Hané—True Value of this Imperial Rescript—Reforms already Commenced—Naval School—Medical School—Military Academy—Defects—Naval Arsenal—Magnificent Machine-Shop—Manufactories—Mr. Hague—Total Failure—Russia and Turkey 46

CHAPTER V.

Bebek Seminary—Patriarch's Efforts to shut it up—Private Warning—Three Vacations—Fierce Contest between Bankers and Artisans—Advanced Position of the People—Progress—Confirmed Position of the Seminary—Jesuit College at Bebek—Jesuit Missions—Armenian Patriarch Avedick—Greek Patriarch Cyril Leucaris—Catholic Missions Compelled to Advocate Toleration......................... 61

CHAPTER VI.

Visit to the Sultan's College in the Old Seraglio—Singular Reception—Martyrdom of Carabet—Course of Sir Stratford Canning—Declaration of the Grand Vizir—Of the Sultan—Conversion of Moslems—Particular Cases—Scene at Brusa—Examination of Mr. and Mrs. Freeman—Treachery of Sir Henry Bulwer—Course of the English Government inexplicable as to Religious Freedom in Turkey.... 77

CHAPTER VII.

Removal to larger Premises—Cheliby Yorgaki and Wife—The old Forms of Oriental Life—The Breadseller and To-

CONTENTS. vii

bacconist—Joannes and Ibrahim—Grand Vizir and Banker—Farewell Blessing and Counsel—Bribery—Bowstring and Safety.. 95

CHAPTER VIII.

Second Night—Dethronement of Selim III—Dethronement of Mustapha—Cheliby Yorgaki and the Kislar Aghassi—Selim Murdered—Mahmûd Concealed, Found, Enthroned—Escape of Yorgaki to Halki—Apprehended in the Night—Yorgaki and the Spoils—Execution of the Kislar Aghassi—Rejection of Gifts—Sent away as a Fool—Joy in Halki. 106

CHAPTER IX.

Third Night—The Greek Revolution—Halet Effendi and the Janizaries—Their three Visits—Communion for Death—Halet Effendi and the Jewish Banker—Persecution—Death by the Bowstring—Confiscation—Firman—College Site—Halet Effendi's Fate—Janizaries Destroyed—Yorgaki's beautiful Daughter—Affiance—Wedding Festival—Elopement — Desolation — Conflagration — Halet Effendi—Advance in Civilization................................... 115

CHAPTER X.

Contest for Religious Freedom—Civil and Spiritual Power of the Patriarch—Anathema and its Results—"Muggerdich and his Bed"—Second escape of the Archives—Persecution at Adabazar—A Mob of Men quelled by one of Moslem Women—Visit to Adabazar and Deliverance from the Mob by Turks—Hassan's Hospitality—Refusal of Reward—Second Visit to Adabazar—The Governor's Conduct, and Consequences to Him—Third Visit—Reception—Growth of a true Christian Civilization—Origin of the Adabazar Movement—Stephan Erginziatsi...... 131

viii   CONTENTS.

CHAPTER XI.

Tour into Southern Macedonia—Cavala—Mt. Athos—Monachism—Salonica—Fugitive Horse Captured by Turkish Woman—Assault of Khan—Retreat—Yeneji—Penlipé—*Gaucherie*—The Bey's Dinner—The Mountains—Nūri Bey and Guard—Brigands—Trojéden—Government Oppressions—Greek Church—Mine and its Prospects—Nūri's Caution—Durzee Bey—Protestant Worship—Temperance—Our Room—Threshing Floor and Instruments—Dinner in Oriental Style—Eating and Drinking together, the Sacrament of Brotherhood—The Sacramental Supper—Suffering from Thirst—Berea—Episcopal Oppression—Pella—Obstacles to Progress.................................. 156

CHAPTER XII.

Morse's Early Telegraph — Mr. Chamberlain — Untimely Death—Prof. J. Lawrence Smith—Presentation of Telegraph to the Sultan—His Interest—Conversation—Peace Principles—Presence of the Sublime Porte—Ceremony of Leave-taking—Decoration to Prof. Morse—No Telegraph Line Constructed till Crimean War—Present Use of Telegraph 185

CHAPTER XIII.

Secular Employments—What Course shall the Missionary take?—Must know the Country—Help the Poor to help Themselves—Promote Industry—Zulu Mission—The Veteran Lindley—Williams of Erromanga—Why have Artisans failed on Mission Ground?—Authority—To be used for Development of Power—Prof. Smyth's Theodolite Screw—Steam Engine—Gen. Neal Dow—Engineers...... 195

CHAPTER XIV.

Condition of Evangelical Armenians—Seminary Students—Workshop—Outsiders Employed—Camphene—Rat-traps

CONTENTS. ix

—Steam Flour-mill—Charles Ede, Esq.—"Capitulations."
—Hon. Geo. P. Marsh—Opposition—Interdict—How Overcome—First Batch—Dressing French Bühr Millstones—
One Year and Results.................................. 212

CHAPTER XV.

Crimean War—Bible Society—Russian Ambassador's Declaration—Hospitals—Bread—Greek Flour Merchants—Confidence in Missionary Character—Sufferings in the Hospital
—Florence Nightingale and her Nurses—Battle of Inkerman—Laundry—Church out of a Beer-barrel—Stolid-looking Workman—Dr. Bartol—Cholera and Storm—Skilful
Boatmen—The Men come up to Duty—Oriental Courage—
Return Home... 226

CHAPTER XVI.

Church-building—Rodosto Chapel—Question of a Church in
Brusa—Building Undertaken by Dr. Dwight and Myself—
Injured by an Earthquake—Sagacity of the Horse—Earthquake at Sea—The Church Destroyed—Terible Destruction at Brusa—Rebuilding, Earthquake-proof—Why Destruction of Life not Great—How Many Destroyed—200?
—6,000?—Discussion about the Sabbath—Lord Napier's
Decision—Vexatious Lawsuit—Ninth Trial—Turkish Law
in the Case—Final Disposal of the Case by Purchase—
Bishop and Judge left out—Church Paid for by Bakery—
Question of the Usefulness of Church Buildings—Growth
of Brusa Church—Winding up of Bakery—Balance of
$25,000—Building Fund—Purchase of College Hill at
Kharpoot—House for the Board...................... 244

CHAPTER XVII.

Bulgarians—Early Knowledge of—Excellent Gardeners—
Meth. Epis. Mission on Danube—Meeting at Palmyra—

Tour South of the Balkans—Gabriel—Adrianople—Bulgarian Teacher—National Awakening as to Language and Education — Greek Bishop and Bulgarian Merchant — Whose Head was broken — A Paulician — Moslems not Turks—Serfage—Final Freedom—Greek Language and Greek Bishops—Orta-keuy—Reception of Pilgrims—Fine Conduct of the Crowd—School Taxation—Greek Teacher and His Story—Jason and the Argonauts—Final Report, and Formation of Mission—Progress of the Bulgarians— Language — Self-government by Exarch — Hope for the Future 261

CHAPTER XVIII.

Education—Extended Discussion of Methods—1st. Vernacular System—2d. No Education—Pres. Seelye—3d. Sound Christian Education—Experience of Missions with regard to second Theory—Burrisal Mission—Dr. Mullens' Testimony upon other Missions—Tendency of Missionary Experience—Testimony of Dr. Wilson and Dr. Duff—Utter Failure of the Vernacular System—Introduction to Mr. Robert—Project of a Christian College in Turkey—Its Fundamental Principles—Resignation of Connection with the Board 274

CHAPTER XIX.

ROBERT COLLEGE.

Purchase of Site—Failure in raising Funds—Accession of Abdul Aziz—Interdict by a Pasha—Purchase of a New Site—Sami Pasha's Confession—Leave Obtained—Jesuit and Russian Influence—Mr. J. P. Brown—The Old Bebek Seminary—*Adet*—Difficulty of Name—Mr. Robert's Interdict—Growth of the College—The Abbé Boré—Direct Appeal—Sir Henry Bulwer and His Treachery—Leave to Build—Imperial Iradé—Gentlemen who had a part in the Work—A'ali Pasha Friendly—Laying of Corner-stone—

CONTENTS. xi

Addresses in Different Languages—Description of Building—Eighteen Nationalities—Other Colleges—Union of Nationalities in the Faculty............................ 287

CHAPTER XX.
SCOURGES OF TURKEY.

Plague—Cholera—Malaria—Medical Treatment............ 302

CHAPTER XXI.

Koran alone not Mohammedan Law—Tradition—Various kinds of Tradition—From Mohammed—From the four Caliphs—Feeble Tradition—Fetvas—Reduced to a Code by Mehmet the Conqueror and by Sulieman the Magnificent, A. D. 1550—Multeka-ul-ubhhur—Confluence of the Seas—Religious Code—Attributes of God—Free will and Fate—Immaculate Conception—Law against Divination, etc.—Ritual—Daily Prayer—Funerals—Tithes upon Luxuries—Spiritual Retreats—Prayer—Pilgrimage—Morals—Subjects of this part of the Code—Political Code—Four Parts—"Exigencies of the Times."—Dethronements—Finance—Strangers in Moslem Lands—Military Code—Declaration of War—Captives—Conquered Lands—Rebels—Condition of People in subject Lands—Property—Costume—Churches—Civil Code—Marriage and Divorce—Parental and Filial Relation—Wills and Real Estate—Slaves—Commerce—Miscellaneous Laws—Mixed Court—Witnesses—Penal Code—Blasphemy—Apostasy—Sedition—Murder—Adultery—Opprobrious Epithets—Drunkenness—Thefts—Robbery................................ 317

CHAPTER XXII.

Islam misunderstood—Koran obscure to the Western Mind—Aimed at Paganism—Taken from O. T.—Mohammedan Religion to be sought in Tradition—Theism—No new Revelation—Reaction against Polytheism—Theism approved by Reason and Conscience—Fatalism—They do not try to reconcile Fate and Free Will—Dr. Draper and Ghazzali—Effect of Fatalism—Opposed to a high Civilization—Ritualism—Severe and exact—Its Influence—Sensualism—In the Koran—More still in Tradition—Islam a strong Religion—Strength from Environment—Influence of Christian Nations upon Turkey—English Influence—Sir Henry Bulwer—Circassians—Loans—Wane of Islam—Revival—Oriental Churches.. 343

CHAPTER XXIII.

Ottomans and Misrepresentation — Turkey Reported by Travellers—Levantine Dragomans—Correspondents—Telegraphs—Associations to collect Faults and Misdeeds—The Savage Tribes of the Empire—Nothing more needed on that Side—Not Immoral to speak the Truth—I. Increase of Religious Liberty—II. Abolition of Confiscation and Bastinado—The Bloody Code Abolished—III. The whole Scheme of Moslem Education Revolutionized—IV. European Law Introduced—Old Law of Church-building Abolished—Progress—V. Material Progress—Increase of Revenue—Progress in the Arts of War—VI. Position of the Government towards Christian Subjects (Rayahs)—The Medjliss, Christians, Rayahs, admitted to high Offices—List of Rayahs in Office—Forces that have produced the Change—Two great Changes necessary—Conclusion..... 356

AMONG THE TURKS.

CHAPTER I.

ORIGIN OF THE EMPIRE.—A. D. 1300.

The origin and growth of the Ottoman empire have attracted the attention and wonder of the civilized world. It sprang from an obscure tribe of about four hundred families dwelling on the banks of the river Sangarius, which flows from the Bithynian Olympus into the Black Sea. There was nothing to suggest the possibility of its coming power. There was nothing new in its faith or its civilization. It had no pre-eminence in arts or arms. It had no knowledge of the world, except of its immediate surroundings. And yet it was destined to control some of the fairest portions of the world, including the whole of Asia Minor, Mesopotamia, Assyria, Armenia, Colchis, the Chersonesus, Dacia, Moesia, Thrace, Illyricum, Macedonia, Greece and all her islands, Syria, Arabia, Egypt, and the African coast; all, and more than all, that was controlled by the Seljukian empire of the Turks and the Byzantine empire of the Greeks. The personal character of Osman, the ambitious and able founder of the empire, may account for the early successes. But neither the personal character of the ruler nor the Mohammedan religion can account for ages of exceptional growth and power. For one ceased with his life, immediately after the taking of Brusa; and the other was an old factor of political life, which could not sustain the Saracenic power, nor the Seljukian, out of which the Ottoman sprang. We must rather look to the institutions of the nascent empire for an explanation of its remarkable success and steady growth.

The founder passed away, just as he had won Brusa for his capital. He transmitted his possessions to his two sons, Orkhan and Alladin. The latter refusing to share the power with his brother, became his grand vizir, and gave himself to the organization of this wild and turbulent empire.

His first and great measure was the organization of a standing army, not for a particular conquest or campaign, but to be devoted thenceforth to the profession of arms. Another original measure for that period (A.D. 1326) was giving the entire army such a uniform that every man should be known, at sight, as to his rank and position in the army, whether officer or private. Thus far the army had been a horde of mounted fighters, of shepherd warriors. They were now divided into infantry and cavalry, and those not competent for service were sent to their homes. Very special attention was given to the turban as an important article of the military uniform, its different forms and colors giving every needed variety. Hence Bashi-bozook (rotten head or irregular head) came to designate any one who, without a uniform, was fighting on his own hook. Every armed mob is a collection of Bashi-bozooks. As every Mohammedan considers himself born to be a soldier, there is no want of Bashi-bozooks, irregular fighters, whenever there is war.

The pursuits of war and agriculture being now separated, a simple form of village government was adopted. A kadi or a chief man, with a council of the notables, appointed by the villagers themselves, regulated all their affairs. This form of municipal government still exists, and, in the hands of an intelligent and virtuous people, would effectually secure them against oppression.

The laws of war were so promulgated as to inspire the army with the lust of conquest. There was one object never lost sight of, which greatly modified them. The object of Orkhan and his brother was to found a great and flourishing empire. Nothing was therefore to be destroyed beyond the exigencies of war. The lands subdued were to be possessed, and therefore not to be desolated. More of rhetoric and imagination than historic truth has been expended upon the blade of grass that doesn't grow after the sultan's horse hás passed. A phrase referring to Attila has been applied to all the sultans. Their guiding principle was preservation for their own use. The value of captives also often arrested the uplifted arm. It was then the universal law of war that the lives of the conquered were at the mercy of the conqueror, and nothing but the value in money saved the lives of those who surrendered. The conquered were reduced to slavery, kept or sold as slaves, the females incorporated into the harem, and thus the wastes of war were at the expense of the enemy.

The advancement of the faith in war was never lost sight of. The Mohammedan is first of all religious. All who professed Islam were restored to freedom and to the possession of their goods. And all who yielded without fighting, were also secure in the possession of their property. Von Hammer affirms that thousands of families passed over from the Byzantine domination to the Turkish on account of the greater security of life and property. The confiscated lands were divided to the army and to the sultan, and large domains were granted to the mosques for the support of the faith.

Both religion and self-interest contributed to make the army submit to its new organization and severe discipline, and to inspire it with the love of conquest. The idea of a standing army, in this sense, had not then entered into the European mind.

Another institution arose under this second sultan; the terrible institution of the Janizaries, the work of Kara Halil Tschendereli. One thousand Christian youth, of the finest and most athletic forms, were selected and torn from their homes, subjected to the severest discipline and the most exact but nutritious diet, their chief officers being named from culinary operations, and the kitchen made a chief magazine of war; all with the design of forming a magnificent bodyguard for the sultan in the field. They were rewarded by high pay and a special share of the booty, and were thus made the very elite of the army. They soon made their name a terror, and their prowess decided many a bloody day when the cross went down before the crescent.

This singular body of troops existed nearly five hundred years. Its numbers increased to twenty, according to some, to forty thousand. It became a hereditary caste, the sons of the soldiers alone being admitted, and by consequence, the tax upon Christian families ceasing. Von Hammer states that, while it lasted, not less than half a million of Christian youth were torn from their homes to recruit this choice body of the Moslem army—an outrage upon human nature which has no parallel, except perhaps in the treatment which Russia has bestowed upon Polish youth.

Orkhan had now a more permanent, better organized, better disciplined, and better paid army than any monarch of Europe possessed. It consisted of horse, foot, and Janizary guards, emulating each other in their bloody work. He proceeded at once to make use of it. Nice fell; and over the altar where the first Christian council was gathered, he carved with his yatagan "God is God and Mohammed is the prophet of God." Nicomedia Cyzicus, and many other places, shared the same fate. The whole country along the southern shore of the Marmora, and almost to the Bosphorus, submitted to his sway.

The new forces of this singular state consisted in its very original institutions. It was organized as no other state had been, both for peace and war.

Orkhan, or perhaps more correctly his brother Alladin, was the true founder of the empire; and intelligent Moslems who study their own history, always speak of him with great admiration. He was the lawgiver, the great administrator, while Orkhan was the leader of the armies to battle.

It thus became an empire consecrated to war. The whole nation was inspired by this one idea of conquest. Both officers and men knew their work, and no sultan could have successfully adopted a policy of peace. The early conquests were not so much due to any great military leader, as to the fact that the whole nation was military, and war its normal work. If "they that take the sword shall perish by the sword," then its present decadence and dismemberment are only the retribution which our Lord himself announced, and which the constitution of the world imposes upon the nation that trusts in war.

The youthful empire had two enemies to oppose and obstruct its ambitious designs. The Seljukian Turkish empire and the Byzantine Greek empire were both in its path. The former was a kingdom divided against itself. Its great sultan, Malek Shah, had made his twelve sons governors of provinces, and their ambition and their internecine wars had reduced that conquering power to such fragments, that it was waiting for some new force to reunite them.

The Byzantine empire was in a still more deplorable state, resembling the present condition of the Turkish empire, but without any solid element, like the Moslem population, to maintain its life.

The Christianity of the empire was lost in drivelling superstitions. Magic and charms and relics and miraculous pictures, and holy fountains and places, were all that remained of the Gospel among the common people. The court was buried in luxury, the people in poverty. The central government had no power over the provinces, and in its internal dissensions often called upon the Turks for aid. Whoever will look over Labeau's, or any other history of the Byzantine empire, will only wonder that it endured so long. If its government was demoralized, its religion was paganized. The time was approaching when it must pass away.

The lamentations often raised over the rich, populous, and happy lands desolated by the Turks, are not justified by history. They had long been the prey to every species of disorder, otherwise the Mohammedan conquests could never have been achieved.

CHAPTER II.

GROWTH OF THE EMPIRE.

The growth of the Ottoman empire is often spoken of as extremely rapid. It was steady, almost uninterrupted, rather than rapid. It gained its capital, Brusa, in 1326. It could not effect a lodgment on European soil until 1357. After this, almost one hundred years of growth and expansion must pass away before it could take Constantinople. During this time, it was by no means idle. It subdued the Seljukian provinces, and enlarged its territories both in Europe and Asia. The taking of Constantinople, in 1453, was only the culmination of the military progress of a whole century. The Christian powers saw this steady advance, but did nothing to check it.

The fall of Constantinople has been considered by many writers as an event disastrous to Christianity and civilization. It gave a shock to Europe and the civilized world. But it was probably the salvation, rather than the destruction of Christianity, even in the East, which was then placed upon the defensive. If it did not lead directly to its reform it arrested its degeneracy. It was humiliated and oppressed, but not destroyed.

The Mohammedan law makes a distinction between the religions which have a divine revelation and those which have not. The men of a book, "Kitablees," as Christians and Jews, are not to be destroyed nor forced to abandon their faith. Nor is military service to be required of them. The soldier is a defender of the true faith, and therefore neither Christian nor Jew could be relied upon as a true soldier. Instead of military service, a special tax was imposed upon all Christian and Jewish subjects. This system has continued to the present day. This is so well known, and has been so universally and uniformly acted upon, and has constituted such a prominent fact in the Ottoman administration, that one may well be surprised to hear one of England's distinguished scholars and statesmen declare that military service has been demanded of all except the five millions of Roumania and Servia! This freedom from military service, while a mark of degradation in the eyes of the Moslem, has had some compensations. It has saved the young men of the Christian races from the wasting influences and destructive diseases of the camp and of the battle-field. It has secured to them more of industry and thrift. No traveller in Turkey can fail to notice, in passing from a Turkish to a Christian village, low as the civilization of both may be, that some signs of growth and progress are to be seen in the Christian village, which will be looked for in vain in the Moslem. Even at this great disadvantage, Christianity is better than Islam.

The Christian populations have steadily increased, and gained upon the Moslem population. The large standing army, drawn exclusively from Moslem young men, makes serious inroads upon population. The camps are badly cared for, and camp diseases ravage them, as well in peace as in war. This makes a preponderance of females, extremely onerous and harassing to the poor Moslem. Not to give his daughter in marriage is a disgrace, and to provide a dowry that shall distance competition is impossible. The birth of a female child is therefore often considered a misfortune. A great deal of covert infanticide results from this. The Moslems are never guilty of the fœticide which is the curse of European civilization; but the female infant often dies a natural death by the agency of the midwife, within a few days after birth. I have met with instances in which evidently some drug had been administered; the mother being anxious and suspicious, and in general not an accomplice. This crime has attracted government attention, but it is one not easily suppressed.

It has also attracted government attention, that their "rayahs" or Christian and Jewish subjects, the Armenians, Greeks, Bulgarians, and Jews, have nearly doubled within this half century, while the Moslem population is stationary. Irresistible forces would change eventually the balance of power without foreign interference.

Certain characteristics of the Moslem faith contribute their share to the effectiveness of all the

INFLUENCE OF FATALISM.

adverse influences from which the Moslems suffer. They are firm believers in destiny. "What is written is written" in the decrees of fate, upon "the preserved tablet" which Allah guards. This induces a serene composure, which makes them put off till to-morrow whatever presses upon them to-day. War finds them half prepared, now that it has ceased to be their constant pursuit. Famine and epidemics, resulting from war or other causes, sweep them away in grand composure. "God is great." "It is written." "Kismet dur." (It is fate). I have witnessed extraordinary instances of apparent satisfaction in death which was simply suicide, the sufferer refusing to take the simplest precaution against impending *fate*. Typhus, plague, cholera, and all their train, have ravaged the Moslem hosts unopposed.

The fall of Constantinople and the overthrow of the Byzantine empire, placed the clergy of the Christian sects upon a new foundation. Mehmet the Conqueror, ruthless and cruel as he was, knew what was necessary to the order and advancement of his empire. He had won a glorious capital, desolated and ruined by war. The country around had been eaten up by its invaders, industry was paralyzed, and starvation threatened to complete the destruction of war. He must rally and reassure the Christian populations both native and foreign.

One of his wisest and most effective measures was the appointment of a Greek bishop to be patriarch of all the Greeks. The Armenians and Jews were also organized under the same system. The sultan himself invested them in their robes of office, and his high officers offered them their felicitations. The patriarch, in addition to his spiritual office, was the civil chief of his community. Great power was given him over all his flock. He could inflict heavy penalties for spiritual offences, and his ingenuity could make almost any offence a spiritual one. As a recognized officer of the imperial government, it also gave him power to do much for the alleviation of the oppressed, and to bring the acts of unjust governors before the sultan. It gave a certain fixed status to Christianity in the realm, and did something to mitigate the sufferings of its followers. A number of important benefits resulted from this organization of the subject religions. It gave them a recognized status before the law. It was not one of equality, but it was something to have the right to claim justice, and always, if wronged, to appeal to the sultan.

It secured also the free enjoyment of religion. The churches and synagogues have been secured by an imperial *Iradè* or "volition," a tenure which is never questioned. Education has also been left in their hands, a privilege for ages lightly prized, but now felt to be of inestimable value.

A certain share in the village government was also accorded to the Christian communities, and they chose their chief men to manage their municipal affairs. This element of democratic freedom, slumbering in these old organizations, is now beginning to bear fruit.

At the fall of Constantinople, certain other immunities and privileges were granted to foreigners, which continue in force to this day. They have been added to by successive sultans, and form the body of Ottoman state papers known in Ottoman diplomacy as the "Capitulations"* not in the military sense, but because reduced to *Chapters* (*capita*).

By these the right is secured to every foreign nationality, locating in Constantinople and the empire, to have its place of worship, its mill and bakery, its consul, and the right to be tried by the consul, in all cases not affecting Ottomans; and to have the presence of its consul in all cases before the Ottoman courts. The foreigner is also secured against arrests and domiciliary visits, except with the concurrence of his consulate or embassy. These, and many other valuable privileges, have been accorded to foreigners, and have been taken advantage of to such an extent as greatly to vex the government. Egypt has succeeded in abolishing them all, in consequence of introducing European law and courts. The Sublime Porte is moving in the same direction. Whether this government stand or fall, the Mohammedan Code, of which some account will be given in another chapter, must be set aside with other antiquated things.

---

* One of these "Capitulation" immunities led to the founding of Robert College, as will be shown.

The assertion that the Koran alone is Mohammedan law, although often made, is only one specimen of European ignorance of Turkish affairs.

Islam has governed the course for more than four hundred years, but has lost in the race. Its Christian subjects are more intelligent, more thrifty, and more progressive than the Moslems. They have borne all their oppressions, and have proved that even a corrupt and oppressed Christianity is better than the purest Islam.

The effect of the fall of Constantinople upon the West is a subject of deep interest, but will be very briefly referred to here.

It coincided so nearly with the invention of printing, that when the treasures of classical and Byzantine learning were poured upon Europe, the press was ready to save and multiply them. The study of Greek spread into the schools of learning. The Greek New Testament became an object of profound interest and study, and it may be said that the fall of Constantinople gave the New Testament to the European mind. The Justinian code, although chiefly in Latin as well as Greek, became an object of increased attention. While the East held the sword, and cultivated the arts of war, the West gave itself to intellectual and industrial pursuits. Printing, Navigation, Commerce, Architecture, Painting, and finally, the Reformation, lifted the West out of its barbarism and ignorance; and its progress in arts and arms has left the East centuries in the rear. Four centuries ago it led the world in arts and arms. Now it gets its cannon from Krupp in Germany, its Martini-Henry rifles from Providence, Rhode Island, and its ammunition from New Haven, Connecticut! The press has proved itself mightier than cannon, and the arts of peace mightier than the arts of war.

CHAPTER III.

EMPIRE OF 1839.

Having been appointed by the American Board, Feb., 1837, to take charge of a high school in Constantinople, and give myself to the work of education, my attention to Ottoman affairs dates from that time, with about thirty-five years of actual residence in the empire.

The condition of the empire, at that time, was in the highest degree critical. For the first three centuries of its existence, it was a menace to Christendom. For two centuries, it had been steadily declining, or, what amounted to the same thing, it had been stationary, while other nations, its enemies, had been making rapid advances. Sultan Mahmûd, the reformer, who had nobly struggled against destiny for thirty years; who had destroyed the Janizaries, and thereby the Turkish army; who had lost Greece, and had lost his navy at the battle of Navarino, and had embarrassed all his resources in wars with Russia, but who still faltered not in his determination-to rescue his empire, was now dying of consumption. The rebellious Pasha of Egypt, who had once been repelled by Russian aid, was again approaching, having possession of Syria, and threatening to advance northward to the Bosphorus. By prodigious efforts, under such embarrassments, the sultan had again a fine navy, constructed chiefly by the distinguished American naval architects, Eckford and Rhodes. It went forth from the Bosphorus with such a thunder of artillery as had never before shaken Constantinople. It was to blockade the Nile and secure the possession of Alexandria.

Far less reliable was the army, commanded by incompetent officers, and destined to meet the disciplined forces of Ibrahim Pasha, whose very name was a terror to the Turks. The sultan was dying, but confident of life till he should hear of splendid victories, so that his soul might be wafted to Paradise on the fumes of blood and the shouts of triumph.

Amid these stirring political scenes, with Europe all attent to the coming phases of the Eastern Question, other forces of a very different character had begun to claim attention.

The evangelistic labors of the American Missionaries at Constantinople had commenced in the year 1831, by the Rev. Wm. Goodell, who was afterwards joined by Rev. Messrs. Dwight, Schauffler, and Holmes. Before recurring to the political aspect of affairs, some account of this early movement may be of interest. The facts to be narrated will illustrate the character of the work.

A decided impression had been made upon education, and a general spirit of inquiry had been awakened. The old unchangeable East had begun to move. The clergy of the oriental churches, at first friendly, had taken the alarm, and were now arrayed in bitter opposition. I became aware of the storm that was rising in a somewhat surprising manner. My Armenian teacher did not appear at the usual hour; but in the afternoon, panting and covered with perspiration, he burst into my room, and throwing a heavy package upon the floor, exclaimed, "This is of God, Mr. Hamlin!" Recovering breath, he explained, that his brother had been seized by the patriarch, and thrown into the patriarch's prison, on account of his well-known evangelical sentiments.

The prisoner had long been the secretary of a secret evangelical union. The Greek revolution, commencing as it did in small associations affiliated with a central body, had filled the Turkish mind with suspicion of all associations and meetings of every kind among the rayahs. The little associated band of evangelicals must of necessity keep their union and their meetings a profound secret. The object of the "Union" was to correspond with all enlightened men in the Armenian church, throughout the empire. The meeting, consisting then of twenty-two members, mostly young men, brought together the correspondence of the week, arranged for replies to important letters, concerted measures, joined in prayer, and encouraged each other in the work. The letters were deposited with the secretary, and a record of all the doings carefully kept.

When the secretary was seized by the patriarch and cast into prison, he apprehended at once the danger that all his papers would be also seized. Through the grating of his cell he saw a friendly neighbor who quickly bore the private warning to his brother, in a distant part of the city, of the impending danger. He repaired immediately to the house, and secured the records and the correspondence, containing the names of many persons who would have been exposed to the fury of the persecution; but delaying too long to fill the place of the abstracted papers with useless and harmless writings, so that no suspicion should be raised, the patriarch's officers were at the door to take possession. He escaped through the garden to a narrow lane, thence to the boat landing, and took a caique which landed him within ten minutes' rapid walk of my residence. He affirmed that he saw the officers in pursuit behind him, and begged me to secure or destroy the papers at once. His terror had probably created the pursuers. I however fastened the gate, took the archives containing the fullest authentic record of this early movement; and entering an old abandoned wine-cellar, into which all the broken and useless articles of an age had been thrown, I dug deep into the debris, and finding an empty cask, I put in the papers, and then packed it full of old tin coffee-pots, and all other refuse of kitchen utensils, old nails, spikes, and links of an iron chain, till I was sure rats could not penetrate it; and then restoring the place to original chaos, left it to darkness and spiders for a whole year. These papers will reappear in a still more exciting scene, when I come to speak of "Muggerdich and his bed." For the present, the revelation, which would have sent many an innocent person into exile, and have subjected every member of "the Evangelical Union" to severe penalties, was avoided.

The frightened teacher did not dare to continue his services, for fear of the patriarch's vengeance. Some six or eight persons were sent into exile, suffering great cruelties by the way, some were thrown out of employment, and anathema was threatened to all who should hold intercourse with these "foreign sectaries" and "apostles of a new faith."

After some weeks, a Greek friend, Mr. Constantinides, to the end of his life a most faithful friend and counsellor, procured a Russian Armenian teacher. Having foreign protection the patriarch could not molest him.

The teacher, Mr. Mesrobe Taliatine, was most cordially welcomed to our house and home. Rather under than over medium size, his beard and eye intensely black, each with a lustre peculiar to itself, with a quiet ease and grace about him, and a knowledge "of men and things" not to be looked for, he was for a time a mystery. But his experience had already been a varied one. He had left his Russian home, where his father wished to train him for the priesthood, in order to join a wealthy

Armenian relative in Calcutta. There he had studied for six years in Bishop's College, established, as he thought, by Bishop Heber, some of whose works he had translated into Armenian.

Hearing, in Calcutta, of a hopeful movement of reform among his countrymen in Turkey, and his relative having died, he came to Constantinople, to find the patriarch and bankers enemies and persecutors of the reform.

His disappointment was very great, and he was glad to find a position where he could do something to help forward the movement.

Every day he was in our family our esteem for him increased. We found him a truly refined and cultured Christian gentleman. He had resided for years in some of the best English families in Calcutta, and had been an enthusiastic and successful student in English history and literature. He was also a man of Christian faith. We resolved never to part with him as an associate in our work. His soul kindled with enthusiasm at the thought of being engaged for life in teaching Armenian youth. It was his perfect ideal of a useful and happy life.

One day, we waited for him at dinner, but he did not come. He had gone out for an hour's walk. In the course of the afternoon, a Persian Armenian, in the service of the Russian embassy, called with an open note from the teacher, asking me to deliver to the bearer his clothes, to destroy his loose papers, to hold his manuscripts subject to his orders, to receive all his books as a donation to the library, and to pray for him while on his unknown and perilous journey. All this was perfectly astounding, but soon explained. The Russian ambassador, M. De Boutineff, had ordered him to be seized and sent to Russia, his real destination being Siberia.

One of the elder missionaries went to remonstrate with the ambassador. He was received with cold and stately courtesy, and his appeal was unheeded. After various proposals had been made in vain, the representative of the autocrat at length said, "While I respect your official character and benevolent intentions, I may as well now assure you that the emperor, my master, will never allow Protestantism to set its foot in Turkey!"

The missionary, rising and bowing low to the ambassador, replied, "Your excellency, the kingdom of Christ, who is my master, will never ask the emperor of all the Russias where it may set its foot!" and then retired. By a singular train of circumstances, into which entered some outside aid, Mr. Taliatine effected his escape and *brought up* at Calcutta instead of Siberia.

An American resident and frequent visitor at my house, Mr. X., was providentially on the same steamer which was to convey Mr. Taliatine to Trebizond, where he would be received by the Russian bishop, and passed on to Russian territory. Noticing him, with surprise, sitting in one corner of the deck amid a crowd of passengers, he exclaimed "Why, Mr. Taliatine, have you left

Plan of Escape from Steamer. 35

Mr. Hamlin?"—and then learned from the despairing man that he was on the way to Siberia. The Turkish steamer was commanded by an English officer and friend of ours, Capt. Benj. Ford. "Does any one know you here?" asked Mr. X. "I have seen no one that I know," replied the Armenian. Mr. X. then took him below into the cabin, and informed Capt. Ford of all the circumstances. As Mr. Taliatine could not escape between the Bosphorus and Trebizond, and as the steamer was Turkish, he was not under guard. The English captain at once proposed to disappoint the Russians of their prey. Mr. Taliatine's Russian passport, and every article that could point to his identity, was made into a bundle and dropped through a cabin window into the sea. His shining black beard was removed, and his face close shaven; and he was dressed in the style of an English servant with long overboots and a stovepipe hat,—a transformation so surprising that he declared that no one would recognize him, as he could not recognize himself! It was agreed that he should appear on deck as Mr. X's servant, and should speak nothing but English.

The intended exile arrived at Trebizond without exciting the least suspicion; the question was, How to land?—for every passenger must present himself at the passport office and show his passport. To evade this difficulty, Mr. X. gave him his own passport, and remained on board himself. Mr. Taliatine thus landed as an American gentleman, presented his passport to the Russian bishop who was there watching for his victim, and was allowed to pass unchallenged. He proceeded at once to the house of the English consul, Mr. Stevens, with a note from Mr. X., saying, "I am on board without a passport, can you get me on shore?" Mr. Stevens kindly went to the pasha, governor of that Eyalet, who sent his own boat and brought Mr. X. ashore, without any regard to the passport office, and the two passengers proceeded on their way as rapidly as possible to Mosul. At the latter place, Mr. Taliatine found an English officer going to Calcutta, and was very glad to serve him as dragoman on the long journey down the Euphrates valley and Persian Gulf to Calcutta, the place in all the world where he most wished to go.

The poor bishop, meanwhile, not finding his prisoner in the passport office, went on board the steamer to claim him, supposing that he had undoubtedly concealed himself there, and intended to return to Constantinople without landing. Captain Ford treated the bishop with the greatest politeness, and as the Siberian criminal could not be found, he offered a large reward to any one, whether of the bishop's party or of the crew, who should find him. After a long and fruitless search, the bishop returned to write the result to the Russian embassy. The Russian agents undoubtedly thought he had jumped overboard and was lost; but I had the pleasure of at length informing

Dark Prospects of Evangelicals. 37

them that Mr. Taliatine had become the editor of an evangelical Armenian newspaper for the enlightment of his countrymen in the East, and of showing them the first number. Their curiosity was never satisfied as to his escape.

At this point, there was little hope of any onward movement. The Armenian church had uttered its voice in anathema. And now the Oriental Orthodox Greek Church added its thunder, threatening excommunication against all who should buy, sell, or read our books, or hold any intercourse with these "false apostles." The Caliph of Islam also joined his voice, and, in a stately and solemn firman, enjoined upon the Christian shepherds to look well to their flocks, lest evil beasts should enter among them. When, before, did ever the supreme authorities of the Greek, the Armenian, and the Moslem churches unite to secure oriental orthodoxy against the influence of a few quiet men?

It was doubtless due to the counsels of Mons. De Boutineff, who, as a gentleman of German education, could better comprehend the danger of these spiritual forces, that an order was obtained from Mahmûd for the expulsion of the missionaries from the empire.

The news fell upon us like thunder unheralded by lightning. I was in Dr. Goodell's study, for discussion of our affairs, when Mr. Brown, the Secretary of Legation, entered. After the usual salutation, by Mr. Goodell, in Turkish, "né war? né yōk?" (what is there? what is there not)—the usual way of introducing conversation. "Guzelik yōk," replied Mr. Brown. "There is no goodness," instead of the usual reply, "The goodness of God." "What is the matter?" said Mr. Goodell, alarmed at the manner more than the matter of the reply. Mr. B. then showed him Com. Porter's dispatch to the Sublime Porte, acknowledging the receipt of the requisition for our departure, and replying that, inasmuch as our treaty was only a commercial one, he could not interfere, but would inform the gentlemen concerned, and he did not doubt they would act accordingly. The situation had become unexpectedly critical. And our fate had been made known to us in a singular manner. The mother of the Secretary, "Lady Brown," as she was called by common consent, Commodore Porter's sister, and, great as he was, superior even to him, a lady to whom the early missionaries were indebted for countless acts of kindness, knew of the dispatch, and, by her influence and intervention, it was thus made known to the missionaries. They immediately took the dispatch, and protested against such a reply being transmitted to the Sublime Porte. All the modification that could be secured was that, inasmuch as this was a grave measure, he wished to consult his government, and would demand the protection of the missionaries in the meantime. They sent immediately to the secretary of state their argument upon the right of protection in common with all the Roman Catholic missionaries, who had been there through all the seventeenth and eighteenth centuries. The brave old commodore was perfectly certain that the reply would be in accordance with his first dispatch.

While we were waiting in this suspense, the sultan himself died, July 1st, 1839. His entire fleet was betrayed into the hands of the pasha of Egypt and added to his own navy; most of the officers however refusing to serve. The Ottoman army, of eighty thousand men, was almost annihilated at the battle of Negib, near Aleppo, in Northern Syria. So sudden and terrible was the rout, that two English savans in the rear of the army barely escaped with their lives, losing instruments, baggage, and journals. This defeat occurred six days before the sultan's death, but the news never reached him. The treason of the fleet was known at the capital nearly at the same time. A startling series of events, which struck every heart with dismay! Would the Moslems rise and slaughter the Christians? Would the Russian navy appear in the Bosphorus, as it did in 1831? Would Ibrahim march as swiftly as possible upon Constantinople, subvert this dynasty, and place his father upon the throne?

However this might be, *I hired another Armenian teacher!* The world was too much absorbed in other and momentous subjects, to think of us, and our Armenian friends drew breath again.

The Russians were not ready. Ibrahim Pasha

did not come. The young sultan, Abdul Medjid, ascended the throne of his father; a new ministry displaced the old; the patriarchs were changed, and consequently the bishops; we looked for our enemies, and they were not to be found. Dr. Goodell had said, in the darkest hour, in his own peculiar way, "The great Sultan of the Universe can change all this"; and lo! it was done. "God blew and they were scattered." The evangelistic work was resumed with new courage. The exiles, with one exception, ere long returned. The banished secretary came a year later, and I delivered to him the buried archives complete, with the addition of some mould and dampness. The reply of the secretary of state was all that could be wished, affirming that we must have the same protection as that accorded to the papal missionaries, or to those of "the most favored nation." It was however not needed, for the execution of the order requiring our departure was never again referred to.

An incident, a sheer accident, of this period may be worth recording. While passing the great Galata Custom-house, one hot day in July, a great crowd attracted my attention; and not having then learned to beware of crowds, I penetrated it, and saw, by the side of the custom-house wall, a poor sailor apparently dying of cholera, in the most revolting and horrible circumstances. His bag of sailor's clothes was near him, and some one had given him a large jug of water for his insatiable thirst. "Do you speak English?" "Yes, damn your eyes." "Are you an Englishman or an American?" "American, damn your eyes!" with still worse expressions of profanity. I appealed in vain for help to carry him to a neighboring boarding-house for sailors, kept by a Maltese. The stupid multitude, the refuse of all nations, wanted to see him die. There is a strange spell in the last hours of human agony, especially to brutal natures.

At length two noble Anglo-African sailors, from the island of Jamaica, offered to take him, and refused all compensation. May the Lord remember it to them in that day. We were refused admittance. Next, we went to the English hospital, whose rules did not allow of his reception, and red tape, the world over, is stronger than human life.

A Maltese boatman, whom I had once employed to nurse a sick American sea-captain at my house, was appealed to, and he received him into his boathouse. The unselfish hospitality of these poor men to each other is quite remarkable; but otherwise, their world could not go on. The profanity of these three men, the suffering man and his bearers, was more shocking than any thing I had experienced. Rebukes had no effect upon them whatever. But they understood the language of the quarter deck, and submitted to a positive order at once. Without this, they were morally unable to control themselves in the use of language which had become their mother tongue. A physician was called, who thought the case hopeless, but wrote a prescription, which the apothecary refused to make up, saying it would kill two healthy men! On my asking him whether he was physician or apothecary, and if he did not know that what might kill two healthy men might save a dying man, he yielded, and the medicine was administered, and the effect watched according to directions. He was afterwards removed to a good room, by the kindness of Dr. Stamatiades, and close to his house. For more than three weeks the case was a doubtful one, having become a typhoid. One evening word was sent that I should be ready to bury him in the morning, as he would not probably live through the night. I went and found him better. The crisis had turned towards life. He afterwards had an alarming relapse, from eating fruit offered to him by a colored sailor. But again he recovered. The Rev. Mr. Hebard of the Beirut Seminary was then with me, in very feeble health. He visited the poor sailor daily, after he was able to talk with one. Dr. Goodell also felt a deep interest in him. He was extremely ignorant, could hardly read, but had that sailor honesty and simplicity that can never be counterfeited. If he called himself "a poor damned sinner," the language was to him the best possible. His profanity was better than some men's put-on piety. It was some weeks before he found a chance to sail for Boston. I remember well the morning he left. He came to thank me, and to say good-by. As he stood lingering for a moment by the door, he said, "I have been a very wicked man, Mr. Hamlin, and have done all the evil I could in the world, and now I am going to do all the good I can"; and so he departed.

Three years after I received a letter from him. It began, "Dear Mr. Hamlin, Thank God I still survive the ded." It was phonetically spelt, but full of life and point. Among other things, he wrote, "I am here workin' and·blowin' the Gospel trumpet on the Eri Kanal." I carried the letter at once to Dr. Goodell, who clapped his hands on reading it. "Let me begin the answer," said the doctor; and taking a sheet of paper, he wrote,

"Dear Mr. Brown.—Blow away, brother, blow!
"Yours in blowing the same Gospel trumpet.
"WILLIAM GOODELL."

After this, twenty-five years passed away in the furnace, often seven times heated, of life's experiences and labors; and the poor sailor was entirely forgotten. In 1867, I was in Paris, at the Great Exposition. Two friends from Whitinsville, Mass., invited me to dine with them at the Hotel Chatham, Rue St. Augustine. At the table d'hote, filled by guests from many nations, we were conversing as by ourselves. At the close of the dinner, as we were about to rise, the gentleman sitting at my right said to me, "You will excuse me, sir, if I ask you a question. I perceive by your conversation that you have been in Constantinople." "Yes, sir, I am directly from there." "Well, sir, while you were there, did you happen to meet with—I do not suppose you did—but I want to ask the question—one Dr. Cyrus Hamlin, a D.D. or an M.D., but I think the latter?" His deliberate, apologetic tone naturally occasioned a laugh, which he as naturally frowned upon, until I said to him, "I am the very person you ask for." "Are you?" said he, "I have often thought I would like to meet you. I am just from Honolulu, Sandwich Islands. I have known a man there by the name of Brown, a man who has done a great deal of good among the sailors, can go anywhere and everywhere with the Bible; and he has told me how he was once dying, *a blasphemous dog* (his own words), in the streets of Constantinople, and you picked him up and saved him, soul and body." Mentioning various other things, he added, "Is this all true, or is it in part a sailor's long yarn?"

In the meantime, memory exhumed from its buried treasures a poor dying sailor of 1839. There was time only for a very brief interview with the Honolulu party, and an appointment was made to meet again, which however failed, and I had unfortunately not taken the name of the gentleman. On my mentioning the circumstance to a friend in this country, he said to me, "One of those gentlemen must be Dr. Wood of Jamaica Plain." At the first opportunity I visited him, and found it was even so. After a pleasant interview, he remarked: "It occurred to Mr. Stillman and myself, in Paris, that you were probably the young missionary who was at the Marlborough Hotel, Bos-

DISTANT PLACES LINKED TOGETHER. 45

ton, and sailed for Constantinople at the same time that we sailed for the Sandwich Islands in 1838." On comparing notes, we found that it was so; although both parties had forgotten the others' names. A short time after, I received from Dr. Wood, through Mr. Farnsworth of Boston, a donation for Robert College of $250.

The Marlborough Hotel, Boston, the Galata Custom-house, the Erie Canal, Honolulu, Hotel Chatham, Rue St. Augustine, Paris, Jamaica Plain, Robert College, all apparently accidental, and scattered through the space of twenty-nine years! How strange the links in the chain of life!

CHAPTER IV.

ACCESSION OF ABDUL MEDJID.

At the accession of Abdul Medjid, a youth of sixteen, the Ottoman empire seemed to have reached the very brink of destruction. It was at the mercy of its rebellious vassal Mahommed Ali. It had neither army nor navy, neither officers nor soldiers, neither money nor credit. Its only advantage was that it had no debt.

The prompt interference of Europe compelled the pasha to give up Syria. The reduction of the strong fortress of St. John d'Acre by the British fleet was a persuasive argument to bring him to terms. He could abolish the sultan; he could not resist Europe.

It was considered an omen for good, that the rising diplomat Reshid Pasha, was made minister of foreign affairs. He was a favorite at the English embassy, and he had the reputation of being very decidedly pro-English. On the 11th of July, 1839, the grand ceremony of girding on the sword of Osman took place, at the Mosque of Eyoub, without the city; and the procession from thence to the palace, through the heart of the city, was the most magnificent which that generation had seen. It answered all that one could imagine of "barbaric gold and pearl."

But while the civil and military dignitaries of the empire were ablaze with diamonds, horse and man, and with all the jewelry the Orient could produce, the Mohammedan clergy brought up the rear in severe and neat simplicity, without an ornament. It was refreshing to look upon men, after the long and weary gaze upon diamonds and pearls.

Shortly after was issued that famous and historic rescript, the Hatti Scheriff of Gûl Hané.* It occasioned a surprise which can not now be understood. It kindled the rage and indignation of the old Mussulmans, and the enthusiastic hopes of the rayahs and of the party of progress among the Turks. The reforms of the late Sultan Mahmûd had been driven forward by his own iron will; but now the whole world was called to participate. Bribery and corruption were to cease, and perfect equality of rights was to be enjoyed. The following is the text of this remarkable document; and it will repay a careful reading to those who wish to understand the subsequent course of events in the empire, and the fruitless attempts to engraft the new upon the old. It must be read, however, with

* Gûl Hané or Rose Garden was the name of the place where it was first promulgated. It is within the walls of Seraglio Point, and is now occupied by a large government printing house.

the constant recollection that it was issued to a people three fourths of whom were still in the middle ages.

"HATTI SCHERIFF OF GÛL HANÉ.

"It is well known that, during the early ages of the Ottoman Monarchy, the glorious precepts of the Koran and the laws of the Empire were ever held in honor. In consequence of this the Empire increased in strength and greatness, and all the population, without exception, acquired a high degree of welfare and prosperity.

"For one hundred and fifty years a succession of incidents and various causes has checked this obedience to the sacred code of the law, and to the regulations which emanate from it, and the previous internal strength and prosperity have been converted into weakness and poverty; for, in truth, an empire loses all its stability when it ceases to observe its laws.

"These considerations have been ever present to our mind, and since the day of our accession to the throne the thought of the public good, of the amelioration of the condition of the provinces, and the alleviation of the national burdens, have not ceased to claim our entire attention. If we take into consideration the geographical position of the Ottoman Provinces, the fertility of the soil, and the aptness and intelligence of the inhabitants, we shall attain the conviction that, by applying ourselves to discover efficacious methods, the result which, with the aid of God, we hope to obtain, will be realized within a few years.

"Thus, then, full of confidence in the help of the Most High, supported by the intercession of our Prophet, we consider it advisable to attempt by new institutions to attain for the provinces composing the Ottoman Empire the benefits of a good administration.

"These institutions will principally refer to these topics:

"1. The guarantees which will insure our subjects perfect security for their lives, their honor, and their property.

"2. A regular method of establishing and collecting the taxes.

"3. An equally regular method of recruiting, levying the army, and fixing duration of the service.

" In truth, are not life and honor the most precious blessings in existence? What man, whatever may be his detestation of violence, would refrain from having recourse to it, and thereby injuring the government and his country, if his life and honor are exposed to danger? If, on the contrary, he enjoys perfect security in this respect, he will not forget his loyalty, and all his acts will conduce to the welfare of the government and his fellow-subjects.

"If there is no security for their fortune, all listen coldly to the voice of their Prince and country; none attend to the progress of the common weal, absorbed as they are in their own troubles. If, on the other hand, the citizen possesses in confidence his property, of whatever kind it may be, then full of ardor for his own affairs, the sphere of which he strives to extend in order to increase that of his own enjoyments, he daily feels his love for his Prince and his country growing more fervent in his heart. These sentiments become within him the source of the most laudable actions.

"It is of the highest importance to regulate the imposition of the taxes, as the State, which in the defence of its territory is forced into various expenses, can not procure the money necessary for the army and other branches of the service, save by contributions levied on its subjects.

"Although, thanks to God, our subjects have been for some time delivered from the scourge of monopolies, falsely regarded hitherto as a source of revenue, a fatal practice still exists, although it can only have the most disastrous consequences: it is that of the venal concessions known by the name of Iltizim.

"Under this system the civil and financial administration of a province is intrusted to the arbitrary will of an individual; that is, at times, to the iron hand of the most violent and covetous passions; for if the administrator is not good, he cares for nothing but his own advantage.

"It is therefore necessary that, in future, each member of the Ottoman Society should be taxed in a ratio to his fortune and his ability, and that nothing further should be demanded from him.

"It is also necessary that special laws should fix and limit the expenses of our forces on land and sea.

"Although, as we have said, the defence of the country is of paramount consideration, and it is the duty of all the inhabitants to furnish soldiers for this end, it is necessary to establish laws to regulate the contingent which each district should furnish, according to the requirements of the moment, and to reduce the time of active military service to four or five years, for it is both committing an injustice and inflicting a deadly blow on the agriculture and industry of the country, to take, without regard to the respective populations of the districts, more from one and less from another than they are able to furnish; at the same time it is reducing the soldiers to despair and contributing to the depopulation of the country to retain them during their whole life in the service.

"In fine, without the various laws, the necessity of which has been recognized, the Empire can neither possess strength, nor wealth, nor prosperity, nor tranquillity. On the contrary, it may hope for them all from the existence of these new laws.

"For this reason, in future, the cause of every accused party will be tried publicly, in conformity with our divine law; and until a regular sentence has been pronounced, no one can put another to death, secretly or publicly, by poison, or any other form of punishment.

"No one will be permitted to assail the honor of any one, whosoever he may be.

"Every person will enjoy the possession of his property of every nature, and dispose of it with the most perfect liberty, without any one being able to impede him. Thus, for example, the innocent heirs of a criminal will not be deprived of their legal rights, and the property of the criminal will not be confiscated.

"These Imperial concessions extend to all our subjects, whatever religion or sect they may belong to, and they will enjoy them without any exception.

"Perfect security, is, therefore, granted by us to the inhabitants of the Empire, with regard to their life, their honor, and their fortune, as the sacred text of our law demands.

"With reference to the other points, as they must be regulated by the concurrence of enlightened opinions, our Council of Justice, augmented by as many new members as may be deemed necessary, to whom will be adjoined on certain days which we shall appoint, our Minister and the notables of the Empire, will meet for the purpose of establishing the fundamental laws on these points relating to the security of life and property and the imposition of the taxes. Every one in these assemblies will state his ideas freely and give his opinion.

TEXT OF THE HATTI SCHERIFF. 53

"The laws relating to the regulations of the military service will be discussed by the Military Council, holding its meeting at the palace of the Seraskier. As soon as the law is decided upon, it will be presented to us, and in order that it may be eternally valid and applicable, we will confirm it by our sanction, written above it, with our Imperial hand.

"As these present institutions are solely intended for the regeneration of religion, government, the nation, and the Empire, we engage to do nothing which may be opposed to them.

"As a pledge for our promise, we intend, after having deposited this in the hall which contains the relics of the Prophet, in the presence of all the Ulema and Grandees of the Empire, to take an oath, in the name of the Almighty, and cause the Ulema and Grandees also to swear to that effect.

"After that, any one of the Ulema or Grandees, or any other person whatsoever who violates these institutions, will undergo, without regard to rank, consideration or credit, a punishment appointed for his guilt when proven. A penal code will be drawn up, to this effect.

"As all the functionaries of the Empire will receive from this day a suitable salary, and those whose functions are not at present sufficiently rewarded will be advanced, a rigorous law will be passed against the traffic in favors and appointments, which the Divine laws reprove, and which is one of the principal causes of the decay of the Empire.

"The enactments thus made being a complete renovation and alteration in ancient usages, this Imperial Rescript will be published at Constantinople and in all the towns of our Empire, and will be officially communicated to all the Ambassadors of friendly Powers, residing in Constantinople, in order that there may be witnesses of the concession of these institutions, which, with the favor of the Almighty, will endure forever.

"May the All-Powerful God have us all in His holy keeping!

"May those who commit any act contrary to the present institutions, be the objects of the Divine malediction, and eternally deprived of every kind of happiness!"

A number of points in this document are worthy of remark. It wears very decidedly that air of Moslem piety, and regard for the divine law, which has characterized all Moslem state papers. But it contradicts itself. For, in opposition to that law, it declares the perfect equality of all citizens, without regard to their religion. It also declares these enactments to be "a complete alteration and renovation in ancient usages." The sultan also renounces a fundamental right of the caliphate as defined by the law. One of his titles is "the hunkiar" — the blood-letter. The Mohammedan commentators accord to him the right to put to death up to fourteen persons a day, without giving any account of the act, or asking any advice; but, beyond this number, he must consult the Divan. In this imperial rescript, he renounces that right, and declares that no one shall be executed without having had a public trial. Personally he kept this promise, and could hardly be induced to sign the death warrant of the greatest criminal legally condemned to death. This paper represents the end of government to be the safety, happiness, and well-being of the people; the exact reverse of the oriental idea of government and people.

The rayahs were not slow to notice the contradictions and the admissions of this remarkable paper. It was both praised and ridiculed. The old Mussulmans cursed it as a flagrant sacrificing of the divine law it so much praised, and the Christian subjects looked upon it as the introduction of a new era. It was an open confession, before all the world, of the miserable condition of the empire, and that nothing but reform could save it. English policy had triumphed; and, for the time, Russia was supposed to be held in check. In point of fact, Turkish diplomacy was then driven hither and thither by the opposing forces of Russia and England; and Turkey, sometimes leaning to one, and sometimes to the other, could carry forward nothing to any permanent result.

Soon after the issue of this "hatt," one of my Greek neighbors knocked down a Mussulman for cursing his grandmother and his religion. Both had to appear before the pasha at Chinili Kiosk, where both were fined, and put under bonds to keep the peace. The Greeks claimed the day, and said they were willing to be fined for knocking down a Mussulman. The Mussulman thought it hard if he could not curse a ghiaour and his religion without being knocked down and fined. Very many such instances occurred, in which, often, the rayah had the worst of it, and yet considered it a great improvement upon old times.

The true value of this document is to be sought in its effects upon the people more than in the administration of government. It went through the empire. It woke up the slumbering East. It was the first voice that announced to the people the true object of government, and the legitimate ends to be attained.

While this imperial rescript was, in general, a disappointing failure, it can not be denied that it accomplished some good in the administration. It stopped summary executions, and since then no government in Europe has condemned so few criminals to extreme penalties. It gave the rayahs courage to contend for their rights, and brought forward the novel idea that men are equal before the law, and that all are entitled to a fair and public trial. It changed to some small degree the administration by introducing salaries. For so it set aside the powerful and pernicious clique of government bankers, it diminished the civil power of the clergy, and at all events it changed the cur-

FOREIGN TEACHERS.   57

rent of thought into new channels, never to revert again to the old.

A naval school, a medical school, and a military academy, already established, received a great impulse. Foreign teachers were introduced, with high salaries, and the attendance of students was large. There were many inherent obstacles to be overcome. The pupils were never so rigidly trained in French as to be able to use it with freedom as an instrument of education. The lectures and text-books in French were imperfectly understood. The Turks despise foreign languages. If the lectures were translated *vivâ voce* by a dragoman, that was wearisome and uninteresting. The course of instruction was divided between two languages, Turkish and French, and was imperfect in both. Owing to the defects of the system, these institutions have accomplished far less than could be justly demanded in view of the vast sums expended upon them by the government. One language and one system of text books should have been the rule in the work of instruction. Often neither pupil nor teacher understood each other.

In the haste to make every thing new, the naval arsenal passed from the hands of Mr. Rhodes to English direction, but with no gain to its efficiency.

Another scheme also attracted great attention, and swallowed up many millions. It was to develop the iron and coal mines, and establish manufactories that would vie with England.

Mr. Hague, a very accomplished and able English engineer, a gentleman of excellent character and of true mechanical genius, was the chief of all these works. Over him was a certain Boghos Agha, chief of the Imperial Powder Works, and over him again there was some pasha who did not usually retain his office long enough to learn its duties, had he been studiously inclined. The whole scheme proved a total failure, after swallowing up many millions. Mr. Hague attributed the failure to "*jobbery.*" He found no fault with the mechanical ability of the workmen. He thought that decidedly good. But no one had the previous education to prepare him for being the head of a department. This was often tried, and as often it failed. A certain degree of civilization, a certain degree of the general education of the public mind, seem necessary to great mechanical progress. Without this, the mental fibre that can bear the strain imposed upon it is not to be found.

Besides, the Turks ascribe mechanical invention to *Satan*, the "stoned devil," against whom they pray five times a day. I have myself, for some supposed mechanical ability, been seriously introduced by one Ottoman to another as "the most *Satanic* man in the empire!" This superstition, although many will laugh at it, is not favorable to mechanical progress.

Many of the first efforts of a similar nature in Russia failed in like manner. As soon as the American or English chief engineers departed, the enterprises which they inaugurated failed. But

Russia has now introduced such a rigid system of technological instruction, that she can not fail of producing competent mechanics and engineers in time.

But another more serious blow was struck to Turkish enterprise than the failure of these expensive efforts. France and England persuaded the Turks that free trade would renovate all theidisordered affairs. The Moslems have a vast capacity for believing what they can not understand, and it is moreover probable that French and English gold added strength to the argument. As soon as the products of English and French industry were admitted, at a tariff of six per cent ad valorem, the Ottoman workmen were astounded to see their own products imitated, made more attractive to the eye, and sold at twenty-five to thirty per cent cheaper. Soon five thousand weavers in Scutari were without employ, and reduced to the most deplorable beggary. The fast colors and firm material of Diarbekr disappeared, the comb-makers and cutlers shut up their shops, Brusa silks and Brusa towels came from Lyons and Manchester.

A few years since, although Brusa was full of Brusa towels, they were all from *Manchester*. I found one only of the old manufactories existing, and in that but three looms at work. A few will still buy the home-made article; for, if twice as dear, it will last four times as long. Thus all the industries of Turkey have perished, except such as, in the nature of the case, like carpenters and masons, can not be supplied from abroad. There is neither capital nor intelligence enough to place any industry upon its feet against foreign competition.

Comparatively few of the Ottomans have paid the slightest attention to the laws of political economy. Being under the necessity of getting some revenue from their custom-houses, they taxed all exports twelve per cent! The beautiful silken goat's hair of Angora is exported now to England, and comes back in fabrics which are enhanced from twenty to fifty or even one hundred times. If one part goes to the raw producer in Turkey, and forty-nine to the manufacturer in England, it hardly admits of a doubt as to which party, England or Turkey, gets the most from the Angora goats. The reason then why the Turkish government has lavished so many millions in vain efforts to promote manufactures is not entirely the incompetence of her people, for they are naturally good mechanics, but it is owing to a system which makes success impossible. Russia has followed the example of the United States, and protected her industries with some degree of success. Turkey has followed the lead of England and France, and destroyed them. In both countries, the "jobbery" which has weighted down all government experiments in manufactures is probably about equal, and in the comparison may be eliminated. The difference in results seems due to the different systems. Free trade, while a beautiful theory, has evidently certain limitations in its applications.

CHAPTER V.

BEBEK SEMINARY.

The political events of 1839, above referred to, had diverted attention from the evangelical movement in the Oriental churches. The changes had been such in the aspect of affairs, that it was deemed safe, in 1840, to open the Seminary of the American Board at Bebek, on the Bosphorus. It is a retired village, five miles from the city, and on the European side. It has a beautiful level at the water's edge, and then rises upon the two sides of a ravine to the height of three hundred and fifty feet.

The beautiful Kiosk of Conference, where all treaties were signed, which then adorned the shore, has since disappeared. There was no foreign resident in the village. I obtained a house which had been occupied by an English gentleman who had married a Greek lady contrary to the wishes of her father. The father manifested his displeasure by hiring two Montenegrins to assassinate him. For some reason their daggers, which rarely fail, did not prove fatal. As soon as he recovered, he changed his business to Smyrna, for greater safety. One day, his two Montenegrin friends found him alone in his counting room, and said, "We were hired by your father-in-law to assassinate you, at the price of twenty liras (nearly $100.) As we failed, he has not paid us a piastre. Give us the twenty liras, and your life shall be safe from any and every Montenegrin dagger. Otherwise, we can't be surety for you." Mr. P. immediately paid the amount, and ordered coffee, which they drank together, and parted eternal friends!

The people of the village were not pleased with having a heretic in the midst of them. They had a pleasant way of throwing stones upon the roof of the house, and breaking up the tiles, which made it rather leaky, as the autumn rains had already commenced. The high land in the rear of the house gave them a great advantage, as a boy of twelve could hurl upon the roof a stone that would break up three or four tiles. It was evidently a great amusement to them to see me upon the roof, the next day, repairing damages.

A Frank dress, smoothly shaven face, and stove-pipe hat so evidently excited either scorn or mirth, that I changed all that, with good effect. Sometimes a stone from some roguish fellow would come unpleasantly near; but no one of the family was ever seriously hurt; and generally they went so wide of the mark as to suggest that probably there was no evil intention. The Armenian patriarch was petitioned to remove me. He replied that he couldn't. The Turks wouldn't. So I stayed. We ate meat in Lent. This was a great abomination, as the quarter was a Christian and not a Turkish quarter. A poor honest woman came one day, and demanded pay for two pullets she had lost. "But what makes you come to me?" "Because we Christians don't eat meat in Lent, and they tell me you do, and you must have taken them." Here was circumstantial evidence quite difficult to get around. "But," I replied, "I am a Christian, and I do eat meat in Lent. But it is meat which I buy and pay for. I would much rather give you two pullets than take two from you. Go home, and when you hear of my not paying a full price for every thing I have, then come and I will give you four times the worth of your pullets." She turned away in a maze and never made the demand.

The vigilance of the Turkish police mitigated very much the various annoyances which otherwise might have been quite serious.

As every Frank was then supposed to be more or less of a doctor, the poor people began to come to me in their distress for aid. I had a few medical books, and a little smattering knowledge of the treatment of some diseases. I always went and did what I could for them. They often needed suitable diet as much as medicine; and as Mrs. H. was very skilful in preparing things for the sick room, we found eventually that this was better than the Turkish police in abating nuisances. I became at length the village doctor for the poor. Ignorance, superstition and prejudice were sometimes annoying. I was once called to a woman who had lost considerable blood from the nose, and had become very much alarmed, as were all the family and neighbors, some twenty of whom were in the room, recommending all sorts of remedies. I immediately found, by compression, that the bleeding was from the little artery passing through the lip, and stopped it at once by a compress under the lip, as large as the lip will retain. The ice at the back of the neck, the wet cloths on the head and on the stomach, and the things stuffed into the nostrils, were all removed and the poor woman made comfortable. In their fright, they had already sent for a famous native doctor from another village. He arrived after I left. He declared to them that I was little better than an assassin. I had suddenly stopped the blood in the rush towards the head, and now it would fill into the brain, and the woman would die of apoplexy before morning! He asked her if she did not already feel faint and headachy like? He frightened her so that she begged him, for the love of the Holy Virgin, to save her life. He accordingly bled her from both feet in order to *turn the blood currents back from the brain*, and save her life! The woman was months in recovering from this loss of blood, and had no doubt but that doctor saved her life! Such was the character of native doctors. The medical school has furnished a large number of men far in advance of these. The fatal use of leeches and the lancet has mainly disappeared.

ATTEMPT TO CLOSE THE SEMINARY. 65

The Armenian patriarch and his advisers were greatly annoyed by the progress of the seminary, and he determined to break it up. I had become acquainted with, and deeply interested in, a young man of splendid talents who had lost his father, and been cheated out of his inheritance. He had become the patriarch's private secretary.

One afternoon, about an hour before sundown, a singular person called, and said hurriedly, "A few words with you in private if you please." On entering my study, he said hastily, and in a hoarse whisper, "His holiness' secretary informs you that to-morrow, which is a great feast day, the parents of all your scholars, whose names some traitor has given, will be called to the patriarchate, and all imprisoned until their sons leave. Think what you will do, but never betray this confidence. Abide in peace." He slipped away. He was miserably clad. His voice was feigned, his language that of an educated man. Was it the secretary himself? I never knew.

I had not a moment to lose; and I decided at once what I would do. I would bend before the storm which I could not resist. I rang the bell; the students came rushing in. I ordered them to take each a bundle of clothes, and depart, so as to get into the city before the gates were closed, and to go in the morning with their parents to the patriarch, present him my compliments, and say that I wished to aid his people, and especially his young men, but not by force. And since he re-

5

jected the aid, I had yielded and closed the school. Some of the boys wept and protested, but I forced them all to depart, and said to them, "Go, and trust in God. It will all come right." The patriarch was astonished, but delighted. He said to them, "I did not want to throw you into prison, but the primates forced me to it. I know Mr. H. is a good man, and he has done wisely. Go my children, and I will see that you have a school of your own. Let us not go to foreigners." In the evening, one of the students came stealthily back, with great joy, and told me how nicely it had all passed off.

A storm was just bursting upon the patriarchate, which, in the course of three weeks, so agitated the whole community, that I quietly reopened the seminary with an increase of students. The patriarch had given us a vacation. Twice after this, the seminary bent before the coming storm and finally became strong enough to resist it.

The storm referred to was the result in part of the Hatti Scheriff, and shows in what way it became an educator of the people. It was one of the first of those movements which have agitated the capital and the empire, at intervals, for almost forty years; and those who do not go back to this period can not fully understand the march of events.

The change in the administration had thrown the great Armenian bankers very much into the background. They had been ordered to settle up their accounts, and the fiscal administration would pass into other hands. The great artisan and trading class of the Armenian community now came forward, and demanded a share in the administration of their national affairs. In that strange *imperium in imperio* which every organized religion constituted in the Ottoman empire, every subject spoke of his organization as a nation; so that you would hear Armenians, Greeks, and Armeno-Catholics speaking of their *national affairs*, meaning thereby those affairs of religion, church-building, education, hospitals and trades' unions, which they were permitted to manage for themselves. The Armenian tradesmen now demanded that their representatives should constitute a part of the patriarch's council, called by them the national council. It was a democratic movement, attributed by its enemies to all sorts of causes, to American influence, to Russian, to infidelity, to any thing that would discredit it.

The Ottoman government was alarmed lest another revolution should be brewing, and imprisoned all the newly appointed representatives. Upon this, the tradesmen and artisans of every class rose *en masse*, and rushed to the Sublime Porte, by thousands, blocking up all its avenues, so that neither pasha nor ambassador could get in or out. They all demanded to be imprisoned or to have their representatives set free. The government called out two regiments of soldiers, hesitated, then yielded and ordered the release of the delegates. The contest with the ecclesiastics and bankers continued, in some form or other, for some months, but resulted in the triumph of the people. At a later date, they adopted a constitution regulating the powers of the representatives of the people, and the mode of choosing them, and also defining the power of the clergy. The anniversary of its sanction by the Sublime Porte is now kept every year with as much enthusiasm, and more rhetoric, than our Fourth of July.

This conflict and triumph deeply affected all the other communities, and they one by one have followed in the same path. One must understand these conflicts and triumphs of the people, or he will wholly fail in his efforts to comprehend the course of things in Turkey.

It is not to be supposed that the Turks approved of all that was done. They undoubtedly felt uneasy to see the people rising up with so much spirit. But while Reshid Pasha's influence was dominant it could not be helped. From such movements as these, helped forward, incited and guided by some hundreds of Protestant organizations in the empire, a large amount of democratic freedom is enjoyed under a very despotic government.

At the close of a year's experience, it was felt that the seminary could not be shut up by patriarch or bankers. A larger establishment was rented; attractive philosophical apparatus, and stated lectures with experiments, drew many intelligent persons within its influence.

THE JESUIT COLLEGE AT BEBEK. 63

About six months after the opening of the Bebek Seminary, our friends, the Jesuits, opened, in the same village, their French college. Every Protestant school, college, or seminary in Turkey shares in the same experience. Whether it is all entirely accidental, or whether that indefatigable body tracks all our efforts, the world over, need not be said. I do not think the college was ever of the slightest injury to the seminary, and I am sure the latter was a benefit to the former, in compelling it to adopt a higher and better curriculum of study.

The Jesuit missions in Turkey were already in existence at the close of the seventeenth century, and they must have had at least two centuries of labor among the Eastern churches and probably more.

In 1706, the French monarch ordered his ambassador, Ferrioul, to favor the work of the holy fathers. Although a man of bad character, if not always partially insane, he had a fierce religious zeal.

The Armenian patriarch, Avedik, was a prelate greatly venerated and beloved in the Armenian church. From the natural suavity of his own character, and also in accordance with that liberality towards other sects which the Armenians have pre-eminently shown, he had treated the Jesuit missionaries with great kindness and attention. He had even allowed them to perform divine service in his church, and had counselled peace and brotherhood between them and his own people.

The Jesuits used the opportunity thus given them, to assume a violent and domineering tone. They had wholly mistaken the mildness of the prelate for want of firmness. When at length they found him firmly opposed to their designs of domination, they resolved to remove him out of their way. Then (as always since) the French ambassador took up their quarrel, and showed himself throughout a fit tool of the Jesuits. The unfortunate patriarch was inveigled on board a French ship, under friendly pretences, and borne away into hopeless captivity and solitary imprisonment in France.

Ferrioul, the ambassador, stiffly denied all knowledge of the fact of which he was the author. The Turkish government peremptorily demanded his restoration. But he was dead, he had been taken by pirates, his fate was unknown, and many things of that kind, while the poor prelate was all the time kept in dark, damp and loathsome dungeons in France. The Porte, perfectly convinced that the whole affair was one of outrage and deception, seized about a dozen of the holy fathers, and threatened them with death if the patriarch was not restored. He was however now beyond their reach and jurisdiction; and Ferrioul left them to their fate. About half saved themselves by professing Islam, and the rest were cruelly put to death. The patriarch, in absolute solitude and darkness, suffering much from cold and want, maintained for years his patience and fortitude, until at length, broken in mind and body, he pro-

THE GREEK PATRIARCH. 71

fessed the papal faith, and died in a convent. The whole painful and moving history is given in "The Man with the Iron Mask," by Marius Topin, translated from the French, Smith Elder and Co., London, 1870.

"The Society of Jesus" triumphed over the Ottoman government in the contest, but it was a moral defeat. The indignation of the whole Armenian nation was such as wholly to defeat their missions among the Armenians for almost a century.

The "fathers" however learned nothing by this experience. Another more positive influence threatened their cherished plan of restoring the Eastern orthodox church to "unity." It was in that region towards which their labors were mainly directed— the Greek church. The Greek patriarch, Cyril Leucaris, had travelled in Europe, and had become tainted with the doctrines of the Reformation. He had felt also the quickening impulse of Western life; he had witnessed the work and power of the press in Europe, and he resolved to reform his own church. In furtherance of these views, he established a press in Galata; and the Jesuit fathers took the alarm. They easily hired a band of Janizaries to destroy it. They did their work roughly, and broke heads as well as presses. The sultan was so incensed that he banished the Jesuits from the empire. If this irrepressible society *goes*, it always *returns;* and, in a short time, through the mediation of France, it returned to the contest. They finally succeeded, by their superhuman craft and bribery, in bringing such accusations against the noble and patriotic Leucaris, that he was seized by the Janizaries, conveyed to the "Tower of Oblivion" at Rūmelie Hissar, strangled, and thrown into the Bosphorus. Its deep currents carried him off into the Sea of Marmora, and the body was thrown up on the shore, twenty miles distant from the fatal tower.

While this most atrocious deed stopped all the reform projects of Leucaris, it also incensed the Greek mind against the Jesuits.

A Roman element has always remained in the maritime cities of the Ottoman empire, from the days of the crusades. And as a portion of the Slavic race belongs to Rome from pagan times, this gives them a strong foothold in European Turkey. Had their early missions been conducted in a more Christian spirit it can not be doubted that they would have met with far greater success. But they still believed in the doctrine of force, taught by their great master, Xavier, that "missions without muskets" are a failure.

During the present century, their missions have pursued a different course, and have been conducted by men of a very different character.

While always leaning upon and enjoying the political support of the Catholic powers, more especially of France and Austria, they have established schools, convents, nunneries, hospitals, and orphanages, and through these charitable institutions they have made considerable progress among the people.

EXILE OF PAPAL ARMENIANS. 73

In 1828, the Armenian patriarch became alarmed at the progress of the papal missions among his people. He easily persuaded the Turkish government that another revolution like the Greek, the *sequela* of which, an impending war with Russia, was agitating the empire, lay couched under this papal organization. The papal converts, about 10,000 in number, were given over to his power, and banished to a distant place in the interior. It was in the winter, and their sufferings were great, both on their journey and after their arrival. The Catholic powers immediately interfered on their behalf, and their recall and indemnification for losses were strenuously demanded. The Jesuit missionaries now put in a strong plea for toleration. What historical argument they could urge from their own example when in power, is not clear. The Turks are so entirely ignorant, as a general thing, of European history, that if the fathers strained a point there, for the greater glory of God and the good of the church, they only obeyed the teachings of their order.

It was nevertheless an excellent thing to have this powerful voice raised on behalf of universal toleration. The question was referred to the Sheikh-ul-Islam, and as chief of the faith he must give his "fetva" or formal decision according to the sacred law.

It is a mistake to suppose that this law has any thing derogatory to the person of our Lord.

The twenty-fifth article of the religious code, as

given by D'Ohsson,* has the following Mohammedan commentary:

"Jesus, the Son of Mary, was born in Beyth'ul Cahhm (Cattle Market). Mary, the daughter of Amram, and of Anna, was desçended, like Zacharia and John the Baptist, from the tribe of Yehhoud by Solomon.

"Jesus Christ, the great prophet, was born of a virgin by the breath of the archangel Gabriel, on the 25th December, 5584, under the reign of Herod, and in the forty-second year of Augustus, the first of the Cesars. He received his mission at the age of thirty, after his baptism by St. John the Baptist in the waters of Erdenn. He called the people to repentance. God gave him power to work great miracles. He healed lepers, gave sight to the blind, raised the dead, walked upon the waters, and even gave life by his breath to a bird made of clay. Pressed by hunger, in the midst of anguish and fervent prayers, he and his disciples received from heaven a table covered with a cloth, and provided with a baked fish, five loaves of bread, salt, vinegar, dates, olives, pomegranates, and all kinds of fresh herbs. They all ate and this celestial table presented itself to them in the same state for forty consecutive nights. This Messiah of the nations thus proved his apostleship by a multitude of wonderful works. The simplicity of his appearance, the humility of his conduct, the austerity of his

* D'Ohsson, Vol. 1, page 33.

Moslem Theory of the Crucifixion. 75

life, the wisdom of his precepts, the purity of his morals, are above the reach of humanity. He is therefore known by the sacred and glorious name of *Rauhh Ullah*—Spirit of God.

"But the corrupt and perverse Jews persecuted him, even to demanding his death. Betrayed by Judas, and ready to succumb to the fury of his enemies, he was snatched away to heaven; and that infidel apostle, transfigured into the person of his Master, is taken for the Messiah, undergoes the punishment of the cross, with all the ignominies designed for that supernatural man, that great saint, that glorious prophet. Thus Enoch, Khidir, Elias and Jesus Christ are the four prophets which had the distinguished favor of being taken alive to heaven. However, many imams believe in the real death of Jesus Christ, and his resurrection and ascension as he himself predicted to his twelve apostles, charged to preach the word of God to all the peoples of the earth."

In the penal code, to blaspheme the name of Jesus is declared worthy of death; and it is a form of profanity never heard from a Mussulman.

The Moslem jurist therefore comes to such a question as was proposed to the grand mufti, without any violent prejudice. The Christian is not hated for believing in Christ, but for being an enemy to Mohammed, and still more for worshipping pictures, and believing that bread is changed into God, and then, that the eating of it brings salvation. The terms "Ghiaour," "Christian dog," etc., are freely bestowed in view of these things, which are specially abhorred, and which are unfortunately regarded as essentials of Christianity.

The fetva of the Sheikh-ul-Islam was brief, but to the point. It was, in effect, that all Christians were viewed by the Mussulman law without any regard to their sects or differences; that, therefore, all Christians were entitled to the same protection, and no one sect could be persecuted by another with any sanction from the law.

All the banished persons were recalled, and this fetva stands as a decision in common law to appeal to. It has often been used by the persecuted for their relief.

The Jesuit college was opened with great *eclat* May, 1841. It did not have the effect of closing our seminary. There was no apparent evil resulting from it. The seminary had more applicants than it could receive, and the two went on side by side for many years, until the French institution ceased to exist for want of patronage.

CHAPTER VI.

RELIGIOUS FREEDOM.

During the years 1842-43, many visitors came to see the American institution at Bebek, and among them was quite a number of young Turkish gentlemen of high standing. Four of the most frequent visitors were young men from an imperial school in the Old Seraglio grounds. As I had performed many experiments in physics for their gratification and enlightment, they were bound by the laws of oriental civilization to make some return. The school was expressly intended to educate young men for the sultan's household, to be his personal attendants, with the expectation of ultimate appointment to desirable offices. Two of these young men were sons of the custodian of the imperial jewels. Their father would show me the jewels, in return for my kindness to his sons. I was invited to see the school first, and I would lunch with them, and after that, be admitted to the splendid display. I had seen them once, in the party of the Duke of Cambridge, a few years before, but with time all too short; and I was glad to accept the invitation, and gaze again upon the wondrous splendor and beauty of diamonds and pearls and turquoises and amethysts and garnets—indeed, upon all the sacred jewelled wealth of this dynasty. It had the reputation, I know not with what justice, of equalling any thing which European monarchies can show.

I went on the day appointed, and landed, as directed, on the Marmora side of Seraglio Point, and was there met by my young friends. I was surprised and interested in our path to this royal institution. We entered, first, a very spacious but entirely empty magazine of Byzantine construction. It was of unknown extent, its arches supported upon massive square columns of brick. From this, a subterranean passage carried us up to the light of day. We emerged into a beautiful flower garden; and near by was the college and the treasury.

The whole establishment was kept with the most scrupulous neatness, but the simplicity of living was such as no American student could endure. Each student had a space about six feet by eight, and in that were all his books and furniture for day and night, viz., a bed, which by day was a sofa, a wardrobe, a chest, and a small desk. There was no chair; you slipped off your shoes, stepped up upon the sofa, and sat down cross-legged. A glass of sherbet was offered, with good wishes, and after a little conversation, we adjourned to the dining-hall for pipes and coffee; smoking not being allowed in their rooms, which they esteemed a great hardship. The dining-hall was grand, and must have been, in ancient days,

Mode of Life in Imperial School. 79

the refectory of a convent. It was lofty, to the summit of the solid arch was well lighted, and at one end were the cooking ranges, a cook and two servants. Each student had his own cupboard and simple table furniture. The cold-water drinking cup, the chibouk, coffee and sweetmeat apparatus, were the only articles indicating wealth and artistic taste. The Ottoman never practices economy here. The justification of extravagance is very peculiar. "I gave a hundred liras for it, but thereupon I gave ten liras to the poor." *

The lunch was excellent, but untainted by a breath of European customs. First, a large bowl of most excellent soup, with boxwood spoons, and a piece of bread, which to the Orientals is pre-eminently the staff of life. We all ate from a common dish, having all first washed at a marble fountain in the dining-hall. To omit this would be as clownish and more disgusting, than sitting down to dine with hats on would be to us. The table might be called a large, round, copper tray, say two and a half or three feet in diameter. The students lunched in *messes* of three, four, or five, as they chose. All was quiet and orderly, the boisterousness of the Anglo-Saxon never having penetrated those thick old walls. After soup came another tray with bread, olives, cheese, and fruit; and then the chibouk and coffee.

The elder of our hosts then excused himself in

* The Mohammedan code taxes all luxuries on behalf of the poor.

order to see if the treasury was opened. He tarried long, came back and whispered to his brother. Both left together, and the remaining two cast inquiring looks at each other. "What is it"? "Wallah bilmem." (The Lord knows, I don't.) Soon they were both called out by a sign from the door; and, contrary to all etiquette, I was left alone in no enviable circumstances; but I felt sure no personal injury could be intended to myself, because there could be no motive for it, and nothing to be gained by it.

There was a mystery beyond my comprehension. Soon one returned. "Nothing at all," was his only reply; but he was moody, silent, and troubled. I rose to leave, but he insisted upon my remaining till Osman Bey should come. He only could grant leave. I did not wait long when he appeared, with a servant bearing on a silver plate three parcels of sugar plums beautifully arranged in white, red, and yellow muslin bags, adorned and tied up with ribbons. His father sent them to my "house" and "chicks," and would always pray for our welfare. He had been engaged in very embarrassing public business, and must beg that I would have the goodness to excuse him till another day. I left with the stiffest and most precise formality possible, and was accompanied by an attendant, another way from that we came, to the boat.

Whatever theories I formed upon this interesting and vexatious affair were soon proven false.

The Armenian Carabet had in the meantime

EXECUTION OF CARABET.

been executed as an apostate from Islam, and his headless body was lying in a public street on the other side of the Seraglio walls, his head beside him with a *Frank cap stuck on it!*

This shocking and atrocious event explained the whole mystery of the reception. I can not recall an event which produced so profound an impression. The old Mussulman party had triumphed in the most disgraceful manner, the grand vizir having given assurances to Sir Stratford Canning that whatever penalty should be inflicted, his life should be spared. The act divided Turkish sentiment and feeling; the old Turks commending it, the young Turkish party, already forming, cursing it as a needless insult to Europe, and a supreme folly of old fools. All the Christian inhabitants, foreign and native, of every rite, were moved with indignation that the Hatti Scheriff should be so defiantly trampled upon. It was asserted, and was probably true, though denied by the government, that two other similar cases occurred in the provinces.

Sir Stratford Canning, backed up by all the embassies, except that of Russia, who preferred to reserve her action, demanded in the most positive manner the definitive renunciation of the law with regard to apostates, and a solemn promise that no similar case should ever occur; otherwise England would join the enemies of Turkey to secure her destruction. He farther urged, that this infamous law was no part of the Koran, but derived wholly from an uncertain tradition. After much *wriggling* on the part of the Turks, the grand vizir gave the required assurance. Sir Stratford then demanded a personal interview with the sultan, that he, as *caliph*, successor of the prophet, should himself sanction it. The vizerial declaration was "The Sublime Porte engages to take effectual measures to prevent henceforward the execution and putting to death of the Christian who is an apostate." The next day the sultan gave his assent in a public audience, adding, "neither shall Christianity be insulted in my dominions, nor shall Christians be in any way persecuted for their religion."

A copy of the correspondence with the Porte on this subject was furnished to each of the patriarchs, to which was also appended the sultan's pledge. Although not then printed, it was translated and recopied many times, and widely circulated among all men of distinction in the empire.

A lively discussion immediately arose all over the Mussulman and Christian world, whether this, after all, meant any thing? Could the sultan abrogate or set aside a law of the Koran? It was clearly proved, first, that the law is not in the Koran. And second, that the Koran is not law. It is useless, however to assert this latter. All the world, excepting those who have resided in Turkey and have there examined the subject, knows beyond all possibility of doubt that the Koran is the law of Mussulmans, and that it is administered by priests! The most respectable Reviews assert it almost every month. Mr. Bosworth Smith, an ardent friend of the Mussulmans, and Mr. Freeman, an ardent enemy, both receive it as true. Both are guilty of the same degree of ignorance. The Mussulman code of law as reduced by Ibrahim Haleby by direction of Solyman the Magnificent, is accepted as law by all Mussulmans. With its accepted commentaries, it forms many volumes, each one larger than the Koran, and treating upon scores of subjects not referred to in the Koran. The Koran has but little in it that is capable of being law. Where it states a principle capable of being so viewed, it stands as the highest authority, and the codified law will be in accord with it. But how can it be authority in those things to which it makes no reference? Even the whole ritual of prayer is governed by this code and not by the Koran; and so of very many of the religious observances most strictly held.

The law of succession in the caliphate is not from the Koran. Different laws have prevailed upon this point of supreme importance, and the one universally accepted, until the khedive changed it for Egypt, was established by this dynasty, in the reign of Ahmed I. But still, when a notion is once fixed in the public mind, it matters not how false the notion may be, it has almost the permanence of a law of nature.

The law requiring the apostate to be put to death is the first article in the second chapter of the penal code, and is in these words: "Apostasy is an enormous crime in the eyes of God. The

Mussulman who is guilty of it must be condemned to death, if he do not immediately abjure his error."

Many have maintained that this law is unchangeable, and that the sultan himself has no power over it. They forget that Mussulman law has changed immensely in the course of a thousand years. It is founded upon various traditions and commentaries, and is no part of the Koran. The khedive has set the whole of it entirely aside, and introduced in its stead the Napoleon code. The law against impiety and blasphemy, held still more rigidly than that against apostasy, is wholly set aside and abolished. Yet no Mussulman state has objected. The Sheikh-ul-Islam has not condemned it, and the Sublime Porte is preparing to follow his example. All this does not invalidate, except indirectly, the Koran as the book of the true faith. But it proves, whatever may be said to the contrary, that Mussulman law can change, has changed, and therefore will change.

There was much to attract universal sympathy to Carabet, who had been so basely put to death. He was a poor and ignorant man. He professed Islam in order to get revenge for wrongs sustained in a drunken brawl. He immediately repented and fled, and was not circumcised. He returned, after a year or so, trusting to his obscurity. He was discovered, apprehended, exhorted to recant; but he was firm. Twice he was brought before the executioner, and life and death set before him. He firmly chose death, and the third time he was executed. He had no spiritual adviser, no human comforter, and was entirely in the hands of those who were determined that he should recant or die. One can not but think there was divine light in his darkness, and divine strength in his weakness. He was executed in strict accordance with Mussulman law, and in strict violation of the Hatti Scheriff. The reaction against the "Old Turkish" party was effective, and it brought Reshid Pasha to the front as grand vizir. The final result was unquestionably a step forward in favor of religious freedom.

We may as well call up here the question, how far there is freedom *for Moslems* to change their faith and openly profess Christianity. While it has been granted that there is some degree of religious freedom for Christians, it has been strongly denied that there is any for Mussulmans. The general subject of religious freedom in Turkey may be referred to in another place.

The first noted test of this question occurred in 1852, in the conversion of Selim Agha and his household. "Baron Bedros," a native helper in the evangelic work, had aroused his attention to the Christian Scriptures, and Dr. Schauffler had crowned the work. He was a resident of Salonica, the ancient Thessalonica. His conversion was well known. Some of his Moslem friends advised him to leave, lest the fanatical mob should do him injury; and there is hardly a more fanatical place in the empire, as the late murder of the two consuls shows (in 1876). He escaped, with his whole family, in 1853, to Malta, where he was baptized with the name of Edward Williams. His wife and children, and his wife's sister, were baptized with him. In 1855 he came, with all his household, to Constantinople, and entered with zeal and boldness, and yet with great discretion, into Christian work. He was everywhere known among the Mussulmans as an apostate; and had he taken a residence in a Moslem quarter, he would have suffered persecution in all probability from the mob. But, residing in a Christian quarter, he was undisturbed for years.

At a period some years later, I took him with me to Brusa on a special service, not intending however to attract any attention among the Mussulmans. It turned out quite otherwise. On the deck of the steamer, all the Mussulmans gathered round him until we arrived at Modania, the port of Brusa, but sixteen miles distant from it. We rode hard, and reached Brusa first, that no one of our fellow passengers might know for that night our stopping place. What followed the next day was unique. While examining the Armenian school beneath the church, three Turkish officials appeared at the door, followed by an armed guard. The native pastor invited them in. They replied, they wished to see him and his guests in the church above. The three persons were the governor of the province of Bithynia, the chief justice, and the collector of the revenues. There was no alternative, and we went in. After seating ourselves, and passing back and forth the usual salutations, conversation commenced about the Scriptures, suggested by the large Bible on the pulpit in front of us. The chief justice absorbed the conversation with Mr. Williams. His reputation for learning and ability was very high, both among Moslems and foreigners. Mr. Sanderson, the English consul, pronounced him the ablest Moslem and the sharpest reasoner he had ever known among them. The armed guard remained in the middle of the church, and seemed intent upon the conversation, which was very free and interesting, showing on the part of the judge no little knowledge of the Old Testament Scriptures. At length he turned full upon Mr. Williams, and said, "I have had the pleasure of conversing with many foreign gentlemen who spoke our language very well, but I never met with one before who spoke exactly like a Mussulman, *as you do!* I knew the battery was now to be opened. For a moment Mr. Williams's eye fell to the ground; and then, looking the chief justice calmly in the face, he replied, smilingly, "You may well say that I speak Turkish like a Mussulman, for so I was till I was forty-five years old. Then I became a Christian, and I am now a preacher of the Gospel!" The guard stepped forward. The chief justice bent suddenly forward, his fore-arms upon his knees, his face reddened with sudden confusion, running his tesbeh (ninety-nine beads representing ninety-nine attributes of God) rapidly through his fingers. The governor looked straight into the air. The collector, a perfect Gallio, shook his fat sides with suppressed and silent mirth at the confusion of the judge. It was a moment of great and painful suspense. What would be the next move? Would he be arrested and imprisoned?

The judge relieved the tension by throwing himself into an easy, careless attitude, his confusion gone, and remarking, "There is one thing in your faith that always surprises me. How can intelligent men believe that one God is three Gods, and three Gods are one God, one is three and three are one?"

Mr. W. replied, "We do not so believe. You can not hold the unity of God with more fervor than I do. As creator and author of all things, he is called God the Father, but not in any human sense. In some way, God visits the human soul, to enlighten, purify, and guide it. He does not appear in any visible form but he acts directly and spiritually upon our spirits, and we call him God the Spirit. But our greatest of all mysteries is that God became incarnate in Christ our Lord. He took upon himself our nature. As we do not know how our souls dwell in flesh, much less can we understand how God came into flesh for our salvation. But this is not another God. It is one and the same God, still manifesting himself in such a way that he is called the Son of God. But these three divine manifestations, personal in view of their work and office, are still the one only living and true God."

The judge turned to the pastor and myself for our assent, and then remarked, that whenever he had inquired about this dogma of the Trinity, the only reply given had been, "It is a mystery, mystery;" but now he could see there is a way in which an intelligent man may receive it. He had never heard any thing intelligible about it before. After a little random conversation, they rose to take leave; which, with them, has forms of etiquette unknown to the West. Would they retire in proud and formal disdain? The judge led the way, and each one of the officials gave to the pastor and myself the salam of honor. There was no significance in this. The Turks are naturally polite in such matters, there was nothing in it worth notice. But now they were to pass the "apostate," one who had openly declared his apostasy in their presence. Had they passed him as though unconscious of his presence, no one would have wondered. Still we should have said, with a deeper meaning than the Moslem knows, "God is great!" But each one exchanged with him also the salam of honor! All passed out, and I turned to Mr. W. and said, "What does this all mean?" "Doubt not," he replied with emotion, "the power of Hazaretli Isa has done it!"

It is not unlikely they had come out of curiosity, and to enjoy themselves in driving the renegade through all possible subterfuges, and at length unmasking him in spite of himself. His frank, unlooked-for confession confounded them. The subsequent conversation interested them, and the judge decided to pass it off in the most friendly way.

But, however interpreted, it was a proof of progress. The ignorant multitude are still fanatical and bigoted, but the governing class has wonderfully changed. Such a scene would have been impossible, a dozen years before. The Scriptures, newspapers, books, education, and the course of things are working slowly down into the mass, and religious freedom is coming in slowly, and in the only way possible, by *enlightenment*. Government can do much but our own country proves that it can not do every thing against fanatical and ignorant masses.

Passing by three young men without families, baptized from Islam, the next test case was the baptism, by Dr. Schauffler, of a cadi and his wife from Philippopolis. His name assumed at baptism was Freeman. He was an educated man, and became a teacher of Turkish in the seminary. Mrs. Freeman's mother followed her to Constantinople, resolved to recover her to the faith or destroy her. She proved herself a most able and persevering diplomat, and neither the grand vizir nor the sultan could shake her off.

At length, a commission came to my house from the Porte, to examine into the truth of the old lady's accusations. When the preliminaries of the

CASES OF MOSLEMS BAPTIZED. 91

examination were satisfactorily settled, I sent for Mr. and Mrs. Freeman. The commission were surprised to find them not held under guard, but in their own hired house, on the opposite side of the village. The examination was long, patient, with some curious and amusing episodes. At length the commission rose. The falsehoods of the old lady had been so thoroughly exposed, that they administered to her a sharp rebuke, and declared their conviction that it was a case of honest persuasion, and therefore *the government had no ground whatever of complaint.*

The third case was that of Ahmed Agha of Kaisery, who, with his family, reside in the capital. His daughters are married to Christian husbands.

There are a few other families of Mussulmans converted to Christianity. Perhaps, all told, the list of baptisms from Islam counting men, women and children, would amount to fifty during the last twenty years. It may be regarded as an insignificant number, but considering there are no missions to the Moslems, that these conversions are from contact with other missions, the number is not to be despised. It is more than have occurred in all other lands,—Russian, English, Dutch, —where many millions of Moslems are under Christian governments.

It is doubtless true that these conversions would not be tolerated in the midst of a Moslem population. The government can not protect them against a fanatical mob if it would. The convert must remove to some place like Constantinople, Smyrna, or to Egypt, and he can have protection. The sphere of freedom is gradually widening, and so far as an evangelical Christianity reaches the Moslem mind, it disarms half its prejudices.

In the year 1864, some ten or twelve of these Moslem converts were suddenly seized and thrown into prison. The exciting cause appeared to be a book published by Rev. Dr. Pfander of the English Church Missionary Society, in which he boldly attacked Islam. He published it against the strongly expressed advice of his American friends. They knew the country too well to believe that no fanatical movement was possible.

The persons imprisoned were soon released, because they had no connection with that book, and they witnessed a good confession with regard to Gospel truth. The most annoying fact that came out of this sudden burst of fanaticism was that Sir Henry Bulwer, the English ambassador, justified it and probably *instigated* it.

In removing Lord Stratford de Redcliffe, "the great Elchi," it was the policy or the destiny of the English government to send a man in almost every respect the opposite in character; and he set himself to undo whatever Lord Stratford had done. As to morals, Sir Henry Bulwer had none, either Christian, Turkish, or Pagan. With an unequalled talent at intrigue, he despised truth and principle, but could practice hypocrisy with the skill of him who can appear as an angel of light. He lost his place in consequence of intrigues which, though profitable to himself, were not consistent with the interests of England. He was more successful in his intrigues for a title, by which he was styled Lord Dalling and Bulwer.

It is not at all surprising that such a man should be a bitter enemy to any movement so absurd as he must regard every religious movement. He openly accused the American missionaries of intemperate and abusive conduct towards the Turks, with whom they had no missions; and displayed a reckless disregard of facts which one would not expect from so wily a diplomat. His recall did not undo his work. England's flag of religious liberty in Turkey had been struck, and her influence since then has been weak and wavering.

The case of persecution of a Moslem family for becoming Christian which occasioned a deputation from the Evangelical Alliance to Constantinople, was arranged by sending the persecuted persons, father and son, to reside in Smyrna, the Porte confessing its inability to protect them in their native place. This is better than death, but is not what we call toleration. The government was then wholly under the power of Russia, and Gen. Ignatieff ruled the palace. It remains to be seen what course the present government will pursue. There are thousands of Turkish Moslems whose faith in the Koran is shaken, and perfect religious freedom has become an absolute necessity.

The course of England with regard to this question seems to be inexplicable. In order to maintain her influence in Turkey, she must be the champion of religious freedom. This would unite the sympathies of all the Christian races. Nothing less than this can by any possibility bring the Turkish administration into harmony with its environment. If not half its numbers, half its power and wealth, is non-Mussulman. The necessary course of things has been to bring the Christian element forward, and previous to the present war, there were many Christian officials in different departments of government, six of them raised to the grade of pasha. But the England of Lord Stratford and Cowley has ceased to exist since the Crimean war; and it has made no difference whether Gladstone or Disraeli was in the ascendant; religious liberty has been weakly defended. Neither of them has cared for it until the imperious march of events has forced it upon their attention, or party conflicts have introduced it. As a great Mohammedan power, she has enforced her Christian ideas of religious liberties in India; it is a very mistaken policy to do any thing less in Turkey.

CHAPTER VII.

THE OLD ORIENTAL LIFE.

The growth of the seminary necessitated a removal to larger premises; and I hired, in the same village of Bebek, the large house and grounds of Cheliby Yorgaki, merchant of the palace under five sultans: Hamed I., Selim III., Mustapha IV., Mahmûd II., and nominally, not really, Abdul Medjid.

As the house was larger than would be wanted, the first year, Cheliby Yorgaki and his family occupied one story and the terrace belonging to it. His family consisted of himself, wife, and adopted son Demetri. This latter was a genius in his way, a fine mathematician and linguist. His first introduction to me was with an algebraic equation for discussion. He had many excellent qualities, but no business tact. The old lady retained signs of the great beauty she once undoubtedly possessed, her husband loyally declaring that, at the time of their marriage, she was the most beautiful young lady the Greek community contained; and she was from one of their chief families.

The old gentleman, past threescore and ten, was the grandest and best of the Orientals of the old school. More than six feet in height, portly as age drew on, with a large and well-formed head, a clear complexion, a majestic white beard, and a countenance of singular dignity, calmness, and repose, he was an object that would fix the attention of any passer-by. He was most scrupulously neat in person, and, in the summer, was dressed in the most brilliant white; his large vest and loose jacket, being of French piqué. Nothing could be conceived of more purely oriental and *distingué*.

The old people were very social, and as Mrs. Hamlin spoke the Greek with freedom, and I with unfreedom, my language being wholly Armenian, we were often solicited to pass the evening with them, and did so as often as we could.

Our chief annoyance was the sugar plums with which they persistently stuffed the children, regarding all our protests as absurd, until we absolutely refused to let them have the children at all.

They were very religious old people. He read the church service every morning, and no word of the whole liturgy was omitted. Notwithstanding the errors that pervade it, he seemed to find the truth, and to love the truth.

We esteemed it a rare good fortune to have such free and pleasant intercourse with persons of so much intelligence and kind feeling, who knew so well the oriental world of the past, and who had so many stories, tragic, strange, or humorous, illustrative of a condition of society that had forever passed away. He often said, "We live now in a new world. When I built this house, which I entered March 17, 1779 (o. s.), the Osmanlee world was following all its old customs. But Sultan Mahmùd changed it all."

One evening, while talking about that old state of government and society, he said, "Perhaps you would like to hear the story of my family. It will show you how things used to go." We of course assented, and he gave us, in the most graphic manner, the following account, which he was always ready to repeat, and which we enjoyed, like many other of his narratives, more than once.

"You know," said he, "the upper gate of the Egyptian Bazar. Well, just outside of that, in that crowded street, my grandfather had a breadshop. His name was Joannes Giras, but always known as Joannes Ekmekgi—Joannes the breadseller. Right opposite was Ibrahim Tūtûngi—Ibrahim the Tobacconist. They were both old men, always on friendly terms, although one was a Christian, the other a Moslem. Each took his son, a lad of fourteen or fifteen, into his shop. The Christian boy, Joannes, was my father. The Turkish boy, right opposite, Ibrahim, became his chief friend. The two boys, Moslem and Christian, were always together when the store would allow, and finally, each was considered derelict to his faith and race by forming such a close friendship. As counsel was disregarded, and the two youth had made a vow of eternal friendship, the Moslem father determined to cut it short forever, although the doing of this would deprive him forever of seeing again his beloved and only son. 'A *Moslem* will do such a thing—' said the old gentleman, with an emphasis, meaning that a Christian would not find it in his heart to do it.

"One day, Ibrahim came to Joannes and said, 'I have come to bid you good-by, Joannes, I sha'n't see you again for a long time.'

"'Wherever you go,' said Joannes, 'I shall go too.'

"'Yes, but now you can't. My father has made me chibûkgi to the pasha of Bagdad, and I am going right off.' Then they fell upon each other's necks, and kissed, and wept, and separated. Ibrahim's last words were, 'I shall come back to Constantinople, and I shall not come back to be Ibrahim Tūtûngi nor Ibrahim chibûkgi, but Ibrahim your friend.'

"The young Ibrahim rose rapidly in favor with the pasha. After a time, he promoted him to be a writer in his great office at Bagdad, and afterwards to be a paid secretary. Next he made him his private secretary, gave him a wife and a house, and thus Ibrahim, while yet a young man, had reached a position of honor and influence.

"After a few years, he made him his second in office. The Kurds (Wolves) on the eastern border were often to be chastised, and the great and turbulent pashalic required a firm and vigorous hand. Ibrahim was the man for the place, and pasha and sultan were satisfied.

"The next change came from the death of the old pasha. Ibrahim was appointed in his place; and thus. the *tūtûngi* had become the great pasha of Bagdad. He now petitioned for leave to visit Constantinople; but the sultan replied, 'When you leave, the Kurds will come down. Stay and keep your pashalic in order.' So he could not see his old home.

"After a while, the pashalic of Aleppo, in Northern Syria, had become disturbed, and one pasha after another had failed to set things to rights. At length the sultan said, 'I will send my pasha of Bagdad there;' and accordingly he went and straightened things out immediately. Again he petitioned for leave to visit Stambool, and was, as before, refused.

"He was finally called home in a most unexpected manner. The Hunkiar (emperor, literally, the Blood-letter) was angry with his grand vizir, and cut off his head. The next thing was, to call Ibrahim to take his place.

"He was hardly installed in the grand vizirate at Constantinople, when he sent two of his bodyguard, with instructions to inquire for Joannes Giras the breadseller, formerly near the upper gate of the Egyptian Bazar. If alive, to bring him with them. If dead, to ascertain if he left a family; and who, and where; and bring him exact word.

"The street was a narrow one, and all the shops open in front. The people were all astounded to see the officers enter the bread store of Joannes. 'Are you Joannes Giras, Ekmekgi?' 'I am.' 'How long have you been here?' 'My father and grandfather were here before me.' 'Then you are the man! The grand vizir orders that we take you before him.' Terror and dismay seized him. He protested that he had committed no crime. He had never been guilty of theft, murder, robbery, or any thing else to be arrested for! All the people from the shops, Mussulmans and Christians, gathered round to testify that Joannes was a good and honest man, and that his accuser, whoever he might be, was the criminal. 'We know nothing about it,' said the officers, 'shut up your shop, and come with us.'

"It was the arrest of fate. Poor Joannes departed, and the terrors of death got hold of him. He met a neighbor from the Fanar, the Greek quarter, two or three miles distant. 'Tell my wife and my two little boys what has happened to me. I am going to my death. The Holy Virgin help them!'

"Bad news travels swiftly. The wife tore her hair and garments. The neighbors crowded in, and added their death wails to the shrieks of the widow.

"Joannes, arrived at the vizirate, waited two mortal hours, unable to ascertain his accuser, or why he had been arrested. At length he was called into the august presence. Throwing himself flat upon his face, he protested his innocence, and begged for his life, and said, 'Shed not so much innocent blood! for who will care for my wife and children? They also will perish.' 'Get up!' said the grand vizir. 'I do not want your life. I wish to talk with you.' He rose upon his knees, with folded arms; not daring to look up. After some other questions, the grand vizir said to him, 'Do you remember Ibrahim Tūtûngi?' 'He was my greatest friend in my youth, but he went away, and never returned.' 'Do you think I am Ibrahim Tūtûngi?' 'Why does your highness make sport of a poor man like me? I know that you are his majesty's grand vizir!' 'But I *am* Ibrahim Tūtûngi, and you are Joannes Ekmekgi,' and he arose, and fell upon his neck, and kissed him! Joannes stepped out of death into life as suddenly as he had experienced the reverse.

"After talking awhile Ibrahim said, 'Time presses, come with me. Do you remember the last words I said to you nearly forty years ago?' 'I remember well,' said Joannes. 'You said you should come back to Constantinople, not Ibrahim Tūtûngi nor Ibrahim Chibūkgi, but Ibrahim my friend; and so God has wonderfully fulfilled!'

"The vizir took him to his treasury, gave him an account book saying, 'Here is recorded all that is here deposited. I hold an exact copy. You will take this, keep an exact account of all my revenues and disbursements, and manage all my financial affairs. You are to be my *saraff*' (banker). 'Remember,' said Joannes, 'that I am only a poor breadseller. Give me some humble office, and I will serve you faithfully; but I can not be your saraff.' 'You are a man of good sense, and an honest man,' replied Ibrahim; 'and you can be my banker just as well as to be a breadseller! When you get into any difficulty, come directly to me. If you send a third person, he will be your enemy. I shall always be your friend.'

"Then, clapping his hands to call his steward, he said to him, 'Take my friend here, give him a fur robe, a Persian girdle, a saraff's turban, a horse, ostler, chibûkgi, all in the uniform of my department, and send him to his home.'

"So they arrayed him, mounted him, and in that style of splendor, he issued from the grand vizir's gate.

"Once in the street, he was looked upon with searching eyes. Which of the old bankers has the good fortune to get the office? Recognized by no one, all bowed down to do him honor. Armenians, Greeks, Jews, Turks, Franks, all saluted him with the respect due to his master and to his place of dignity and power. For, being in constant communication with the first officer of the realm, it was often a great political as well as financial office. Occasionally, one would approach the chibûkgi, and ask, 'Who is this new saraff?' 'Joannes Giras Ekmekgi!' 'God is great!' he would reply, and march on."

As he reached his home, his son Yorgaki, my narrator, saw him first, and cried out, "They haven't killed papa! Here he is, mamma, all alive." The desolated widow saw him dismount at their humble door—the caparisoned horse, the servants, the rich array! She fainted at the real or unreal sight, and fell upon the floor. She soon revived, and all sorrow was changed to joy and exultation, in which the whole neighborhood joined. But what was he to do with horse and servants in his small and humble home. He sent them away for the night; and the following day he could have any establishment in the Greek quarter.

Pleasing as a story of remarkable friendship between a Moslem and a Christian youth, carried through a long life, it illustrates well the changes, possible and frequent, in life, under the old regime. In the morning, this man went out from his obscure home a poor breadseller. Towards noon, he went, as he supposed, to be bowstrung and flung into the Bosphorus. At night, he returned to his home the first Christian citizen of the empire.

"What was his after history?" we asked, charmed with the story. Our aged friend replied, "My father was a good and just man. He was content with his regular gains, which were a certain per cent., or commission, on all his transactions. He remained saraff to a good old age. His friend died, and he retired, rich and honored.

"When he felt that his end could not be far off, he called his sons, me and my elder brother Joannes, and said to us, 'I am now old and feeble. I shall not live long, I want to give you my last blessing and counsel, while I have strength to do it. I have only one thing to say, but it has a great weight of meaning. *Never give nor take a bribe;* and God will bless you, and the Holy Virgin will watch over you, and you will die in peace in your own homes, as I do in mine. My contemporaries have lived by another rule, and they generally died by the bowstring.'"

"Did you both follow this rule?" we asked.

"I have always followed it; but my brother Joannes forgot the wise counsel of his father. He fell into the ways of others. He took large gifts, became very rich, but was beheaded, as his tombstone indicates by a sculptured head and knife, and his property was mostly confiscated."

"But did the government compel you to put that sign of capital punishment on the tombstone?"

"Oh no," he said, laughing, "We esteem it rather a sign of honor. You must be somebody, to have your head cut off!"

It is not difficult to see why bribery brings danger, and absolute freedom from it safety. When you give a bribe, it is for the purpose of gaining something which others also are after. You secure their enmity, but you gain no friend. You are in the same case, if you do work for a bribe. It is all laying up wrath against the day of wrath; and the time will come when the penalty will fall suddenly.

We asked our friend if, in the course of his life, he had often felt in any personal danger? Both the old people laughed heartily at this. "Until the destruction of the Janizaries who was safe? They sometimes killed men out of mere caprice, as I have seen with my own eyes, many a time."

We begged him, at a future time, to give us something of his own history, which he agreed to do with evident pleasure; and we adjourned the Arabian Nights' Entertainment.

CHAPTER VIII.

DETHRONEMENT OF SULTANS.

When again we spent an evening with our Greek friends, the conversation commenced about the sultans he had served. Of all the five, he pronounced Selim III. incomparably the best. Yorgaki's father obtained for his son the position of merchant of the palace, when he was very young for such responsible duties. The palace meant about 10,000 persons; and he supplied every thing connected with apparel and furniture.

Selim would often talk with him in the most familiar manner, knew perfectly well the disorders of the empire resulting from Janizary rule, and wanted to find a remedy. The sultan never addressed to him a word that would remind him that he was a rayah, but always called him "Cheliby Yorgaki" (equivalent to "Esquire Yorgaki"), and would even say to him, on leaving, "Allah emanet oloon!" (I give you into God's keeping.)

The Janizaries were incensed by the attempted reforms of Selim, and at length, in 1807, they dethroned him, and placed Mustapha IV. upon the throne. Much blood was shed, and for two or three days terror reigned in Constantinople.

The Surprise in the Palace.

Yorgaki remained at home until he was called to the palace; and he went, full of evil forebodings; for Mustapha IV. was as wicked as he was weak.

The chief eunuch, who was the sultan's treasurer, introduced him. "Tell this Ghiaour," said the sultan to the eunuch, "that I hear he is a quiet, decent peddler, and never concerns himself with what don't belong to him. That is the right way. While he does so, he will serve me. Tell him so, and clear out!"

"But, would you serve him, after such an insulting reception?"

"What else could I do, if I wished to keep my head on my shoulders? Besides, I never saw him again. My business was with the old eunuch, who had more wit and wisdom than a score of Mustaphas. With him I got along very well indeed. But now I must tell you of the terrible events of 1808. Alas! Alas! Accursed day! I went to the palace at Seraglio Point, with a heavy bill—about 30,000 '*columnars*' (the name by which the Spanish dollar was known). The old eunuch was in excellent humor. His secretaries copied off the bill, possibly doubling the amount, for they all lived luxuriously by stealing: and the money was counted out and ranged in different coins, gold and silver; and I was about to call my servants to sack it up and carry it to my room in Vezir Khan; when a strange noise, a rush of men, a clang of arms! Confusion and tumult changed us all to stone! The servants went wild. The eunuch sank down in despair. 'It's all up with us, Cheliby Yorgaki! We shall never see another day!' 'But let us flee! let us flee!' I said; 'let the money go, and let us escape!' 'Well, escape then!' said he, 'The moment you leave this room, you will be killed!' And then suddenly he thought of his master, the sultan, and rushed away.

"Now I must tell you what had happened. There was, at Adrianople, a pasha, general of the army of Rumelia, who greatly loved Selim, and resolved to reinstate him upon the throne. This Bairactar Pasha was a very able and fearless man. He laid a conspiracy, with three thousand faithful soldiers, to surprise the palace; and this was what had taken place."

"But would not the Janizaries immediately overcome so small a number?" I asked.

"The Janizaries were devils," he replied. "They, as well as the people, had become disgusted with the miserable Mustapha, and without doubt he had secretly gained over some of their chiefs. But I must continue my story. The eunuch having fled, and the servants having all disappeared from the first, I was there alone with my worthless gold, every para of which I would give for a safe exit. But soon the noise ceased. Bairactar Pasha was caught in a trap. The wretch Mustapha sent to him, 'Don't shed blood! Give me half an hour to collect my household and retire; and the palace shall be given up in peace.' This arrested for a

SULTAN SELIM BEATEN TO DEATH.

few minutes the possession of the palace. The crafty Mustapha ordered his eunuchs instantly to kill the two only heirs to the Ottoman throne, Selim III., held in the palace as prisoner, and young Mahmûd.

"Selim was cruelly beaten to death with clubs, no one daring to give him a mortal blow.

"Mahmûd's faithful nurse (once a nurse always a nurse, in the imperial family), at the first sign of trouble, instinctively fearing danger to him, had persuaded him to crawl into an old oven in one of the outbuildings, and to answer no voice but hers; and she then successfully concealed herself. Neither of them could be found. Mustapha had only insured his own ruin.

"The body of the murdered Selim was dragged into the garden, and a rug thrown over it. The pasha soon came and threw himself upon it, and wept and groaned like a lion. I could see him, through the lattices of the window; and I knew it must be the body of Selim. I dared not fly. I awaited death there. Springing from his place of lamentation the pasha cried out, 'Let no one escape!' The palace was soon in his hands. Many were put to death. Mustapha was put under guard, and Mahmûd sought for everywhere. Great rewards were offered for his discovery; and this search caused a long delay. Evening drew on. I could no longer endure my position. I left the money, except what gold I could easily carry about my person, and I sallied out into a long corridor, and met a person of Bairactar's force, who knew me. 'Yorgaki! why are you here?' I told him, and putting some gold in his hand, begged him to get me out. 'But the Janizaries will kill you.' 'Let me out by the little gate, close to the water, and I will risk it.' So, after a while, he found means to let me out, telling me I should undoubtedly be killed.

"I crept to that great boat-house which still exists close by the sea-wall, waked the boatmen, and rowed off to Halki (one of the Princes' Islands), where my family was staying at the Convent of the Holy Trinity."

"I have been there," said I. "Do the same buildings now remain?"

"Precisely," he said; "and I had some rooms on the high wall nearest to the gate. My family and friends were in great distress about me, knowing of the revolution, and that I had gone to the palace."

"Ah!" said the wife, "what a night was that! I never wish to think of it. But I have passed many worse nights, since; although, when you came home safe, I declared I should never be unhappy again in this life."

"The following day nobody dared to move. Nobody left the island for the city, and nobody came to it. But in the evening, one or two boats came, and said Mahmûd had been proclaimed by public cries sultan, *vice* Mustapha dethroned. When the old nurse, at length, had become convinced that he was wanted for life and not for death, she brought him forth from the oven where he had suffered not a little, and so he was proclaimed sultan; and the miserable Mustapha, not long after, ended his days by poison.

"I did not mind much the loss of the money. I had still enough to live upon—something in foreign funds, this house, another in Beshiktash, and the most splendid of all in the Fanar. I had escaped with my life. But, that very night, as the day was about to dawn, I heard a heavy knock at the convent gate. I felt it was my death knell! I opened the window, and asked from the wall 'who was there?' 'Spahis from the palace.' 'What do you want?' 'Cheliby Yorgaki.' 'Wait a little, and I will come.' I hastily received the last sacrament, and left my poor wife, more dead than alive, on the stones of the pavement inside the gate. The new officers and members of the household wanted me to divide the spoils. Many had been put to death. Many had been condemned to exile. Confiscation of goods and properties had thrown together a vast amount to be divided, and they thought I could tell the value of every thing at a glance."

His description of this part of his work was too long to repeat. He had five accumulations of spoils to subdivide to individuals, and, at the close, he did not doubt he should be bowstrung. The last heap was close by the place where palace criminals or supernumeraries were disposed of. All day long he was nearing the terrible spot. He saw the poor eunuch with whom, forty-eight hours before, he had been so happily settling accounts, borne along by the executioners to that accursed place.

"'Ah!' said he, 'Cheliby Yorgaki, how bitter is the last hour of life!' and tears rolled down his great black cheeks. He had always treated me well," said Yorgaki, "and I felt that I could almost die for him; but in a few minutes his body rolled down that plank-shoot into the water; and I knew that soon mine would follow. Did you ever visit that place?"

"Yes," I replied, "the water is deep and the current strong, and whatever falls there goes out into the Marmora."

"Well," he added, "I at length came to that last lot of the confiscated goods. I had learned what pasha presided over it, I knew him as a connoisseur of diamonds; and, in a division of some diamonds, I ventured to propose one for that pasha. It was agreed to, and I was the bearer of it. 'You have done well, Yorgaki, to bring me this,' said he; and as he turned it to the light, he descanted upon its beauties. I then besought him to intercede for me. 'Nobody thinks of hurting you, Yorgaki, we all know you.' 'That is the feast you prepare for the dying,' said I; but he only replied, 'Finish your work, and you shall see.' With trembling heart I finished; and he then said, seeing how exhausted I was—for I had neither eaten bread nor drank water all day long—'My lamb, don't die just yet! You are now to be rewarded. There are three confiscated houses, of which you shall have your choice.' He sent me away with a fluttering heart, that perhaps after all, my life would still be spared! When I turned my back upon that throat of hell, I began to hope. My feet would hardly carry me to the place indicated, which was not far from the boat-place. I protested that I would not take the offered gift. 'But,' said the pasha, 'the house we have selected for you has a fine garden, excellent water, a pleasant view, and is moreover a safe place.'* 'I doubt not in the least its value,' I replied, 'but I never give nor take gifts. In doing so I only follow the footsteps of my father.' 'Then go home, for a fool as you are! You have done our work well, and we wanted to reward you well.'

"I departed for my boat. I drank at a fountain by the way. I bought some bread, cheese, and a bottle of wine. As my boat came round Seraglio Point, and the pure fresh breeze came into my soul, I said 'Glory to thee, O God!' I then felt that I must eat instantly or perish. Never before, never since, did I make such a meal as that! The

---

* I had heard this word *safe* often used in describing or commending places; and I asked a native gentleman what the precise idea was. "A place that is not *overlooked by another*, not easily *accessible to thieves*, and is *in a good neighborhood*, we call *safe*. What would you have us call it?" These are the first things to look after, the next is the water.

evening was setting in, the breeze directly ahead, and it was a long row of three hours to Halki. I laid down and slept profoundly, while this *side-rib* (wife) was weeping over my death. As we approached within hail of the island, my boatmen raised Yorgaki's boat-cry; and I awoke to hear it answered with cheer upon cheer from the island; and I was carried up to the convent with shoutings and rejoicings! The next day, I sacrificed some sheep for a feast and a thank-offering. In a few days the new Sultan Mahmûd called me, spoke very kindly to me, and reinstated me in my office. He assured me no one should ever take it from me. He had much of the kindness of Selim. But he had a terrible force of character; and *such an eye* that I always felt overawed. He struggled with great misfortunes all his days. May his son have a kinder fate!"

CHAPTER IX.

HALET EFFENDI AND JANIZARIES.

"My greatest troubles began with the Greek Revolution, although I had no part in it whatever. I was an officer of the palace. My sovereign trusted me, and I was loyal to him. My people sometimes accused me of being only half a Greek, because I am of Armenian parentage."

"Are you then an Armenian by race?" said I.

"Yes. There are a few of our sort, in the interior, who have always belonged to the Greek Church. We have nearly lost the Armenian language, and we more or less intermarry with Greeks; but we are called by the Armenians Hi-Herome-Armeno-Greeks.

"When hostilities had commenced, and there had been much bloody work, the Janizaries began to seize and put to death suspected Greeks, in the most barbarous manner. Then Sultan Mahmûd called me, and told me that I must keep within my own premises for a time, unless I had a special and responsible Moslem guard, which, when necessary for my business in the palace, would be furnished me. On no account should I go abroad in any other way. For although he had given special instructions that I was not to be molested by any one, the Janizaries would rob and kill without his knowledge. He said to me, moreover, that any body taking refuge in my house at Bebek, whom I wished to protect, should be safe. He would give the most special instructions that my house should not be visited.

"For a while, I got along very well for such times. There were occasional outbreaks; but, after all, the Janizaries feared Mahmûd as much as he feared them. Revolt against him was out of the question, for they had no one to put upon the throne except a little boy. There was a certain Halet Effendi, the worst man the Osmanlees ever produced, who was the leader of the Janizaries, and who had obtained a wonderful power over the sultan. He feared nothing, had no conscience, no feelings of mercy, delighted in blood and confiscation, and committed enormous outrages never known to the sultan. The whole world feared him far more than they feared the sultan. He was passing through Beshiktash one day, in Ramazan, and he saw, or pretended he saw, a poor Turk smoking; which is forbidden during the fast. He had him seized, and his head cut off upon the spot. A label was put upon the body, 'Sent to Gehenna by Halet Effendi, for smoking in Ramazan. Take warning, O ye faithful!'

"One day there came a messenger to me, saying, Halet Effendi wants you at the kiosk, the Kiosk of Conference, at the foot of our street. I

HALET'S GRIM HUMOR. 117

knew my fate. I should go from thence to the Tower of Oblivion, just above us, and all my goods would be seized. He had recently committed just such outrages. I hastily partook of the sacrament; we all asked pardon and granted forgiveness; and I went down to meet the monster.

"He seemed to be in very good humor. He received me with mockery and jokes; but they all had a sinister meaning. 'You are in excellent health Cheliby Yorgaki! I am glad to see you looking so well. They say you are very rich, that you have oceans of money; don't know what to do with it. Well, if you like, we shall help you a little. You are a man that values life, Yorgaki! And the sultan has insured your safety. He has put you under my keeping. I shall look out for you. Don't be afraid, but I'll keep watch upon you. I shall send some of my men with you, and what they bring will show how much you value your life.' Then, whispering to one of his men, he sent him, with a dozen others, up to this house with me.

"I knew the man. I threw open every thing in the house, but my wife's room; and the rascals had decency enough to make no allusions to that.

"They took down all my rich curtains and embroidered sofa coverings, all my sweetmeat and coffee service, my expensive chibūks, and all the silks, satins, and embroidered work which I had for the palace. They made up twelve packages, worth many thousands of dollars; and departed, leaving my house stripped of all its luxuries.

"I knew the insatiate monster would come again, and would not depart empty without blood. So I filled up again, and he made me a second and a third visit before peace was made. I lost also my beautiful winter house in the Fanar, and my house in Beshiktash. Both were burned, with all their contents. But these were not our greatest troubles. Our lives were safe, while our enemies perished. Every one of them came to a miserable end."

"Ah!" said Madam Yorgaki, "our loss of property has been great, but it was nothing compared with our other griefs!"

"And what were they!" said Mrs. H. to her. "You have told me that God never gave you children, and you have had no family griefs, I am sure."

She buried her face in her hands, and said, sobbingly, "We had an adopted daughter; but he must tell you the story, I can not!"

The oriental world holds in readiness a large supply of tears for every suitable occasion; but we felt that the grief of the dear old lady was unfeigned. She was in feeble health, her constitution broken down; and she could never speak of that daughter without tears, and often not without sobs.

He began, "I went one morning early to the church, where I was often the first to arrive. I found a beautiful and singular looking package on the door-sill. I took it up to examine it, and behold there was a sleeping infant within, very nicely dressed. I carried it home, and said to my wife, 'Has not God given us our heart's desire? See what I have found at the church door!' She pronounced the child a perfect beauty, and joyfully agreed to call the priest, and consult about the adoption.

"Nothing ever came to light about its parentage, and it seemed not only to us, but to all our friends, like a gift from heaven. We celebrated its baptism, and gave it the name of good omen, Maria. Every body gave us their felicitations, and could hardly be persuaded it was not our own child. It was so beautiful and lovely, it was every body's favorite."

"But you don't tell," interrupted the wife with flowing tears, "how intelligent the child was. At three years old, it was more forward than other children at six."

"Don't interrupt me, wife, and I will tell it all! As the child grew up, and promised to be a maiden of rare beauty, we resolved to educate her, and marry her into some position higher than mercantile life. She was trained in music and dancing, was taught the French and Italian languages, and ancient Greek. If we thought her the most beautiful girl in Constantinople, we resolved that she should be the best educated. All were proud of her attainments in ancient Greek, and none but educated men could converse with her about the works of our immortal ancestors."

"Of what use was it all?" broke in the wife;

"how we erred, how we erred! We meant it for good, but God mixed us a bitter cup for our sins. We sought things too high, and God gave us things too low."

The old man stopped, and seemed for a while to forget himself in thought. He then resumed. "The full time had come when she should be affianced. We looked around among all the young men who were not engaged, and we found M. C. of the Russian embassy; an under dragoman, but sure to rise and come into the first society. His mother was delighted with our proposal, she knew our daughter, and said that of all the maidens in the city of Constantinople there was no one she would so gladly choose. We arranged all the terms, and agreed upon the dowry without any difficulty; for, as we had only one daughter, we intended to be liberal with her."

"But did the young people know each other, and did they agree to your choice?"

"It would have been highly improper to ask them!" said the good old lady, with spirit.

We saw a discussion would follow; and we begged our friend to proceed.

"When the time for the wedding came, I determined that as I should make only one, it should in every respect be worthy of us. All those cooking ranges, the remains of which are still seen along the wall of the inner court, were made expressly for that occasion. I employed twelve of the most skilful cooks I could find, and, that no nation might complain of not finding its own choicest food, my cooks were Armenians, Greeks and Turks.

"The festival lasted a week. On Monday, I invited the boatmen of this village and neighborhood. The outer court was covered with an awning. The food was abundant, the wine flowed, and the guests were joyous. Tuesday, I had another rank of guests; and so on, during the week. Sunday evening, there was a great assembly. No rayah merchant ever had a more brilliant one. The prelates of our church, merchants and bankers of different nationalities and religions, and members of the Turkish government were there. We had the choicest music of the capital, and the greatest delicacies and luxuries of the table.

"At a late hour of the evening, the bishop called for the bridegroom and the bride, in order to perform the final ceremony. The service proceeded to that point where the magnificent cushion, prepared and embroidered expressly for the occasion, was brought in for the affianced to kneel upon, and be made man and wife. The bridegroom was brought in by his fellows; but the bride could not be found. This often happens out of modesty. The maiden hides herself, and must be searched for. This occasioned only amusement at first; but as the delay was long, the guests lost their good-humor, and all began to search for her. As there are some twenty closets in the house, and many outbuildings and terraces, no one, for a long time, was alarmed, but much provoked; and the search extended to the neighbor's houses.

"I was getting very impatient and angry, when my wife called to me, and said 'Search no more! Come to my room!' She there showed me that all her jewels which she was not wearing, and various choice and valuable articles, were gone! My wife threw herself upon the sofa in despair. I could not yet believe that our beloved, idolized, beautiful daughter could prove herself to be so base a traitor! I went down, with some friends, to the boat scala, and inquired if any one had left in a boat? I was answered, 'People have been going and coming all the evening.' But one man said, 'Yani, the Sciote, left in an island boat, with a woman closely veiled.'

"Then I comprehended the whole! I had known the wretch hanging about our village, and our daughter had eloped with him, and plunged us into wretchedness and woe! The assembly broke up. The chief of the police was informed. Couriers were dispatched to all the landing places; and the next morning, the guilty pair were arrested at Halki, just in time to prevent their marriage.

"Our daughter was sent back to us, but we would not receive her. She had disgraced us. She had made us the talk of the whole city. She had plotted against us. She had stolen from us, in return for all we had lavished upon her. She had also disgraced and ruined the young man to whom she was affianced. He never married, never showed

The Sad Results. 123

any ambition to rise, and became a misanthrope. And we, we were ruined. All the joy of life fled with that black night. My wife has been an invalid from that time to this. Was ever a family visited with grief like this? Every thing else was transient, this never passes away."

The old people wept, and we could not restrain our tears.

"What became of the poor girl?" said Mrs. H.

"A neighbor down street took her in. One of our own servants had helped the culprits to a secret correspondence, and had conveyed the letters back and forth. She had fixed more than one time for the elopement and failed, and then accomplished it at the last moment.

"She came again, and threw herself at our feet —confessed her great sin against us, and entreated that we would take her back again, if only to be a servant. We forbade her coming again, and ordered the doorkeeper never to admit her!

"Once she threw herself at my feet in the street; but when I threatened to call a policeman, she went away, and we have never seen her since.

"The family that took her in married her, after a while, to a grocer at Hissar. She has six children, has never had a servant, has to do all her work, and to work like a slave from morning to night. She has no associates but people of that low class."

"But would you not have been happier," said Mrs. H., to the weeping mother, "had you taken her back? Perhaps she truly repented; and I think her faithful, toilsome life shows that she was not a wicked girl, not wholly lost!"

"We should have been a great deal happier," was the united confession; "but we could not do it. We should have entirely sacrificed our own standing had we done it. She had to bear her part of the evil consequences of her own doings, and it was much lighter than ours."

"What became of the Sciote who carried her off?"

"He was kept in prison for a while and then banished from Constantinople and vicinity under menace of a heavy punishment should he be caught here again. He had friends who bought him off. Never expect justice in such cases! It was after all this that we lost our three houses: one in the city, one at Beshiktask, and one at Therapia. Our city house was princely. It was destroyed in a fire that broke out so near that nothing was saved, I being away at the time, and only a watchman in the house. I expended eighteen thousand piastres upon the reception room, when three piastres paid for a day's work of carpenter, mason, or painter. The ceiling represented the heavens, blue with silver stars; and there was richly carved wood-work which our artisans now can not make. I do not speak of these losses as griefs. Others have them to bear as well as we. But our own beloved Maria has brought the cloud over our old age!"

It was an oppressively sad narration. I would not have given it, except that it illustrates oriental

THE ENGLISHMAN'S NOVEL. 125

life, and shows that its boasted wisdom, in taking the management of the marriage relation entirely out of the hands of inexperienced youth, and committing it entirely to wise and unselfish mothers, does not always work to perfection.*

HALET EFFENDI.

As he has entered into this narration, I will here dispose of him. I crossed his destructive path at another point. In 1859 I purchased the first site for Robert College. The deeds were accompanied by a special firman of Sultan Mahmûd, indicating, in reserved terms, some previous *taking off* and *confiscation*, which led to an inquiry.

The land which was thus deeded, had belonged to a Jewish banker of vast wealth, and a bold successful *operator* with the Turkish officials in government loans. The Jewish banker has this

---

* A novel called "The Armenian" was written by an Englishman, Macfarlane by name, founded on the events above narrated. It is full of stupidities, crudities, and strange misapprehensions of oriental life. The same Macfarlane, having grown old in taking imagination for fact, came to Constantinople and wrote the book called "Turkey and its Destinies." He was sent, according to his statement, to write down Turkey; and he was not expected to be particular as to truth. While writing the book, he undertook to impose himself upon absolute strangers to whom he could obtain an introduction, and he made himself so excessively disagreeable that I think he was turned out of every house after a little experience of him. There is this general truth in the book, that Turkey was in a bad way; but the facts by which he sustains the position are largely fabrications, and some of them very stupid and absurd.

pre-eminence of position, that every Israelite will loan him, in case of need, every cent in his power. The poor and the rich alike will help him to the utmost of their ability, knowing that he will always keep faith with them. In any great operation, the Jewish banker of distinction has his entire people to back him. In this way, the banker S. had prospered and became great. He was also of "the straitest sect of the Pharisees." A few young Jews had professed Christianity; and, according to the account given me, which I can not vouch for, were baptized, half of them into the Armenian Church, and half into the Greek, the design being to secure a better protection by the united influence of the two communities.

The banker S. resolved upon the destruction of every one of these converts. He was much too sagacious to attack them on the ground of their faith. They were falsely accused of crimes, and, by suborned witnesses, Jewish, Christian, Moslem, they were speedily delivered over to cruel punishments. Patriarchs and ambassadors interfered, and they were released. After a short time, they would be arrested again, and the same experience gone over with. Two of them fled to the Jesuit College of St. Benoit, Galata, and entering the Catholic church, were safe. Two of them died in consequence of their treatment, the rest fled to Smyrna; but the Jewish community there was in the hands of their enemy; and finally they fled to Athens, where he could no longer reach them.

SPLENDID LIFE AT HOME. 127

This banker always appeared abroad like a poor humble Jew of the lowest class. His "Jewish gabardine" was always old, his turban old and soiled, his shoes about *to depart;* and, with a shuffling gait, he would slip slyly into his house on the Bosphorus, when he returned at night from the city. Once within, he threw off this old array, was clothed "in purple and fine linen," and was treated by his household and obsequious servants with all the deference ever granted to despots.

His house was a large wooden structure, so built as to appear like two houses, and the halves were daubed with different colors. I supposed, myself, the building was for two houses, until I entered it. Within, the scene changed like magic. Wealth, luxury, magnificence, saluted you in surprise. I once visited the son of this man, in the same house, and he received me *in state*. The array of reverence that stood around him was comical in the extreme, and produced an impression far different from the one intended. In his boyhood he had learned it from his father, and had not sense enough to unlearn it.

Halet Effendi had been a willing instrument of the banker S. in persecuting the Jewish converts. His insatiate greed made him a terrible force for any one's use, who would *pay*. He fixed his eye upon the wealth of this Jew, and resolved to have it. His operations with the government, whether honest or not, were a ground for accusation and condemnation, without a trial.

One evening, when the banker had returned from the city, and doffed his gabardine for rich apparel, in the same room where I saw his son, and doubtless in the same magnificence, a servant announced three Turks at the gate. "Are they gentlemen, or common fellows?" "Gentlemen, your Highness." "Then show them up." They requested a private interview; and supposing them to be government agents after a loan, or something of that nature, he sent away his servants without suspicion. They must have strangely deceived him, and sprung upon him so suddenly that no cry was heard. They departed quietly; and when his servants went uncalled, and wondering at the silence, they found him bowstrung, and dead upon his sofa. Amid the consternation and woe that followed, the family had presence of mind enough to collect their jewels and flee. Aside from this, all his estates, loans, moneys, goods, and chattels were seized and confiscated.

But Halet Effendi had filled up the measure of his iniquities. Mahmûd at length became aware of his atrocities, and that his zeal for the government only covered up a coarse bloody greed. He instantly banished him to Brusa.

As soon as he was away from the capital, the revelation of his iniquities filled Mahmûd with rage. He had given him a "*Birat*," diploma, that he would never sign his death-warrant; but notwithstanding this, he sent an executioner to cut off his head immediately, with only time enough for an ablution and a prayer. I have conversed with persons in Brusa who remembered well Halet Effendi and the manner of his death. Although described with some variations, all the legends substantially agreed. The executioner appeared, and summoned him to prepare for death. "You can't deceive me," replied Halet, taking from his bosom the *birat* and pointing to the sultan's own signature.

The executioner then took from his bosom the wrathful order, and bade him read and mark the date. He made the lowest *salam* of reverence to the imperial document—read it with careful scrutiny, and said, "One ablution and prayer! It is all I ask! A thousand years to the sultan my master?"

After carefully performing his ablution according to the minutest demand of the ritual, and saying his last prayer with composure, he returned to the sofa, laid aside his turban, bent forward his head, and, with a firm voice, exclaimed, "STRIKE WITH POWER?" In a moment his life-blood was gushing out upon the floor. Thus the banker and the favorite, each guilty in his own way, came to a sudden, disgraceful end. "A man that doeth violence to the blood of any person, shall flee to the pit. Let no man stay him."

With the execution of Halet Effendi, and the destruction of the Janizaries, the long age of irresponsible shedding of blood came to an end. Since then, the executions in the Ottoman empire have been comparatively few, considering the low state of civilization and morals. Life has grown safer, and government more inefficient. The temperance of the people saves them from many temptations to crimes of violence. Oriental fatalism produces a quietude not easily disturbed. The simplicity of life, outside of the cities, reduces human wants to a small list. However these and kindred causes may have co-operated, the termination of the Janizary period marked a great era in Ottoman history. No second Halet Effendi has risen since, or can rise again. Government and people, when the passions are not roused by war, have grown milder, and no one who has long resided in Turkey can deny a general advance in civilization. Islam has a capacity of progress up to a certain point, and there it stops. It has no high ideal to work by, or to draw inspiration from.

CHAPTER X.

ANATHEMA AND ITS RESULTS.

Another step was now to be taken in the contest for religious freedom.

We have before referred to that peculiar constitution of the Turkish government by which, from the times of Mehmet the conqueror, the patriarchs of the Christian sects became high officers of the empire, and had great civil as well as political power over their people. A brief note, with the patriarch's official seal stamped upon it, would send any one of his people into exile or to prison without any inquiry whatever into the truth of the alleged reason. This gave them great power for good, but also for evil. It gave them official access, at any time, to any member of the Divan; and their views were received as authoritative with respect to their own people. They had the power to bind and to loose on earth as well as in in heaven. They had both spiritual and temporal power to such a degree, that the office was sought by all ambitious prelates, and immense sums were expended to attain it. Then, when attained, bishoprics must be sold to repay the bankers who had advanced the money; and the bishops must get it from their flocks. Simony became universal. The Hatti Scheriff was designed to limit this power, by assigning salaries. The people also had come into power, and the financial evils of the system were in the process of correction. But the spiritual power was intact, and "the great anathema" still carried all its civil penalties into every interest of social life.

As the evangelic movement was plainly increasing, not only in the capital, but in other cities, and as the clergy in immense majority refused to listen to any proposals of reform, there was in their view but one course left—to try the power of the great anathema, to be uttered with all solemnity upon the condemned persons, by name, in the patriarchal church, and afterwards by all the bishops in their dioceses.

Many recanted their errors, and escaped the impending doom. About thirty of those best known as advocates of church reform, and a return to the simplicity of the Gospel, were selected, and with great solemnity were pronounced, on the 12th of January, 1846, accursed of God and man. Had the penalty been merely spiritual, it would not have been minded at all. But, in the first place, every anathematized person was cast out of his *guild*, or trades' union, and his permit to prosecute his industry or mode of living, whatever it was, was taken from him. Secondly, all debtors were released from obligation to pay any debt to one so anathematized. Thirdly, all creditors were re-

FORMATION OF EVANGELICAL CHURCH. 133

quired to enforce immediate payment. Fourthly, all persons were forbidden to transact any business with them, or to return their salutations. Fifthly, they were all immediately driven from their homes and shops into the street. Of course, under all these penalties, many were thrown into prison, and subjected to severe sufferings.

The hope had been, *reform within the church.* The patriarch and his advisers forced the formation of a new church, called the "Evangelical Church of the Armenians." It was not a matter left at all to their choice, but was forced upon them.

Being cut off from the old Gregorian Church, and the Turkish law requiring every man to belong to some organization, their new position, as an evangelical church, may be said to have resulted from the combined action of the Armenian ecclesiastics and the Turkish law. The necessity was regretted by all, because it would for a time arrest the movement within the church. The energetic influence of Sir Stratford Canning softened the violence of the persecution. Mob violence, bastinado, imprisonment, bonds, loss of all things, had to be borne for a time, and they were nobly and quietly borne.

A firman reinvesting them with all the rights of citizens was demanded by the ambassador. Papal and Russian influences strongly opposed it, but finally Lord Cowley, during a visit home of Sir Stratford, obtained it. It was a grand stride forward for freedom of conscience. Given in 1847, it was repeated in 1850 and 1853. So strong were the influences against it, Armenian, Greek, Roman Catholic, and Russian, that the Turkish government itself often faltered in its course. So far as it understood the case, its sympathies were with the persecuted; its interests were with the all-powerful persecutors. The successive firmans, however, braced up the Turkish officials, and made known to the empire at large that religious liberty must be respected.

The Hatti Scheriff of Gûl Hané, the martyrdom of Carabet, and the royal authority organizing the Evangelical Armenian Church, were three distinct steps in the conflict for freedom. Each accomplished its part, and prepared for the next move. Those who demand that every thing should be perfect in order to escape their condemnation, will see no meaning, and find no value, in any or all of these movements; but such persons will not be found among those who have had any personal knowledge of them, or any sympathy with the cause promoted by them.

One result, unlooked for by the patriarch, was, that young men, thrown out of employment by the anathema, joined the seminary, and formed a very choice body of students whose influence has been great and good. In order to stop this, he took advantage of an old order that no one should change his residence without a permit from his head man. As this would always be an Armenian, who would be instructed not to give it, the influx of students would be arrested.

Baron Muggerdich, who had become the Secretary of the Evangelical Union, already referred to, had remained for some time undisturbed in his business. He was at length closed out, and his goods confiscated.

Taking all the archives of the Union, which had in the meantime greatly increased in value and importance, he packed them in his bed, and putting all into an enormous sack, he came to Bebek, and was passing up the street when the priest, on watch, saw him. He called out to him to stop! but Baron Muggerdich marched straight ahead, as though he were deaf. The priest ran and threw the sack from the back of the porter, and then went for a policeman, who took possession. In the meantime B. M. was safe in the seminary, where consternation reigned, when it was found *those archives* would go direct to the patriarch! There was not a moment to be lost. I bought the bed, and paid for it at its full value; and when the owner remarked, "If you recover it we can trade back," I replied, "No! If I get it, it shall be mine forever; if I lose it it shall be my loss forever." I then hastened to the scala, and claimed it as my property. The priest had it in the boat, and was just putting off, declaring that by official order it must go to the patriarch; and the captain of the village guard-house so decided. I turned to him, and said, "That is my property, and I will require every thread of it from you, and not from the priest! You may sink it or burn it, or give it away, but I will require it of you alone, and before that can reach the patriarch, I will accuse you to the American ambassador. I commit it to your keeping!" I then left him, but he called me back, ordered the sack to be carried into the guard-house, and every knot of the rope to be covered with sealing wax, and sealed with four seals; his own, the priest's, the village head man's, and my own. He then piously added, "Now, O Lord, nobody touches this till my superior orders it! This case must be decided by the pasha at Chinili Kiosk." The next day, the captain, the priest, the head man, and the American dragoman appeared before his excellency. The dragoman stated the case, and the pasha, having his mind perfectly clear, did not wait for the other side, but turning fiercely upon the priest, he poured upon him such mild epithets as the Turkish language is very rich in, the mildest of which would be "pig," "ghiaour," "dog"—and asked him if he couldn't find better work in his priestly duties than pushing loads off the backs of porters, and raising quarrels with peaceable foreigners! "Aman! Aman!" said the priest. "'Aman, aman,' won't do now!" said the pasha. "Do you, captain, and the head man, and this jenabet of a priest, accompany the dragoman with the goods to Mr. Hamlin's house. See it there opened, and if he declares that every article is there, then priest and head man shall make an apology, and beg him to pass it over; and if he shall do so, give me notice, captain, and the case is finished. *Haideh git!*" The priest objected that he had duties at the patriarchate; the dragoman kindly interceded for him, and he was excused. The poor priest was not to blame for performing the duty imposed upon him by his superior. He was, on the whole, friendly to me, and I would have regretted the humiliation.

When the cavalcade returned from the judgment hall, the idlers of the village were all assembled at the coffee-shop near the guard-house. The captain beckoned to a porter, and all entered the guard-house. As they came out, and took the street to the seminary, the idlers cried out, "Alas! Alas! The glass-eyed (a kind reference to my spectacles), the glass-eyed has triumphed over our stupid priest!" And, attributing it all to his stupidity, they used up such epithets as the pasha had left them!

The great package was opened, and every thing spread out. "Effendim," said the head man to the captain, "what are all these papers? It was *a bed*, and not papers, that was claimed; and I will take possession of these." "Eshekimuz!" said the captain, "O our donkey! was it not the bed and *every thing in it?* If there were diamonds there, they belong to him! Is every thing here, cheliby?" said the captain. "Every thing," I replied. "Now make your apology," said the captain to the head man, "and let your words be sweet!" The head man stepped forward, and acquitted himself to admiration. I am sure, had I been in his place, I could not have done so well. We all separated the best of friends. This was the affair of *Muggerdich and his bed.* The articles purchased were all of home manufacture, and outlasted all other articles of their kind in the household; or else, from their historic character, they were better used. After this event, the persecuted became a separate community, and the archives could no longer be sought or obtained by patriarchal power, nor could they endanger any one's interest. There were seven years between the two rescues, and in that space of time great changes had occurred in preparation for others still greater.

During the whole of 1846 and 1847, persecution in manifold ways was very busy, and the friends of truth and progress had little rest. Word came from Adabazar that the anathema had swept every thing before it there. A few, who refused to yield to the requirements of the clergy, and curse the evangelical party and demand its extinction, had been compelled to flee to the Turkish quarter to escape the mob. Three of their houses had been nearly destroyed. That is, the walls of sun-dried bricks had been well driven in. The mob, getting some sticks of timber, and using them as battering-rams, soon breached the walls, and every thing within was destroyed. The fourth house was a singularly solid thing, which put an unlooked-for end to their sport. For it was the last house in the Armenian part of the city, and then came the Turkish. While the roaring mob was delayed by the solidity of this house, built of timber dowelled together, the Turkish women, with their shrill and piercing voices, cried out from their verandahs, "See what the ghiaours are doing to the Prots, because they don't worship pictures! Well! *we* don't worship pictures! Next they'll be after us! Come, let every woman take a bean-pole and drive them away!" With incredible swiftness the word travelled from street to street, and hundreds of screaming, yashmacked women, every one armed with a long stick, bore down upon the mob, and dispersed it like fog before a wind!

Then their lords poured out, with yatagan and pistol, and not an Armenian head was to be seen! The tables were turned upon them, with swift amazement.

There being, at the time we heard of this, a vacation in the seminary, and the other missionaries being overburdened with work, I was sent to Adabazar to ascertain the state of things, provide for any in absolute want, and report. I went first to Nicomedia, about sixty miles from the city, and having there obtained all needed information, I proceeded nine hours farther (twenty-seven miles) to Adabazar, so as to arrive in the dusk of the evening, and be unnoticed. I entered the Turkish quarter, and found, as directed, the khan or hotel of Hassan Agha. It was a rough wooden building, the lower story having a large coffee-shop and some storage rooms, and the upper story, empty rooms to let. The villagers of the fertile plain of the Sangarius, upon which Adabazar is built, come here to bring their produce and make their exchanges; and mainly for their accommodation the khan was built.

I found the refugees in these rooms. They were driven from home, anathematized; their goods, whatever they had, destroyed; their permits taken from them; they were outlaws. Hassan was a rough but kind-hearted Turk, of genuine Mussulman piety. From his utter abhorrence of idolatry, into which he supposed all Christianity had fallen, he heartily despised it, and blessed God and the prophet that he was enlightened into the true way.

Finding, to his astonishment, Christians who were persecuted for rejecting this idolatry, he gave them a refuge, and for some weeks had supplied their wants, never expecting or wishing a cent of recompense. Being of the dominant race, he could guard his establishment against the intrusion of enemies, and so long as the refugees did not venture out, they were safe. In the darkness of night, they could cautiously visit some of their friends.

For twelve cents per day each, he agreed to provide the refugees with all they would need until their case should be decided upon by the government.

I kept concealed during the day, as it was not

MIDNIGHT MEETINGS. 141

desirable to have it known that a missionary was in the city. The whole Armenian quarter would be in a blaze of excitement immediately. At night, I held a meeting in that very house which the mob had essayed in vain, and from which they had fled in base retreat. Some twenty persons or more were present, Nicodemuses, who came by night. I resolved to wait for one more night meeting. In the profound stillness of a Turkish city by night, no light in any street, all asleep by eight or nine o'clock—eight in winter, nine in summer—you can go, with a guide, unobserved. You will encounter here and there a sentinel who will stop you. My guide simply said, "Hakem bashi Hamlin, Stambuldan." "May God grant healing!" said the pious watchman; and on we passed.

I accomplished my object of seeing certain individuals, chiefly Steppan Erzingiatsi; but was kindly advised to hasten my departure, and not wait till morning light. All the city knew I was there, and there would be a general rising of the Armenians in the morning. Hassan knew it all, and had engaged the horses for three o'clock in the morning. I believed they were frightened, and did not feel concerned. The scenes through which they had passed had filled all minds with terror.

I resolved, however, to wake and leave at three in the morning!

I slept a little past the time, awoke, dressed hastily, and opened the window. The stars were hardly dimmed by the approaching light; but there was a low and alarming hum of suppressed voices in the street below. I listened with beating heart. There could be no question of the fact. On the other side it was the same. Already hundreds were assembled, and the occasional clink of steel showed they were armed with spades and hoes, or other implements of industry. It is not a pleasant thing to wake up from profound and peaceful sleep to such realities. There is nothing more reckless, cruel, and dangerous than a fanatical mob, even though the individuals may be, as in this case, for the most part kind-hearted and honest men.

I went below, and was glad to find Hassan himself on the ground. I think he must have staid in his coffee-shop during the night. He indignantly refused to go to the governor for a guard; said *he* would take me through that crowd of Christian dogs, and not one should bark!

"Get your breakfast," said he, "if you want any; the horses should have been here half an hour ago!" I had not much appetite just then (so early in the morning), but I drank a cup of bitter coffee; and the horses came. The retinue that came with them would cause a sensation in any other land. It was composed of six tall, swarthy, stalwart Zeibeks. Every man of them seemed to me to be six feet six, and they were armed with a whole battery of pistols and daggers. Hassan mounted the first horse, with a formidable and well-made club secured to his right hand. I mounted next, and the surijie, who must go to Nicomedia to bring back the horses mounted; then the Zeibeks were ranged, three on each side. "Open the gate!" and Hassan's cafégi threw it open, disclosing a compact mass. It was light enough to distinguish lowering and unfriendly countenances; and their long-handled spades were intimations of evil. "Destoor! destoor!" (stand aside!) roared Hassan in no equivocal tones; and we slowly pressed out into the crowd.

Our safety was neither in our number, nor arms, nor prowess, but simply in the fact that the guard were Mussulmans. To attack them would be to arouse instantly the whole Turkish population against the Armenian. There was a real danger that some blow would be struck by the guard, which would rouse the mob to reckless passion. The crowd cursed in Armenian, and the guard, although understanding not a word, answered in no measured terms in Turkish. The scene was unique rather than edifying. A Christian mob of many hundreds. In the midst, a "heretic," to kill whom, that morning, would be doing God service. On each side, a small but most formidable Moslem guard. Both parties cursing; the multitude cursing the heretic, and the guard the multitude! I besought Hassan Agha to stop the invectives of the guard, which he finally did.

About half-way through, a man spat upon the ground, close at my right. It did not seem to me to be a signal, but others followed, and soon all were spitting innocently and energetically upon the ground. The meaning was plain enough, and it was difficult to restrain the guard from striking.

At length, we cleared the multitude, and I breathed freely. The sweet pure breath of the early morning seemed like a special gift of God. I turned to Hassan, and said, "You have saved my life; may God save yours if in danger!" "Koozoom" (my lamb), he replied, "you don't understand these dogs. They are lying in wait for you behind these hedges; and I shall go with you to the river." The natural hedges along the way, thick and entangled, afforded every opportunity; but we saw nobody.

When we reached the river, he said to me, "Now you have an open plain, and your horse is enough for safety. I give you into God's keeping!"—a common but beautiful form of leave-taking—and so we parted.

I had not fully comprehended the spirit in which he had done this, and I offered him a reward, "bakshish." He seemed offended, and refused, saying proudly, "I am a Mussulman! I have not done this for money." On ordinary occasions, nobody is more ready to receive gifts than Mussulmans. Often, you can not satisfy them. The truth is, I was *his guest*. I had eaten with him. He had undertaken the protection of the persecuted, and, in his mind, it was a work of piety and hospitality. It would have ruined the merit of the work, had he then and there received pay. I afterwards sent him a present, which he joyfully received; and I repeatedly *remembered* him, to his great delight. The duties of hospitality are among the most sacred of the oriental world.

The excitement at Adabazar was of good omen. It showed a people with religious convictions. Any thing is better than indifference or cold unbelief. The people there assembled were unenlightened but honest, good men, for the most part. More than thirty years have passed, but some countenances in that crowd are photographed upon memory, both for bad expression and for good.

Three years later, I went, with Dr. Goodell, to assist in ordaining a pastor over an evangelical church which had been formed. Freedom had been secured, and all were quietly working at their various occupations. Still, the chapel, to escape annoyance, was in the Turkish quarter, in a large Turkish house, hired and fitted up as a place of worship.

A large number attended the services. We were not insulted, except by boys, in the streets. The man ordained was the first secretary of the Evangelical Union, the same who was sent into exile in 1839, and whose brother rescued the archives.

The next morning we had a taste of the old sort. Some twenty persons accompanied us from Nicomedia. They had all been thrown into prisons, and all our horses had been taken for government officers passing through; and the people were ordered not to furnish us any more. The clergy and chief men of the Armenians had made over the governor to their purposes.

We went to the konak (official residence), to remonstrate. The governor treated us with scant civility. He said we might go in carts, there were no horses, etc. When you can not persuade a Turkish official to do right, you can often browbeat him; and, if your case is a very plain and clear one, you will generally succeed.

Having tried all mild measures, I went up in front of him, and threatened him with exposure at Constantinople, if he did not immediately give us horses. He yielded with a bad grace, but kept some of our native friends for that day in prison. A formal complaint was made against him, in which many other bad deeds were included; and he was removed from office. Thus, often, an official in the interior will contravene, for a time, the intentions, and indeed the most positive orders, of the central government. This is one of the most damaging weaknesses of the Turkish government. It makes a regular and quiet administration of law impossible, and dependent upon the varying characters and caprices of the officials.

Some years later, I visited Adabazar to aid in dismissing the previous excellent pastor on account of failure of health, and in ordaining his successor, a "prophet *with* honor in his own country," and one of the highly esteemed graduates of the Bebek Seminary.

Our reception was far different from the former

FRIENDLY RECEPTION. 147

one, indicating the advance in public sentiment. There was a cavalcade of some six or eight, pastors and delegates. We arrived late, having been delayed by a heavy shower; and yet there was a large company waiting to receive us before the pastor's house. A hymn of welcome was sung, and there were Turkish boys, who had learned these "Gospel tunes," joining with all their might and main in the ghiaour song!

A church had been erected in the Armenian quarter; the house was crowded to its utmost capacity; the pastors and delegates were saluted in the streets, in the usual manner of oriental politeness; and evidently, the evangelical church had won its recognized position.

I visited my old friend Hassan, and bore him a present from the Rev. Dr. Sprague of Albany, in grateful recognition of his noble conduct in defending a Christian missionary. He was profoundly surprised and delighted. I think, however, it was inexplicable to him, that a distant stranger should either know or care for what he regarded as a mere act of hospitality.

The evangelical church at Adabazar had within it a capacity for growth and development. Having thrown off the superstitions and errors which trammel and cover up the truth, and relying upon the declaration that "one is your Master, even Christ," they went forward fearlessly, as his servants, to do his work. "Self-sustaining, self-governing and self-developing" is the motto which the venerable Secretary of the Board, Rev. Dr. Anderson, had proposed for the guidance of the native churches. This church has nobly followed it; and amidst poverty and oppression, has developed a true Christian civilization.

The pastor is a noble and excellent preacher of the Gospel; a man of thought and power. A system of graded education has been energetically pursued, and the youth are carried along into studies corresponding to those of our high schools. Female education has its due share, and all these influences are extending directly and indirectly into the regions around. This is the only way in which the evangelization of the Eastern world can be accomplished. Central points must be well established, and then left to do their own work.

The Master compared the expansive power of his kingdom to a grain of mustard seed. The origin of this Adabazar movement so beautifully illustrates it, and also gives such an insight into missionary work and experience, that it will be worth narrating. I recur to it also with the more interest, because it was connected, incidentally, with my first missionary tour.

In the summer of 1840, I accompanied Dr. Dwight to Nicomedia. He was already, though but nine years in the field, a veteran traveller and tourist. "Smith and Dwight's Researches" were preliminary to the establishment of the mission. He had gone over the field into the distant interior, and surveyed all its desolations. He was in his element in the field. If somewhat reserved at home, in touring, he was social, genial, and full of good-humor. The discomforts, the strange notions, the unlooked-for obstacles, and the manifold absurdities of the oriental world, as viewed by us, were all met in a spirit that changed dross to gold, and recognized the native gold wherever found. He was a model fellow-traveller. If in another world I should have any touring to do, I would like to do it with him as my guide and teacher. Up to the time of his sudden translation, he was intimately associated with the prosecution of the work in every part of the field and, more than any other one, may be called the father of the Armenian Mission.

Our fellow passengers filled the deck of the vessel which conveyed us to Nicomedia. They were Armenians, Greeks, and Turks. Conversation with them was quite free, and chiefly upon religious topics. It was plain that people, away from the influence of their surroundings, and in the freedom generated by all the circumstances of travel, were not disposed to be suspicious and distant. There were simply good-nature and good fellowship on board. The costumes were strange, and the head-gear extremely *bizarre*, but otherwise I could hardly believe that this was the barbarous East. There were more external acts of politeness than would be met with under similar circumstances at home.

Arrived at Nicomedia, we took a room in a Greek khan, overlooking the city and the gulf with its beautiful opposite shores. Our Armenian friends could drop in and see us without being watched and reported by the neighbors. For no Greek cares what an Armenian does, and no Armenian cares what a Greek does. Neither can be any more of a heretic than he is, in the other's view.

It was Saturday evening, and one of the little evangelical band came to say that he would come in the morning, while yet dark, to guide us to a place of meeting outside of the city, in a garden.

It was so dark, when we started, that we carried paper lanterns to light our way through the narrow streets. The guide stopped suddenly at a house, opened the door, and we all stepped silently in. There was a dying man who wished to see us. He would not receive absolution from the priest, and simply wanted we should pray with and comfort him. His brother, the owner of the house, would not allow heretics to enter it in the daytime, when it would become known; but in the deep slumbers preceding the dawn, he consented to gratify his brother. The invalid was awake, and expecting us. The preternatural brightness of the eye, the emaciation, the bloodless lips and hands, the laboring speech, showed that relief and release were near. He was cheerful, in the full bright hope of immortality. He "ministered" to us as much as we to him.

The day had just dawned over the eastern heights, as we left the city, and entered a wondrously beautiful pathway which led to the garden. It was formed by a channel separating two lands. The earth in excavating this was thrown up on both sides, and the banks thus formed were thickly planted with fruit trees, whose branches met overhead. The dew-drops on every leaf reflected in prismatic hues the morning light, and the whole archway was vocal with the songs of the nightingales. As we entered, they stopped immediately around us, but commenced again in our rear as we advanced; and thus, enveloped in this morning song, to which the quiet of the Sabbath, and the encompassing dangers, added a peculiar charm, we reached the place. Dr. Dwight was always so calm and cheerful and self-possessed, in the midst of plague and cholera and death, that I was quite surprised to see him wiping away the fast-falling tears. Nature sometimes catches us unawares.

We met some fifteen in the garden, under a very large old fig-tree. The wall around it was perhaps seven or eight feet high, the gate three or four feet higher. The Easterners will always build a high gate, a "sublime porte," whatever may be the wall. A man was perched on top of this gate, chibouk in hand, as though he was enjoying the scenery. His attention was often so intently given to the gathering under the fig-tree, that one would break out—" Keep your watch; an enemy may come, and you not know it." Our interview had already been a long one, when he gave the alarm, "A man coming straight towards the gate! Disperse!" The owner of the garden remained, and soon cried out "It's Karaguez Carabet (Black-eyed Carabet)! Come back, all of you!" We reappeared, and he was welcomed with a hearty laugh and cordial salutations. Without loss of time, our work continued, until four hours of incessant effort, together with the long walk and visit to the sick man, compelled us to say, "'The spirit is willing, but the flesh is weak.' We must have refreshment and rest." After this, another long interview; and then, towards evening, in a grove beyond the opposite side of the city, another still. Now what were the subjects of these long interviews, in which we must have spent at least ten hours? Every one of them was a diligent and earnest search of the Scriptures. Every man had many passages presenting real difficulties, and some of easy explanation. Then there were theological questions, sometimes very abstruse. Some were specially interested in the Jews, and wanted the whole argument concerning them thoroughly overhauled and discussed. Others wanted to know what course to pursue with Moslems, to prove to them that Christ is the true prophet and only Saviour; and others brought up the argument with Romanists. We asked them if they could talk with Moslems upon Islam and Christianity. "We can with one alone. But when there are two Moslems, neither will speak freely for fear of the other. But there are many Moslems who privately wish to know about our faith, and who do not have full confidence in their own."

Seeking a Physician. 153

It was a day of intense mental and spiritual work. Uneducated mind, when it gives itself intensely to subjects which it regards of high interest and immense value, becomes rapidly educated and disciplined in those things. It was evident that these men, having but one book, had made admirable use of that. After enduring six years of persecution, this noble band became an evangelical church, which has continued to flourish to the present day. For the singular and interesting origin of the work, see Goodell's "Forty Years in the Turkish Empire," page 221.

As we returned to our room, at one time, an Armenian, a stranger, met and saluted us. "Are you physicians?" said he. "Yes," replied Dr. Dwight. "What diseases do you cure?" "All diseases." "But have you medicines for all diseases?" "Yes, one medicine for all diseases," etc. The man being rather obtuse with regard to Dr. D.'s real meaning, he came to direct terms; and an interesting conversation ensued with regard to the Gospel as the only remedy of sin. The man knew how to read, and Dr. Dwight gave him a New Testament and some tracts.

He was on his way to Constantinople to consult some Frank physician. He had enlarged liver, from malarial fevers. We prescribed for him (see Chap. XX.), and sent him back, with the New Testament, to *Adabazar*—a place we then heard of for the first time. He was Steppan Erzingiatsi, whom I visited in the night.

It was the first New Testament in modern Armenian which had ever appeared in the place. He read it in the coffee-shops. The people listened, and discussed the subjects, so new to them.

A few months after, some of the more intelligent ones, notably he of the strong house, came to Constantinople for more books. The whole work sprang out of that one Testament, as the work at Nicomedia sprang out of the one tract, the "Dairyman's Daughter," left by Mr. Goodell. It went forward, too, mainly by the Word of God. Dr. Van Lennep and Dr. Schneider both visited the place, and rendered useful service, but, for the most part, this evangelic movement was a plant of native planting and growth. At its inception, as in Nicomedia, it was a grain of mustard seed, which is the least of all seeds. And so, in some hundreds of places, the seed is sown. In due time, the hundreds shall become thousands, the thousands a strong nation.

Steppan, who initiated the work, did not endure bravely "when persecution arose." He could stand any thing but the anathema, and consequent loss of his business. He wavered, and then retreated. He could not face the enemy. He had been an earnest advocate for the truth up to the crucial test, "Forsake all and follow me;" and this he could not endure. I visited him in the night. He confessed he was not where he ought to be. Those who had stood firm had done right. But his business, his means of living, would all go and he would be an outcast, a beggar. He could not endure the thought. He would still cherish and enjoy the truth for himself. But the truth would not be thus treated, and finally left him. He grew more and more distant and disappeared. My soul mourns over him as one who knew clearly his Master's will, and did it not.

CHAPTER XI.

TOUR INTO SOUTHERN MACEDONIA.

An incident led to my devoting a vacation in 1847 to a tour in Southern Macedonia. A certain Turk, Nūri Bey, had found in the mountains a mineral which he believed to be rich in silver. He hastened to Constantinople, and went direct to the royal mint. It was subjected to intense heat, but the crucible contained nothing except a little black scoria. Again and again it was tried, with the same result. The chief of the mint assured him it was a *counterfeit mineral*, and contained nothing. Nūri Bey, a sharp but ignorant man, felt some doubts whether Nature manufactured counterfeits; and he went to an Armenian silversmith, who sent him to the Bebek Seminary. The ore was a sulphuret of antimony, and very rich. I gave him the results of the analysis, with the assurance, that, if found as he described, it was a valuable mine. With this certificate, he easily found two partners, a Mr. Charles Brown (of Boston), and a Dr. Spadaro (of Italy), ready to help develop it. They made the whole depend, however, upon my visiting the mine and reporting. Wishing to see the country and the people, and to do any thing I could for the development of neglected resources.

I consented to go, upon the condition of my expenses being paid.

The steamer for Salonica, the ancient Thessalonica, went first to Cavala (Neapolis). Soon after leaving the Hellespont, we saw the shining summit of Samothrace in the horizon, and it arose beautifully to view as "we fetched a straight course" by it to Cavala the port of Philippi. We landed, chiefly to visit the humble house where Mohammed Ali was born, and the magnificent college of white marble which he proudly built close by, and endowed for the education of Mussulman youth. The remarkable quiet of the students showed one step of progress; the old Mussulman, or rather oriental mode of all studying aloud, and the louder the better, having been abandoned. I would gladly have gone to Philippi, and followed the track of the apostle to Thessalonica, but our arrangements would not allow of it. We next touched at Mt. Athos, the *sanctum sanctorum* of Greek monachism. Here we left a company of monks returning from a long begging pilgrimage in Turkey and Russia. Their looks and persons were not attractive, but the bags of coin which they landed surprised the passengers, and occasioned no little comment not complimentary to the monks. "Two things will pay," said one, "brigandage in Greece and Thessaly, and monkery in Mt. Athos." "No," said another, "Monkery alone. The 'Clephts' can't employ steamers to carry their coin." "These lazy devils get money from rich and poor." "Let them work like us for a living," etc. No one offered a word in their defence. That peculiar phase of oriental piety exists more in Russia than Turkey; and seemed to have little honor on board our steamer.

I pass by the usual objects of interest, so often commented upon, in Salonica. In crossing the plain west of Salonica, one of our horses escaped at a stopping place, and made for home. The two best mounted pursued him, and drove him across a field into a parallel road, but could not capture him, though they intercepted his course towards the city. Again he took to the fields, as he was about to meet a Turkish woman in a blue feredjé (cloak). The woman apprehended the situation, and, as we surveyed the scene from a distance, we were surprised to see her also take the field with her horse at the top of his speed, and her blue feredjé streaming horizontally behind her. A crowded road stopped at the sight. She was soon at the side of the fugitive horse, and pressed him round and round in a circle, until he stood still, and surrendered at discretion.. She took the bridle, passed him over to our pursuing party, and trotted nimbly on her way. The whole road sent up a shout of "yoha! yoha!" "mashallah! mashallah!" and we were soon on our way, but with three horses half disabled by this fierce experiment under a July sun. The Turkish woman must have been of the Tartar race, which takes naturally to the horse's back.

The Messrs. Abbott, of Salonica, had cautioned

UNFRIENDLY RECEPTION. 159

us against stopping at the khan on the western side of the plain. The malaria would be dangerous to every one but the natives, whom it half kills, and it was then in the height of its power. Owing to these delays, we did not reach the khan till an hour past sunset.

The heat was still suffocating. We were all exhausted and sleepy, and notwithstanding the danger, must stop to rest a while, and refresh our horses. Our two Turkish guards had passed that way before, and regaled themselves without pay. The keeper was determined not to let them in, and though they knocked and bawled at the gate, all was silent within. I did not suspect the reason. As we had all dismounted, we tied our horses. I proposed to batter down the gate. We each took as large a stone from a pile of marble fragments as we could carry, and forming in Indian file, we ran towards the gate, and each delivered his stone against it. The barking and shouting from within proved no common amount of life to exist there. The keeper opened the gate. I reproved him for his perverseness. He declared he was fast asleep, *and when those accursed Turks called, he didn't hear!*

"What can you get us to eat?"

"Nothing, cheliby; absolutely nothing."

"Well, give us some eggs, and a little fresh butter to fry them in."

"I have no eggs and no butter."

"Then let us have some bread and olives, and a little buttermilk to drink."

"No bread, no olives, no buttermilk."

"And no yoghoort?"

"Not a particle."

I put some money in his hand, and said, "You are telling me lies. Get us something, anyhow."

He took the money, and, without a moment's hesitation, said, "What will you have? I have fresh eggs, and butter, and buttermilk, and excellent cheese, and olives, and yoghoort!"

He then told me that he was afraid our whole party of seven would go away without paying a para. Those Turks had told him that they were from Nūri Bey, and were going after us.

We agreed, after an excellent supper, to risk two or three hours' sleep, for the day had been too much for us. The whole morning had been lost in getting horses, and then the heat of the day, in chasing the fugitive.

To avoid the malaria of the night, all were sleeping inside, some twenty or thirty, in one dormitory. The air was insupportable. We asked for another room. We were all driven from it immediately by the fleas, each one carrying out some thousands with him. Before I became aware, my white pantaloons were black with them up to the knees. We chastised ourselves with bushes to get rid of them, but were compelled to throw off some of our apparel.

The white malarious fog had risen about three feet high over the plain, and, in the brilliant moonlight, was like an expanse of snow, into which we would like to plunge our lively friends. We all laid down under a verandah, but not to sleep. The air was thick with mosquitos. We tried all the means at our command in vain. Badly bitten, and exasperated, we mounted our horses, and rode nine weary miles to Yenidjé, beautifully situated above the plain.

The air was cool and delightful; and it was doubtless well for us all that we did not sleep in that malarious atmosphere. We reached, at dawn, a new and cleanly khan, embowered in a clump of huge plane-trees. We washed our *wounds*, and slept profoundly until ten o'clock. We then had the breakfast we had ordered—a quarter of mutton baked at the public oven, in a pan of rice. It was the perfection of cooking. No mutton, rice, or culinary art ever surpassed what we then enjoyed. We had seven right royal breakfasts for a dollar.

The extremes of discomfort and enjoyment following each other constitute one of the charms of oriental travel.

The next evening we reached Penlipé, passing over a beautiful, well watered region "clothed with flocks." In the distance we could see, as we rose to the crest of a ridge, vast fields of grain.

At the village we had some instructive experience. I inquired at the bey's threshing-floor for a khan. They replied there was none, and we must stop there. I did not believe it, went through the long village to the farther end, and returned—

humble. Generally, unbelief is safe in Eastern travel, but not always. I sent my travelling firman to the bey, with excuses of fatigue for not calling to pay my respects in person. He sent, in return, his two cavasses, with his best wishes, and excuse of illness, to which I replied orientally.

The cavasses, well-dressed, gentlemanly fellows, lingered. My companion became impatient, wished to get his supper, and go to rest. He begged me to send them away. I objected, and said to him that oriental politeness often required more time and patience than we can well spare, but I would prefer they would sit an hour longer, rather than show the least impatience. They demanded what he was saying. I replied, "he is speaking about his supper." "If it please God, he shall have a good supper," one replied; to which the other heartily responded, "If it please God!" I was not a little amused, not fully comprehending it. Soon my fellow traveller started up, and said angrily, "If I could speak their language, I would send them away!" They perceived at once his meaning; and making me a hasty salam, they left in hot displeasure. I was shocked at the conduct of my friend, and set before him some of its possible consequences. While we were talking, two servants entered, with a splendid dinner, in six courses, from the bey. They brought tables and all on their heads, the food in covered dishes, the tables being round waiters, about three feet in diameter. The cavasses whom we had driven away, and who were young men of superior bearing for that grade, had evidently hoped to enjoy the dinner with us. The bey had sent us a good share of his own dinner, for the dishes were full, and contained food for a dozen hungry men.

My friend confessed his folly and impatience. We, by our *gaucherie*, our impoliteness, our stupidity, our ill-temper, had made enemies of those who were disposed to treat us with the greatest kindness and politeness. It is a common fate of travellers. One should lay in a good supply of patience and good feeling, or stay at home.

In order to remedy, so far as possible, our blunder, I called the chief of the threshing-floor, and asked him to select such persons as he chose. He assembled about a dozen, in connection with the servants of our party, and we passed along to them each dish, after taking out what we wanted. The servants of the bey were with them, and it was a merry and good-humored party, without a drop of wine. Giving the servants their bakshishes, with injunctions to explain things to the offended cavasses, and to express our thanks to the bey, we got out of the unpleasant affair as well as we could.

The next day, we crossed the plain of Karajowa, turning northward into the mountains. A cool wind was rushing down through the gorge by which we entered, and waves of mournful sound broke upon us from distant gorges. Steep mountain sides, sadness, and desolation, changed the whole scene of the fruitful plain.

At the village of Borsko, on one of the mountain sides, we met Nūri Bey with nine armed attendants. They were a villanous looking set. A few years before, this whole region had been held by brigands. An enterprising pasha had surrounded them, and driven them into a remarkable and extensive cave which could be approached only in single file. He starved them into surrender, put their chief to death, and settled them and their families in five villages. Rojeden, our "*objectif*," was one of the five. He made the whole community responsible for each and every individual, and killed brigandage at a blow. His rule was watchful and stern. When he heard that our party had gone in, he sent a company of fifty soldiers after us, lest something should happen.

The chief of our guard had been a noted robber; and numerous ugly scars attested to the desperate frays he had shared in. He talked freely about his robber life, confessed he had killed seventeen men and women with his own hand, had no compunctions of conscience, had confessed to a priest, performed penance, received absolution; he was all right. I tried, one whole evening, to reach that man's conscience, and awaken a sense of sin, and need of a Saviour; but all in vain. All these men were of the Greek church, but they had fewer religious ideas, and a more blunted and stupified moral sense than I had ever met with. Military power held them down, but there was nothing whatever done for their enlightment or elevation.

NÛRI BEY'S COOLNESS. 165

There was no school, and not even a priest resident in either of the two villages we visited; and they wanted neither priest nor school.

I asked the bey if there were no Moslems among the brigands. "Oh yes," he said, "brigands are of all sorts. But they are tolerant of each other's religions. The Greek crosses himself and burns a lamp to *mūshamba* (i.e. *oil-cloth;* meaning picture of the Virgin); and the Moslem ablutes and prays. When we catch a Moslem robber, we send him to the army; and if he deserts, we shoot him."

Nūri Bey was a Moslem of Slavic origin; and nearly all the Moslems of this region are either Slavs or Greeks by race. The Turks are chiefly in the army and in public offices. No Moslem was ever a more devoted fatalist than Nūri. He coolly rode his horse along a precipice, where it required a cool head even to walk, and where the path was so insecure that it was simple fool-hardiness. He laughed at our all getting off and walking. I tried the experiment of hurling a stone horizontally from the path where I had secure standing, and noting the seconds of its fall into a little lakelet below. It was seven seconds, as near as I could ascertain; and Nūri and his horse would have fallen about seven hundred feet before they would have found a comfortable stopping place. My friend fell over the precipice, a few hundred yards ahead, in a place not quite so precipitous or deep. He caught upon a beach-tree growing out of a crevice about six feet below the path, and was rescued without much difficulty. But for this tree, he would have gone from one to two hundred feet, and as to any chance of life, might as well have gone seven hundred while he was about it.

We found our village of Rojeden on the escarpment of a mountain, well situated, well watered, with forests near by, and back of the village a quarry of slate, from which the materials for the walls of the houses were easily obtained. Each house was built with the solidity of a fort, with high, sharp roof, well thatched. More than half of every house is a stable; the family part so far elevated as not to interfere with the rights of the live stock.

These hardy and fierce mountaineers complained bitterly of the government. They had to give a sheep for the privilege of keeping a pig. Their flocks were all numbered, and if one died, or was stolen, they had to account for it to government. If one of their number ran away, they were all taxed for him; and although their land was good, they couldn't live. Their healthy, robust look showed that their mere animal wants were provided for. That they were moral and accountable beings, entered into no man's thought. Nūri Bey spread his rug and said his prayers; and this was all the visible sign of religion in the mountains.

The Greek Church has any amount of orthodoxy in her old standards, but, though she possesses Macedonia, there is not a ray of light in these dark regions.

How to Drink when Heated. 167

We found the mine all that Nūri Bey had represented. We traced signs of the ore cropping out, here and there, for a mile and a half along the face of a hill. The access to it was so difficult, and the transportation so expensive, and the state of the country so wretched, that the mine must wait for better times. We reached it by a very circuitous route. A much shorter road is practicable and will some day be made, and the vast riches of these mountains brought into commerce.

On returning from the mine we went around through another gorge about three miles in length, finding nothing but pyrites, which, of course, the natives believed to be gold. The direct and reflected heat of the sun was almost insupportable. As we emerged from this furnace, there was a cry of joy, and the party rushed forward to a fountain gushing out from beneath a cliff, and rolling away, a sparkling brook. Nūri, with a stentorian voice, forbade every one to drink till he had washed himself thoroughly and rinsed his mouth. This bathing and gurgling the water took away half our thirst, cooled our blood, and we could then drink without any bad effect. It was a wise caution for other occasions.

Some of the people spoke freely to me of their intention to assassinate the bey and his father. I warned him to govern more justly or it would in the end be the worse for him. He said every man of them was an arrant coward and if they dared to kill him why didn't they do it? He was among them unarmed every day. A short time after they killed his father and would have killed the bey but he hid in a hollow log till he almost died of hunger and thirst. The pasha at length came in and regulated things in oriental style. The bey still works the mine after his fashion and sends two or three hundred tons of the ore every year to Salonica from whence it goes to Trieste. They lose so much by evaporation that all their efforts to smelt it have been fruitless, and so the ore is transported in its crude state to the port of Salonica. Ignorance, darkness, and oppression go together. The schoolmaster must come abroad in Macedonia and the light of divine truth, now wholly extinguished, must again begin to shine before the land will yield its increase. Nor is it desirable that it should be otherwise. The wealth which lies here in secret had better wait for a better generation. Its development now would only give rise to greater oppression and injustice.

I rescued a Trebizond Armenian miner from the mine, and brought him away, to the displeasure of the bey. I did not suppose he would ever repay me, and I exacted no promise from him. He knew what I paid for him by the way; and, as soon as practicable, he sent me every farthing. One often meets with rectitude and a strong sense of justice, where he least expects it; and the reverse.

I visited the family of the late priest. His three stalwart sons looked as though they would make excellent brigands. They had no idea of religion

No Desire for Change. 169

whatever, except to perform the ritual of the church. That any relation exists between religion and moral conduct, had never entered their minds.

The villagers brought us specimens of copper, iron, and orpiment. The latter we saw repeatedly, in beautiful veins on the mountain sides, but in very thin layers.

Having examined the mine, and more especially its surroundings and embarrassments, and having decided that it was not in a place, at present, inviting capital, we commenced our descent; the same band of thieves guarding us safely through the mountains, and receiving our bakshish with enthusiasm. There is no Macedonian cry from those mountains, except we regard their hopeless condition as such.

It was Saturday when we came upon the plain of Karajowa; and the question was, where we should pass the Sabbath and rest. They assured us there was no village except that of Durzee Bey, the governor of the plain, where we and our horses could be well cared for. The people looked strong and healthy. Their houses, of one story, with high, sharp, thatched roofs, and walls of sun-dried bricks, were dark within, having at most two small windows closed with board shutters. We very rarely saw a pane of glass. In the mountains, and on the borders of the plain, the abundance of pitch pine, which is burned in a *jack*, for both light and heat, has painted every thing within of a jet black; and, while it has a wholesome, it has a sombre effect. In entering such a house, you go right into midnight.

Durzee Bey, they said, is three hours off your road; but from his village you can take a cross road that will bring you to Yenedji without loss.

We had learned to place little confidence in their knowledge of distances or geography. But they extolled the power, glory, and hospitality of Durzee Bey, the governor, to that degree that we resolved to visit him. To see a Mohammedan prince untouched, unvisited, by European civilization, was worth the extra time and fatigue.

We found it four hours instead of three; but that was moderate, and we had time to spare; for the steamer from Salonica did not leave until Thursday evening.

It was evening when we reached the bey's residence. His long, straggling house covered an immense extent of base, but most of it was of one story, with immensely projecting roofs, glazed windows, guarded on the harem department with jalousies, the whole painted red, and showing the peculiar taste and wealth of a Turkish lord of the interior. He welcomed us with dignity, but with some reserve, until he should know who we were. I told him we were Protestant Christians from America, the "Yeni Dunia" (the New World), as it was then called. We had been to visit and examine a mine at Rojeden, in the mountains, belonging to our friend Nūri Bey. We were very weary. We wanted to rest on the Sabbath, and perform the duties of our religion, and go on refreshed Monday morning.

To have his Mohammedan konak turned into a place of Christian worship was evidently embarrassing. He replied, "I do not know the rites of your religion, and I could not therefore prepare a suitable room for you." Knowing that all his ideas of Christianity were from the rites of the Greek church, I replied, "We do not want an altar, nor a crucifix, nor a picture of any kind, nor incense, candles, robes, nor any thing of all that stuff." "Then you are good Mussulmans!" said he. "Oh no," said I, "we do not even want a *mihrab*" (showing direction towards Mecca); "we worship in any direction, believing God to be an infinite spirit, everywhere present."

"I will give you a room," he replied, "after you have dined." After an hour's waiting, we had a most excellent dinner, which no hotel of the western world could surpass. He apologized for not giving us *brandy*, thinking that a necessary part of a *Christian* dinner. The Christianity which the Mohammedan meets with is not such as to command his respect. He was surprised at what we told him of the temperance movement in our land.

European habits of drinking are insinuating themselves into the circle of official Turks. In the commercial cities, where there is a large European element, it is making sad progress; but it may still be said that, as a whole, the Mohammedans of Turkey are the most temperate people in the world. Our room was large and cool and very perplexing in its character. We came to the conclusion that he had given us his private chapel, and if so, it was because we were free from any taint of idolatry. There was a place for the *Mihrab;* but either it had not been made, or it was a movable one, and had been taken away. A Moslem must always have the *Kebleh,* or direction towards Mecca, before he prays.

Beyond the bey's walled premises, was his threshing-floor. It covered more than two acres, and was likewise surrounded by a wall, about eight feet high, against which were built many rooms for storing grain and for the use of the workmen. He had at one end an elevated lodge from whence he could survey the work. Near by, some men were making "the sharp threshing instrument, having teeth" (Isaiah xli. 15). Two planks, each three inches thick and two feet wide, were bolted together, and looked precisely like a New England stone-drag, except that the front ends were more curved upwards, so as to slip over the straw. The wood seemed to be ash, but was very cross-grained and unsplittable. The workman, with a suitable chisel and a heavy mallet, made a deep incision, into which was driven a piece of flint with great force, and the outer edge skilfully trimmed off, so as to be curved and sharp. It was so difficult to detach these flints, that when one was badly trimmed and ruined, the workman let it go. As the whole bottom surface was filled with these

WINNOWING GRAIN—DINNER.

sharp flints, it made an ugly-looking and effective thing. The driver sits upon the drag with a sharp pole which he thrusts down to hold the straw, if it piles up in front, and to thus make the drag slip over it. It cuts up and bruises the straw, and makes excellent fodder of it. Very little hay is used for horses, but instead thereof this comminuted straw and chaff, with barley. One great objection which the people have to threshing machines is, that they leave the straw unfit for fodder.

The most interesting part of the work on this great threshing-floor, was the winnowing. As the surrounding wall kept the wind off the surface, the grain was thrown high into the air, so that the wind took it and carried away the chaff. The shovels for this operation had long elastic handles, the grain was tossed high into the air, and came down with beautiful precision, and very well cleansed.

In the evening the bey had his dinner in the highest style of an oriental prince.

When we went into the dining-hall, the only suggestion of dinner was the large array of servants, in their neatest attire, standing at the farther end of the long room. We all sat down upon the divan at the elevated end of the room; and, at the clap of the master's hands, two men came forward, one bearing two stools about a foot high, and the other a magnificent copper platter, five feet in diameter, by the eye, showing a narrow but heavy raised edge. It was polished to the last degree, and I could not but let the bey know how I admired the beauty of the work. It was placed upon the stools, and covered with a white cloth; some slices of bread and three spoons were placed for each guest: the one of boxwood, for hot food; the one of tortoise shell, for cold food; and a ladle of cocoanut shell for sipping sherbet. We all sat down upon the floor, the cushions alone covering the matting.

With a skill and adroitness I could not comprehend, a servant caused a roll of cotton cloth to descend upon our laps, which we all adjusted so as to cover them. Then came the ceremony of thorough hand-washing, with soap, in running water. An Oriental has inexpressible disgust at washing in a bowl. By the first dip of your hand the water becomes polluted, they say, and so you wash in nasty water! The water is poured upon your hands in a very fine stream, while you use the soap, and then more freely, to carry off the soapy water, which goes through a pierced cover, and disappears in the basin beneath; the very sight being a taint to purity. Then you adjust your napkin; and the first dish is placed upon the table. The kitchen is separate from the house, and the food is brought in covered dishes. These are of copper, tinned within, and sometimes without. The servant places it upon his head, and comes, with a peculiar swing of his arms, as much as to say, "See how fearlessly and safely I bring it." The grace with which he deposits it upon the

Twenty-two Courses—Etiquette. 175

center of the table, and then retires to the end of the hall, marching backwards, is quite amusing. The spoons are changed for each dish; which gave us a variety, both of cold and hot spoons, the latter being always of boxwood, the former of èbony, horn, or shell. There was some display of taste, occasionally, in the workmanship of the handles.

I gave my travelling companion notice that we should probably have not less than fifteen courses of food; and, as we must taste of all, we must act accordingly; and so we did. But we had *twenty-two* courses, and it need not be said that the latter part of the dinner dragged. After dinner, pipes, and a small cup of strong black coffee; and we were soon disposed to sleep.

While eating, the bey asked me if it was true that in Frankistan we all eat at high tables, sitting on high stools, and having every man his plate, knife, fork, spoon, and his food doled out to him as we do to prisoners? I explained, and defended our table habits as well as I could; except the drunkenness, which does sometimes disgrace them.

"But how would you do an *ikram* to a guest" (an act of honor and regard)? "Now *this* is what we do;" he said, as he detached a piece of roast mutton with his fingers, and passed it to me, which I took with my fingers from his, and ate.

"Now do you know what I have done?"

"Perfectly well. You have given me a delicious piece of roast meat, and I have eaten it."

"You have gone far from it. By that act I have

pledged you every drop of my blood, that while you are in my territory no evil shall come to you. For that space of time we are brothers."

"But does it not make a difference whether you eat with a Moslem, a Christian, a Jew, or a pagan?"

"We don't eat with pagans. They are kitabsiz and dinsiz (bookless and faithless). But as to Moslems and kitablis,* it makes no difference. We are all brothers of the dust."

He expressed a very strong dislike to Frank modes and fashions at table. He thought them *uncivilized*, and not susceptible of expressing kindness and good-will. "If they only once knew our customs," he said, "they would adopt them forever." This sacred regard to eating and drinking is such a peculiar trait of the Eastern world, that it will repay a little attention. It has evidently been a kind of sacrament, from very ancient times. It was a sacrament of brotherhood. The bey expressed it, in saying, we are all brothers of the dust, made out of the same clay; but he illiberally excluded the pagan from it. It seems, at this day, to be in greater force among the Moslems than others. The sacrament of the Lord's Supper has taken the place of it among Christians, so that it has almost disappeared from their social life.

I was once coming from Smyrna, and we had on deck two hundred and fifty raw recruits from the

---

* All who have a *revelation* are called *kitablis*.

interior, for the Turkish army. They were strong and healthy young men, from the fields and vineyards of Asia Minor; and they were going to tread the wine-press of God's wrath in war. Just before reaching port, some fifteen or so of these recruits threw off their look of stolid resignation, cleared a place on the deck, as I supposed, for a country dance; and I looked on with interest. I could see, by their costumes, that they were all from the same village, or villages closely associated. Generally the mode of wearing the turban, more than any thing else, indicates neighborhood. They stood in a ring, each man's right hand upon his neighbor's left shoulder. Soon one came to take a vacant place, with a *semeet*, a ring of bread, in his hand. He broke it into bits, and they all ate of it, saying a few words of prayer, probably the first chapter of the Koran. It was a religious act, plainly. About to separate, and be dispersed into the army, they bound themselves to be faithful in memory, and in aid, should it ever become possible. It was to them a kind of sacrament, an oath of brotherhood.

I was once, under peculiar circumstances, in the island of Rhodes, spending the night in a solitary house, with a colored man as the only companion. He was a giant in form and strength. Born in African heathenism, and thoroughly tattooed, he had been made a slave, but became, by the piety of his master, a soldier, to serve Abdel-Kader in his wars with France. When his master was taken, he fled to Turkey, and had become a butcher, thus adhering, so far as he could, to his old trade of blood.

I felt I must test him, and see whether I could trust him. His aspect was huge and rough, but not positively forbidding. I arranged our evening meal, and invited him to partake of it with me. He took food from my hand and ate it, and he returned the compliment. After dinner, I made two cups of Turkish coffee, poured them out in his presence, and gave him one. He rolled up a cigarette and gave me, and we drank and smoked together. I felt perfectly safe with him. We had become "brothers of the dust." We were "of one blood."

At a very late hour, there was a knock at the door. I went down; it was a cavass and note from Mr. Kerr, the English consul, a noble and generous-hearted man, telling me that man would put his knife through me for a shilling; and I must come directly to his house. I felt his kindness and thoughtfulness, but I assured him, in reply, that I could not be safer under his own roof. And so the event proved. He served me with a brother's fidelity, and I have often prayed that the Lord would remember him for good. I have no doubt he would have defended me to the last drop of his blood. He had bound himself by the oath of human brotherhood to do it. Every other feeling of obligation might fail, but this never. To break this would be to consign himself to Gehenna,

The Sacrament of Brotherhood. 179

without redemption. I would not hesitate to risk my life upon it, at any time.

Our Lord, in instituting the Supper, took hold of an institution as old as the human race. David recognized it in saying, "Yea, mine own familiar friend, who *did eat of my bread*, hath lifted up his heel against me!" The Saviour makes the same charge against Judas; and it is also said that *after the sop*, after he had himself sealed the oath of brotherhood, he yielded himself to Satan, and betrayed the Master who had pledged his own life for him.

The Sacramental Supper was not only commemorative of our Lord's sufferings and death, but was also a sacrament of brotherhood. It was in this view that he said to the chosen disciples, "With desire have I desired to eat this passover with you before I suffer." Having loved his own as brethren and friends he "loved them unto the end."

At four o'clock on Monday morning, we left our hospitable host. His venerable imam accompanied us four hours on our way, to show us a nearer route to Yenijé. We took our breakfast and drank up all our water, under a wide-spreading sycamore; and the good imam assured us we were five hours from Yenijé; which we were, *plus* four hours more!

It was a hot July day, and in two hours, our whole party had become thirsty. We passed squads of Bulgarian harvesters. To our surprise, they all used the cradle, while the others, Moslems and

Greeks, used the sickle. The cradling was neatly done, and the workmen looked strong and stolid. I had then seen but few Bulgarians, except ostlers and gardeners at Constantinople; the influx having then hardly commenced. We stopped repeatedly and spoke with them. When we asked what any man used the sickle for, when he could do three times as much with the cradle, they simply replied, "Those others can't work in our way." It is one of the marvels of the East, that a wise and a stupid way of doing a thing can hold on from age to age, side by side.

We liked these Bulgarians. Few of them could speak either Turkish or Greek with freedom, but their countenances lighted up with a smile. They assured us that the water of that plain was bad, and advised us not to drink it. The good water was two miles off our road. Their own supply was short. Repeatedly we made the same inquiry, with the same results; and our suffering became extreme. At twelve o'clock, we were still an hour from the village of "Durt Armūd" (Four Peartrees), where we would find excellent water. The Armenian miner had accompanied us all the way on foot. His strength utterly gave out; and for the first time I saw a man's tongue hanging out of his mouth from exhaustion and thirst. Each horseman gave him a ride, and so we reached Durt Armūd. In dismounting, he fell upon the turf, utterly demoralized, his tongue still out. I now followed the example of Nūri in the mountains, and made them all wash and gargle the mouth before drinking. I dashed water upon the poor man's face, with but little effect.

In the mean time, a huge *testeh* (or jug) of buttermilk had been brought. The owner claimed it was sixteen okes (forty-four pounds) and I gave him four piastres, or sixteen cents, for it. We lifted up the fallen, pushed back his tongue, and made him drink a tin cup of buttermilk. This enlightened his eyes, and he said "bir dahah," (one more). When we had all drunk round, every one was saying the same thing, "bir dahah." I insisted upon five minutes' interval; but after two minutes, I saw there would be a "strike"; and not having any regular army to enforce orders, I yielded. Even one minute seemed long, and I had to hold my watch in view to convince them that two minutes were not ten. When we had drunk all round five times, we all agreed to give half an hour to sleep before dinner. The poor miner was quite restored and jovial.

After three hours given to dinner, buttermilk, and sleep, we were ready to mount again. I called the party to look at the small remains of our forty-four pints. They exclaimed "bir dahah!" and not a drop of the buttermilk was left! During the four hours to Yenijé each one willingly gave the miner a lift, and enjoyed it. The surigi at first refused, but the threat of a good caning from one of our party brought him to the ground, and he had as long a walk as any of us. And yet these poor fellows will often help each other with the most devoted unselfishness. I fear he did not like to see the miner made so much of. I am sure he would have helped him, had they been alone.

After four hours' ride, the khan at Yenijé again refreshed us with its excellent food and profound sleep. Few objects, after a space of thirty years, remain so clearly defined in memory as that rûde Eastern hotel, beneath its magnificent trees, with the everlasting beauty of the scenery before it, and within, the rugged good-natured keeper who kindly served us.

On our way to Salonica, we stopped at Berea. There were four Greeks of the place at the coffee-shop. They knew nothing about Paul's having preached the Gospel to the Jew in that place, or his having commended the Bereans as "more noble than the Thessalonians." Their fierce hatred of the Jews is such that they naturally would ignore any thing commendatory. We saw one poor Jew, but he did not belong to Berea, and he certainly was not "noble.". Finding I was an American, the Greeks became more sociable. They had heard of America. They complained freely of the oppressive taxation under which they groaned. Their bishop and their pasha both fleeced them. The account of what they paid the bishop was probably exaggerated. They declared that the bishop and the pasha had a good understanding, and helped each other, and there was no redress. Their condition was hopeless.

We made a brief stop to examine some of the remains of Pella, the birthplace of Alexander the Great. The object of greatest interest is the remains of the old aqueduct. The buildings around it have disappeared, heaps of decayed walls, here and there a fragment of marble; but in the aqueduct the water was flowing pure and clear, after so many centuries. It is now used for irrigation. The mortar in all these works is Greek and not Roman. That is, its hydraulic quality is derived from pounded brick, and not from puzzolana. The same is true of all Byzantine structures. It makes a very durable cement, and often stands the wear of time better than the stone or brick around it. Wars, and consequent famines and pestilences, have so desolated these regions, that the malaria has got the upper hand, and nothing but large outlays, with scientific engineering, will ever restore them. The peasants themselves suffer not a little, as indeed they did in ancient times, intermittent being among the earliest topics of medical discussion. A grain of quinine with every meal, or else some constitutional indifference, preserved me; but I saw a plenty of *shaking* at every stopping-place. Generally the first questions were, "Are you a doctor? Have you any ague medicines?"

It is difficult to find an entering wedge to do any thing for this people. They are under a double oppression, of the Mohammedan government and of the Greek church. The latter, having both temporal and spiritual power, is the worst.

It stands right across your path, and uses the Moslem power to close the doors against you.

We had as fellow passenger to Constantinople Emin Pasha, educated in England, where he distinguished himself in mathematics. His European culture had made him a skeptic and a misanthrope. He was a pre-Darwinite, believing in "the forces of nature" and "the reign of law"—nothing else. I endeavored to show him that the human mind demands a first cause, and an intelligent cause, for the universe. He finally gave it up, saying "The whole question is dark, inexplicable! One does not know what to believe." His mind had "fallen among thieves" who had stripped him of faith—a frequent result with the Turk in Europe.

CHAPTER XII.

MORSE'S TELEGRAPH.

Professor Morse, while at work upon his telegraph in Paris, in .1839, had as an associate a Mr. Chamberlain, of Maine. Mr. C. having a set of the newly invented instruments, came to Constantinople, hoping to obtain a patent from the Turkish government, and after that, from the Austrian. Finding that I had a galvanic battery, he set it up in my study, and a few gentlemen there witnessed its operation. The instrument had many faults of construction, and did not work with precision, nor with very satisfactory results. Instead of the steel point marking the paper, the pens for lining off paper were used, three of them, side by side.

Sometimes the mark was blurred, and sometimes there was no mark at all. Still, it was a demonstration of what could be done, and as such it was extremely interesting. It was agreed, however, that Mr. Chamberlain had better go on to Vienna, employ the best workmen to make an entirely new set of instruments, with various improvements which had suggested themselves, and after finishing whatever he might be able to do there, to return and see the Turkish government. At the opening of the Danube, he departed, with high hopes and enthusiasm; the boat was capsized in the rapids of the Danube, and Mr. Chamberlain, with five others, lost his life. Thus perished this early attempt to introduce the telegraph into the East.

In 1847, another attempt was made.

Prof. J. Lawrence Smith, of Nashville, Tenn., a gentleman of superior scientific attainments, and for a time employed by the Turkish government as geologist, with the design of establishing a school of mines, ordered a set of instruments from America, with the hope and expectation of establishing some telegraphic line from the capital to a neighboring city.

Some parts having been unfortunately left out, they were supplied in the little seminary workshop, where I was accustomed to repair our philosophical instruments.

As he did not wish to employ any of the crafty "ring" that surrounds the palace, I readily consented to aid him; and we first put up the telegraph in the seminary, in order that I might practise upon it till I could send a telegram.

The instrument was very different from the crude one in the hands of Mr. Chamberlain. It was an American invention, and it was gratifying to us all that an American gentleman, Prof. Smith, should have the honor of introducing it into Turkey, and of presenting it to the sultan.

In the Sultan's Palace. 187

After three days' practise, entirely unfitted as I was, we had to go to the palace, at the sultan's call. It was a rare thing for unofficial persons to enter the sultan's presence, at that day, and the etiquette of the occasion is worth preserving.

Mr. J. P. Brown, Secretary of the American Legation, accompanied us as interpreter.

On arriving at the palace, we were received by the chamberlain and, in his reception room, awaited his majesty's orders. After being regaled with the inevitable sweetmeats, pipes, and coffee, we were called to the throne-room. It was in the Yellow Palace of Beylerbey, a wooden structure of immense length, since then taken down to make room for one of stone, as much smaller as it is more solid and beautiful. The room was so large that I dare not give any estimate of its dimensions.

The sultan had entered from the opposite end where we were ushered in. Advancing about twenty steps, we all made a low and formal bow, which he acknowledged by a slight inclination of the head. We advanced again, and bowed as before, while he was also advancing to meet us. The third salute brought us into *presence*. He passed a few words of compliment to Mr. Brown, commended Prof. Smith's zeal in his service, inquired who I was, and hoped I had found a pleasant residence in his capital.

Prof. Smith then proceeded to show him the instruments, and explain to him the alphabet of signs. The sultan readily apprehended its use, and remarked, "It will apply to any language, and we shall have the advantage, as we have but twenty-two letters." The working of the instrument perplexed him more. Prof. Smith had taken with him such of our galvanic apparatus as he wanted for illustration. The sultan was not satisfied with the fact that the electric current magnetizes the iron only when it circulates round it. He took the iron semicircles, laid them on the coil, laid the coil on them, and placed them in every possible position, with no result; but when he passed the ends within the coil, they instantly cohered with a *click* that surprised him. At length, throwing them down, he turned to me, and said, "Why is this so?" I replied, "Your majesty, science makes known to us facts, but God only knows the reasons of those facts." He immediately bowed his head reverentially, and said no more.

He watched Prof. Smith's arranging of the instruments with unflagging interest, and often delayed him by asking questions. He was plainly and simply dressed, and intended that we should feel perfectly at ease. In a word, he had the bearing of a gentleman.

One telegraph station was at the upper end of the throne-room, the other in a corner room of the palace. While we were thus at work, he was often talking with Mr. Brown, and expressed great surprise at our uniform success in Mexico, against superior numbers. Mr. Brown told him the Mexicans were an ignorant people, and Papists, and

The Sultan a Man of Peace. 189

they could never stand against educated Protestants. "Is that so?" said the sultan, with a Turkish phrase indicating doubt or surprise. And then he added, "If I could do any thing for such a purpose, I should like to have a congress of nations to settle all international disputes, and man should never shed the blood of his fellow-man!" One of his titles of honor is *Hunkiar* (*Blood-letter*), and to recall the history of his dynasty, and then hear him announce the favorite principle of Capt. Ladd, then known as the apostle of peace, was a true surprise. This dislike to blood, which prevents one from executing murderers and brigands, while there are no moral forces to take the place of fear, is not conducive to an energetic administration in any thing.

When Prof. Smith announced to him that the instruments were ready, he thought a moment, and then asked Mr. Smith to go to the other station. He wished to send away the great magician, and retain myself as the less, whom he could easily penetrate. His private secretary and French teacher had said to me, "You must not sit in his majesty's presence, but if you wish a cushion to kneel upon, I will have one brought." I declined; and when all was ready, I asked his majesty for a chair, in order to work the instrument with precision. "*Mettez une chaise! Mettez une chaise!*" he replied with evident pleasure; and his attendants sprang to execute the order, wondering that a ghiaour should have the temerity to ask, and thê sultan the condescension to grant, such a favor.

Mr. Brown then asked him for a message, and he gave—"Has the French steamer arrived? and what is the news from Europe?" For a short time, he looked carefully at the work upon the key, and then went off in great strides to the other station, leaving his attendants far behind, determined that no one should be able to communicate with that before himself. As he entered, demanding what it was, Prof. Smith read off to him the same words he had just given. He threw up both arms, saying, "Mashallah! mashallah!"

The return telegram was much longer, and he returned to my station to see it come off. I was putting, with a pencil, each letter under its sign, so that he might be able to read it. As he was reading it off, he said, "Have you not made a mistake here? This should be *l*, to make sense," and then added, "I see there might be many errors, and yet it would not obscure the sense." He sent for Prof. Smith, and expressed to him his great gratification, and asked him when he could come and show it to the Sublime Porte. "Any time when your majesty commands." "Then come to-morrow at one o'clock;" and we departed, with the same etiquette with which we came, bowing as we retired. Prof. Smith had every reason to be satisfied. He could not have wished to make a more favorable impression. An oriental despot generally holds himself superior to the ordinary range of human feelings. But in this case it was not so at all. The sultan was evidently delighted. The next day, we were careful to be in good season to witness the assembling of the whole Sublime Porte at the palace; a sight we had much desired to see. In the magnificence of a Turkish palace, there are always some things wanting, some things unfinished. About the grounds there were corners not neatly kept; and the lower class of servants were in shabby uniform. There was but one guard of honor detailed to receive the pashas as they arrived. But, as some came by water and some by land, the guard was needed in two different places at the same time; and the distracted manner in which they rushed from the land gate to the water-side and back again, as successive arrivals demanded their services, was very amusing. We were conducted into the throne-room. Soon the sultan entered at the head of the grand *cortége.*

There were present the Sheikh-ul-Islam, the Chief Justices of Roumelia and Anatolia, the Grand Vizir, the Minister of Foreign Affairs, the Ministers of War and of the Navy, and all the other dignitaries of the Sublime Porte. As they were listening to an explanation of the instrument, there was a fine opportunity to view the men. There were some who were truly noble in form and countenance; and some who carried decidedly too much weight. There was one who reminded us of the Irishman's wall, which he built five feet wide and four feet high—so that when it tumbled down it might be higher than it was before!

Before commencing work, the grand vizir asked

Mr. Brown "if that was one of those American missionaries who were turning the world upside down?" and added, "He does not look like a dangerous man!"

When at length they were ready to see the instrument at work, the grand vizir gave a telegram of a number of sentences; and Prof. Smith sent it through. The strip of paper was examined with very great interest and astonishment. No second telegram was required, and very fortunately; for we afterwards found one of the wires separated; and strongly suspected this was done by the malice of some one who did not wish the telegraph to be introduced.

The extreme deference shown to the sultan was one of the marked features of the interview. "Evvet effendim" (Yes, my lord)! was the reply of the whole body to every remark of the sultan; each one bowing down and giving the salam of honor. When he proposed to establish a line to Adrianople, they were all delighted; and when he inquired of Prof. Smith the expense, they thought it wonderfully cheap—a mere trifle.

The ceremony by which the Porte took leave of its sovereign was peculiar, and is a sight not often witnessed by foreigners. The pashas took their places, about forty in number, in the anteroom of the great hall, and the sultan stood, languid and weary, in the door-way, with the right foot a little advanced. The grand vizir placed himself before him, and momentarily assumed the fixedness

FORM OF LEAVE-TAKING. 193

of a statue; then suddenly fell upon his knees, and forward, as though to kiss the foot; which, however, the sultan withdrew, leaving the left advanced, which became the objective of the next prostration.

The man of great diameter, whose rich sword belt seemed to do good service in holding him together, must take his turn. "My stars!" whispered Mr. Brown, "Is *he* going through with that?" Of course he must. The pillars of state would tremble, were he to be excused. He fell with force but rose painfully, the big drops of perspiration standing on his face. Otherwise, the prostrations were most gracefully executed. The devout Moslem keeps himself in practice from his childhood, and the grace of the ceremony is the result of a life's training. The canonical prayer comes five times a day, and each prayer of three *rikaats* has six kneelings, and throwing forward of the person to touch the earth with the forehead. The postulant must rise without touching any thing with the hand to aid him. This will give him 10,950 experiments every year, leaving out special mercies; and no wonder that after thirty, forty, fifty years' practice, he rises with an ease and grace no unbeliever can attain.

After the Sublime Porte had departed, and we had made our salams, and retired to a parlor below, the sultan sent his secretary to ask Prof. Smith how he should express to us his gratification; the occult meaning being a purse? or a decoration? The reply had been agreed upon. Whatever his majesty chose to do, let it be for Prof. Morse, the inventor. Accordingly, an imperial *Birat* or diploma was sent him, and a decoration in diamonds, the first decoration which he received. Many other potentates followed the sultan's example, and decorations and orders were showered upon him.

At a later date, Prof. Smith received one, but no telegraphic line was built. The pashas united against it. They wanted no such tell-tale to report their doings every day, while in the distant interior.

Six years later, the Crimean war made it a necessity; and the lines have become numerous, uniting Constantinople with all the world. From the distant parts of the empire, from India, from America, from all parts of Europe, the telegrams pour into the capital, and are published morning and evening.

My connection with these two efforts to introduce the American telegraph into Turkey was incidental and unimportant; but there is always an interest in looking back to the beginning of things which have fought their way up from weakness to power. The customs of the Ottoman court, and indeed every thing peculiarly oriental, are so rapidly changing, that the above record will not be without some historic interest.

CHAPTER XIII.

SECULAR EMPLOYMENTS.

Secular employments are, to some extent, forced upon every missionary. He finds himself in new circumstances, where almost every thing is out of joint. He is tempted to take hold of every thing that is crooked and *straighten it out.* The man who goes to a foreign land to labor for the regeneration of an unevangelized people, will find few questions more perplexing than this.

Some of the people who gather round him are living in great poverty. Some suffer in their wordly affairs from persecution, and are often at their wit's end for daily bread; sometimes actually suffer the pains of hunger. Their children cry for bread, and they have none to give them. In some communities there is general comfort among the converts, in others, general distress. What shall the missionary do? He is living in comfort which seems to these sons of misery not only abundance but luxury. He has a horse with which he travels on his preaching tours. He has a servant to help in his household. He has food, clothing, and books. He sends out colporteurs and pays them wages. Poverty and misery will count over all these things; and indolence and incompetency desire to have all things in common. That the course to be pursued is not always clear, is plain, from the fact that missionaries differ among themselves, both in theory and practice.

Some hold themselves entirely aloof from every thing secular. They will even refuse to do an act of common kindness, in order to keep themselves aloof from all secular complications. I once wished to pay a small sum which I owed to a man who had gone into the interior. I drew an order upon the treasurer of the station where this man was, and paid the money into the central treasury. But the treasurer refused to honor the draft, because it was secular, and not missionary, business. He was doubtless very conscientious.

But others have been lavish of aid, beyond their resources; which is unmitigatedly bad in principle, and bad in results.

But then—what should the missionary do?

He is not to use commerce, and the arts and industries of civilized life, as a substitute for the Gospel. May he not sometimes use them in aid? It is with this question as with education. It has a subordinate place. In one field it may be a very important one; in another, it will hardly appear at all. In every field, as the mission grows strong, all such questions will be reduced to a very manageable quantity.

I will make a few suggestions and references to certain missions, and then give my own experience.

I would say, first, that the missionary should make all the converts, that is, all who profess to follow the truth, church members or not, feel that they have his sympathy and thoughtful regard. He can do this only by visiting them, seeing just how they live and what their surroundings are. He will soon be able to judge whether there is any hypocrisy or exaggeration in the case, and will have his own sympathies healthfully enlisted. It is very unsafe to endeavor to aid a man, before you know, in common phrase, "all about him."

Secondly, it is equally important to know all the laws and customs of the country. This is not so easy and simple a thing. Unevangelized lands, generally, have no full-written code of laws. What answers somewhat to our common law, is a tangled mass of precedents, out of which almost every thing can be extracted. One must be able, in protecting the right and thwarting injustice, to oppose precedent to precedent, and to fight the oppressor with his own weapons. Without something of this knowledge, one is always in danger of getting into trouble which he had better avoid. One can never get fully into the native life, and become a wise adviser, without a knowledge of the laws and administration of the government.

This is secular work. But the first twenty years of the mission at Constantinople threw upon those who occupied that station so many cases of persecution to be redressed at the Sublime Porte, that much time was of necessity given to that work, and to an acquaintance with the administration of the interior. Dr. Goodell's testimony (see "Forty Years in the Turkish Empire," p. 402) is in point.* One must know the country in which he lives. He will always know too little of it, never too much.

There is no unity to any of the interests of society. Land is embarrassed by a great variety of tenures, and lies here and there under disabilities perplexing and injurious. Industries are loaded down in the same way. The laws of inheritance are an abomination. It requires infinite address to remove one's family (native family) from one place to another. Every thing is embarrassed on all sides. One can not move without running against something and bumping his head. Unless, then, a missionary is acquainted with his surroundings, his course will often embarrass those whom he wishes to aid, and his advice will be absurd or injurious.

Thirdly, the object of the missionary must always be to help the needy to help themselves. The giving or loaning of money is not often beneficial in its final results. I have made four loans, with money placed in my hands for that purpose. One of these gave me no trouble at all, and answered perfectly the end in view. Two others gave me not a little trouble, but resulted well. The fourth

---

* "Much of our time and strength were taken up, and all our wisdom and influence were employed in endeavoring to secure protection for those who were persecuted for righteousness' sake."

ended in bankruptcy, with a loss of three hundred dollars, which has finally been repaid, at the rate of forty or fifty dollars a year. This repayment, however, has been peculiarly gratifying, because I could not legally enforce it.

These loans were all made with every possible precaution, with abundant securities, with an accurate knowledge of all the circumstances, and with a full conviction that no trouble would result therefrom. And yet, only one of the four fully answered my expectations. I consider it, now, rather a piece of good fortune, that no one of them was attended with final loss.

Aiding the poor with money direct is so bad a policy, that nothing but necessity can ever justify it. The late famine in Asia Minor was such a necessity. The persecution of 1846 in Constantinople and neighborhood was another; bringing with it, however, many difficulties and much morbid action, to which I shall hereafter refer.

Now, whatever the missionary can do to promote industry, and to guide to the right objects of industry, is in the line of his calling, and places him in the apostolic succession, although he may not be a tent-maker.

The Zulu Mission in Africa is an example of what intelligent and devoted missionaries can do for the wretched and ignorant, in secular matters. The people in their heathen state were naked savages; woman was held in a state of abject slavery. Revolting cruelty characterized many of the relations of life. There was no such thing as industry. The forced labor of women was the chief source of the means of living. In such a condition of things, the missionary must evidently go very largely into secular employments. It would never do for him to preach the simple Gospel, and leave the converts in the simplicity of nature. He must insist upon their being clothed; and then there must follow a complete change of life, greater to them than any thing we can easily conceive of.

And this is just what the missionaries there have done. They have taught their converts the use of the spade and the plow, and many other implements of agriculture. They have taught them how to make bricks, to build comfortable houses, to have decent furniture, to cook their food properly, to eat at tables, with the blessing of God implored upon their food. They have taught them to build school-houses and churches. Masonry, carpentry, and blacksmithing, have all entered into missionary labors. In developing these industries, they have taught the converts the invaluable lessons of self-support, self-reliance, and division of labor, which puts woman at the head of the household, and man in the workshop and the field.

Commerce has been initiated, and some have been taught to devote themselves to the work of managing the exchanges which the dawning civilization demands. Some are already able to forward their bills of exchange, and to send their own orders for goods to Boston, or to some other port. And so on, with the whole organization of civilized life, these missionaries have given themselves to all varieties of secular labors with a diligence, zeal, ability, and success worthy of all admiration. Under their guidance, a civilized, Christianized society is springing up, with all the blessings of the Christian home, right along the edge of the most infernal heathenism; on the same plains, the Shekinah of the Gospel on one side, the darkness of Egypt on the other. Whoever has listened to the veteran Lindley has been filled with admiration of both the secular and spiritual work there accomplished.

If you have read of Williams, the martyr missionary of Erromanga, you have seen the same process of transition from heathenism to civilization; from utter and hopeless indolence to industry; from a beastly life to a Christian manhood.

So also with the Sandwich and the Fiji Islands, and wherever the Gospel has gone to the debased, ignorant, and degraded, the missionary has had a great secular work to do. And it has not been found practicable to dissever this from his spiritual work. The farmer, the carpenter, the blacksmith accompanying him have been a failure. The reason is plain. They were not the teachers sent from God. They were not clothed with authority to say, "Thus saith the Lord," and to bind and loose in the name of the King of Heaven. Nothing but authoritative teaching will do the heathen the least good. These artisans were not themselves inspired by the recognized possession and use of any such authority. The church did not ordain them to preach the Gospel, and *therefore* they could not teach the heathen to make or drive a nail.

Reliance was placed upon the advantages accruing, upon self-interest, upon the desire for a civilized life. But selfishness ran in strong currents the contrary way. Some of the artisans were discouraged and went home; some fell into heathenism, and were sent home; and some few were ordained to the ministry of the Gospel; and, after that, they could make the lazy scamps work!

If we consider the condition of a mind stupefied by heathenism, just awakened and brought to the knowledge of God, its dependence upon its recognized religious teacher is perfectly natural. It is, in some respects, in childhood. Kind, unselfish, paternal *authority* meets its condition and wants. This authority must be used for the development of power. Just as we train up children to become independent men and women, and are anxious to clothe them with all capacities and powers necessary to their well-being, so must we do with ignorant, uncivilized, or half-civilized converts. We must guide and help them in all things pertaining to a decent, civilized life, until they can go alone; and then, *let them go alone.* The danger is, we shall trust them too late, rather than too soon.

Nor is there much danger in thus introducing civilization, when it is accompanied by the organization of the converts into a Christian church; and the work of bearing testimony to the truth properly committed to it. *Benevolent, self-sacrificing Christian work* is the great and only remedy for the many evils that so often result from a change to a higher state and condition of living.

Our Saviour said, "Give alms of such things as ye have, and behold, all things are clean unto you.' This Christian alms-giving has saved the sudden civilization of the heathen as nothing else could. Commerce and the arts have no corrupting influence, when introduced to help forward a Christian life, and Christian work. Deeply and fearfully corrupting under some circumstances, they are pure and elevating under others.

And this is what our Saviour meant, in that bold and remarkable declaration that alms-giving according to one's ability—"of such things as ye have"—should purify all things. It is a principle of universal application. It is not the possession, but the *use* of money, that determines its moral effects for good or evil. Wealth is everywhere corrupting if not rightly used; it is everywhere purifying and elevating, when consecrated to Christ and the Gospel. Were missionaries, everywhere, to stand upon the spirituality of their work and message, and actually have nothing to do with any secular labors whatever, the first impression might be much greater. But, would the converts, left to themselves, work out a Christian civilization? Would they rise up into a perfect manhood in Christ Jesus? I trow not. No experiment of that nature has ever succeeded. Education, and the common industries of civilized life, must accompany, but not precede the Gospel, in order to have a church with the three grand characteristics,—"self-governing," "self-supporting," "self-developing."

Some suppose that I have gone into secular and especially mechanical industries, in the evangelizing work, from a natural tendency that way. Nothing could be further from the truth. What I have done has been from the *imperious force of circumstances;* and naturally I am no mechanic, and no business man. Every boy brought up on a farm till he is sixteen, as I was, gets a certain use of tools. With a brother two years older than myself, and no father to take the heavy work, we tried to be men while we were yet mere boys. We essayed to make ox-yokes, wood-sleds, bobsleds (the name and thing are now unknown), ox-bows, cart-bodies, etc. My brother had marvellous skill and taste. I was clumsy and blundering, but with considerable perseverance. There was nothing else. Two years in the silversmith and jewelry shop of my brother-in-law, let me into some of the mysteries of the metallic world; and I had nothing more to do with wood, if I could avoid it.

I was glad to abandon the shop when I commenced my studies. A sheer accident, while a member of Bowdoin College, led to some other things of more importance; and on their account, is worth narrating.

As I was passing along in front of "Maine Hall," a gang of students, who had been out surveying, were just presenting to Prof. Smyth his theodolite, with a screw lost. It was the binding screw, used in clamping the disks in taking horizontal angles. Professor Smyth never disguised a feeling, any more than a principle. He had been accused of saying, on receiving the beautiful instrument from England, that it was "handsomer than any lady in Brunswick!" He was just saying to the luckless students, "The beauty of this instrument is ruined! What sort of a screw will Jackson make!" I stopped, and said to him, "I think I can make a better screw than Jackson." "I don't doubt that you can, if you can make any," he said; and to my surprise, gave up the precious instrument to my care. I found excellent brass and all needed tools at Mr. Cary's (the watch-maker of Brunswick); and made a screw that in general was like the one lost. Having the use of the lathe well learned, and finding a screw plate to fit, there was not the slightest difficulty. Could I produce a polish that would equal the English, and surpass Brunswick beauty? With a piece of a razor hone, letting water drip on, I ground the surface to a dead evenness, leaving not a trace of the turning tool. By taking sulphate of iron, and subjecting it to red heat in a closed crucible, until the sulphuric acid was expelled, and then "levigating" it, an excellent polishing powder was obtained, and a satisfactory polish produced. The Professor expressed his gratification as frankly as he had expressed his disgust. It was a worthless incident, but life is made up of such. We know what we do to-day, but we know nothing of its bearing upon the future. This affair, trifling as it was, led to that kind of friendship which a college youth so highly values, which indeed both value. The youth, with love and reverence, thinks, how shall I rise to any distant approach to him—and the man, with yearning heart, thinks, "What shall the harvest be" in this young soul? No shadow ever passed over that friendship; and it ripens still.

When Prof. Smyth lectured to our class on the steam engine, few of us had ever seen one. Few of us had any clear idea of its essential parts, mode of working, and power. I had myself seen the engine of the steamer Chancellor Livingston for a few minutes only, as she was about to leave the wharf in Portland. A man told me which was the cylinder, and which the piston, and then said, "you had better jump ashore, if you don't mean to go to Boston!" I was not very much enlightened, but then *I had seen a steam engine!*

After the lecture, I said to Prof. Smyth, "It seems to me I could make a working model that would illustrate the thing to the class; and if the college would buy it, in case of success, I would spend the winter vacation upon it, instead of teaching a school." "I believe you can make any thing you undertake, Hamlin, and I have no doubt the college will buy it." I was in for it, knowing nothing of what I had undertaken; but Prof. Smyth's confidence was an inspiration to me; and at all events, there could be no backing out. I said to him, "There will be some expense for material, and I have not a dollar to meet it." "How much will it be?" "I'm sure I don't know. Ten dollars, perhaps." "You may draw upon me for that," he replied; and so, within five minutes of the first inception of the idea, the bargain was sealed. In certain things, ignorance accomplishes more than knowledge. Had I known the difficulties before me, I would have chosen school-keeping!

I obtained Lardner on the steam engine, and began to read up on the subject. I was alarmed at having undertaken to do it in two months. When reviews commenced, I obtained two weeks' grace, as I could prepare my reviews in the evenings; and away I went to Portland.

I found a place to work in Mr. Edward Grueby's clock-factory; a bench, a small forge, and a good foot-lathe being the chief privileges. Ten dollars' rent went *at a slap*, and I knew the learned Professor's scant salary must not be drawn upon for more. I had made my plan. A cylinder giving ten-inch stroke, with two-inch diameter of piston-head. I turned out a model for the cylinder. The first casting did not suit me, on trial, and I had to pay for recasting. Eight dollars more went; and that was only the beginning of troubles; for it was to be a low pressure or condensing engine, and there would be many more castings, and more models to be made. The boring out of the cylinder was the chief difficulty. I contrived a way of doing it, and General Neal Dow, then full of the enthusiasm of youth, which he has also carried into age, helped me in this operation. Mr. Sparrow was putting up a little second-hand high pressure engine, which he had bought in New York, and he had a lathe which we used for the boring.

The bore was a thing to laugh at, but by patient use of a fine, half-round file, and emery and oil, I obtained a uniform and beautiful surface. I had then never seen emery glued to a surface of wheel or stick for polishing, and had not wit enough to invent it. I soon found I must work evenings, or the ten weeks would not suffice. Mr. Grueby very kindly allowed me the use of the shop, often working till nine himself. Each week I advanced an hour until ten, eleven, twelve, and sometimes one o'clock, if I could keep awake. Ten weeks passed, and the work was not done. Prof. Smyth came up from Brunswick to look after it. He said, "Go on, success is sure," and he obtained two weeks more for me, in which I finished it. I was *seventy-two dollars in debt!!* Lyceums then paid ten dollars per lecture. I gave two in Portland, and engaged one in Saco. Mr. Nichols, of the machine-shop, said, "Let us have a ticket lecture here, and my men alone will give you more than ten dollars. You can just as well go away with twenty-five or

LYCEUM LECTURES OF 1832.   209

thirty dollars." The change was made, and golden dreams haunted me. The evening came with a fearful snow-storm. I have friends in Saco (Dr. Goodell for one) who still remember that evening, and the lecture. Some twenty-five or thirty men came; but with pay of hall and travelling expenses I was one dollar and fifty cents out of pocket. Prof. Smyth, who thought in mathematics, told me I could now form a clear conception of a *minus quantity!* In Hallowell and Augusta, I had better fortune. Brunswick gave me ten dollars at the Lyceum, and thirty-two dollars at a ticket lecture! My debts were paid and the college gave me one hundred and seventy-five dollars for the engine, to use as a model in lectures. It is now placed in the Cleaveland Cabinet. The skilled mechanic would smile at it, and would need to remember that it is the first steam engine ever made in the state of Maine, and that it was made by a student, not by a mechanic; and by one who had never seen a steam engine except as mentioned above. If it had led to nothing farther, this history would not have been worth giving.

The knowledge of the philosophy and use of steam, which I thus acquired, has often been a pleasant thing to have. I once visited a steam saw-mill, and noticed what I thought a mistaken mode of saving heat from the waste steam. Knowing the man to be a very profane and scornful fellow, I said nothing; but afterwards meeting him on a steamboat, I called his attention to that point, and we had a long and pleasant discussion. He said I was probably right, and he should apply the remedy immediately. When he left, he shook hands with me, and said in all honesty and simplicity, "I don't often talk with men of your cloth, but when I meet one who knows as much about steam as you do I'll be damned if I don't respect him!"

Thirty-nine years ago, when I first went to Constantinople there was but one English store where good English articles could be obtained. It was a store for every thing, and the missionaries went there occasionally for supplies. It was the rendezvous for English engineers from steamers and government works, when off duty; and no missionary could happen in, when they were there, without hearing a great deal of profane and insulting slang, spoken to each other, but really intended for him. I resolved to have a discussion with them, some day, upon steam; and fixed upon certain points about *superheated* steam, then attracting attention, and about the philosophy of high steam used expansively. It was not long before I found the desired opportunity. A good number was present when I went in. While I was making my purchases, they were talking with each other about *sanctification*, the *conversion of the heathen*, etc. When I had finished my business in the store, I turned to the chief one among them, and asked him if I might propose to him and his friends some questions about steam and steam engines. "Oh yes, yes; certainly, certainly." They all looked quite ready to laugh, and answered some questions very incautiously, until they began to suspect that they had fallen into a trap. They were compelled to admit their mistakes, and they never invited any more catechetical exercises on steam; but treated us all with invariable respect. With two of them I formed a pleasant acquaintance. Thus I often felt that the time I had given to steam was worth something, besides the one hundred and seventy-five dollars which was, at first, its sole measure.

CHAPTER XIV.

INDUSTRIES AND INTERDICTS.

During the years of trial from 1839 to 1849, the evangelical Armenians had suffered much, and in many ways. The anathema had done its work, but could not obliterate them. The firman of organization and equal rights had been obtained, but with the numerous and combined opposition of Greeks, Armenians, and Catholics, the firman was often powerless. The persecuted could not establish successful trade among such numerous enemies. They could not get into remunerative employments. Many were living in enforced idleness, and were, of course, being demoralized by it; for "Satan finds some mischief still, for idle hands to do." He is a great worker himself!

The students in the seminary felt this condition of the community. Many of them could not provide for themselves decent clothing, and their friends could do nothing to aid them. Some who had not joined the anathematized body at all, were cut off from aid by the mere fact of their being in this "heretical" establishment. Gratuitous aid was becoming a failure and a disease.

To remedy this state of things, and to provide

for pressing wants, I applied to my friend, Mr. Hague, the accomplished engineer of the Imperial Works at Zeitūn Bornou. He and his workmen furnished forty pounds sterling for fitting up a workshop, among the columns on which the front part of the seminary stood. No money of the American Board was invested in it. It was a workshop for sheet-iron stoves and stove-pipe, then coming largely into use. We learned the business as we went along. Three hours every day were given to the shop, and the boys took hold of it with enthusiasm and success. One result was, that bare feet and rags disappeared; another, habits of study improved; and another, the work furnished outside employment for those who went round setting up stoves. This was not so simple a matter, where there were no chimneys to the houses, and the stove-pipe must pass through the window, and run up outside far enough to produce a draught.

Some of the students attempted other industries, as silvering and gilding, and developed not a little chemical knowledge and tact in various ways. I constructed three small assaying furnaces, and something was done in the assaying of ores, by fluxes, as well as by chemical solution.

This scheme of doing things encountered great opposition. It would secularize the whole work, and turn young men from the ministry of the Gospel to worldly pursuits.

My own view was, that minds born into society destitute of all spirituality, would not be greatly corrupted by being taught to work instead of beg, and especially in a country where work is so unpopular as in the East.

Another thought had much weight with me. Ability to engage in some secular pursuit, the conscious power to live by one's own exertions, is a necessary safeguard to the purity of the native ministry. He who enters the ministry because there is nothing else for him to do, will hardly be a very spiritually minded worker.

The students of that seminary did not all enter the ministry. Those who did, are noble men. They and their pupils can hardly be equalled in the ranks of the native ministry. Some of the very best workmen in the shop have become "workmen that need not to be ashamed in rightly dividing the word of truth." Were they not still living I should like to delineate some of them, whom I hold in love and honor. Of Zenope, the teacher of the high-school in Aintab, I may speak, for he has passed away.

In addition to mechanical skill, he seemed to have a true genius in chemistry, and I thought Providence meant him for a manufacturing chemist. The Jesuits, from their great pharmacy in Galata, were then the chief purveyors to the pharmacies of all that part of the empire which, commercially, centres at Constantinople.

The Hon. Austin H. Layard, then in England, and always a warm friend to our educational establishments in Turkey, obtained for him a place with

A Splendid Position. 215

a distinguished manufacturing chemist and friend of missions, offering him every facility for mastering his profession, and promising him all needed aid to establish himself in Constantinople, should he prove himself a faithful and competent man. It seemed to open a great future to him, that would make him an honor and a blessing to the poor struggling community, which was fighting its almost hopeless way through the long lines of the enemy.

I had not intimated to him what I was doing, until the result was secured. When I told him, he seemed deeply moved, even shed tears, but said, firmly, that he had covenanted with God to be a teacher to his poor ignorant countrymen. I placed the question fully and fairly before him, and advised him to reflect upon it, and seek for light from the Father of lights. He remained immovable, though deeply tried; and went to Aintab on a salary of twelve dollars a month, and to find himself. His memory is fragrant in all that region, to this day. I have never known a purer, nobler, instance of entire abnegation of self.

Some of those students have made their mark in business life, and some in the medical profession. One is the civil head (vekil) of the Protestant community of Turkey, and dared, in the Turkish parliament, to speak for peace, against the tumultuous outcry for war. One, a Christian merchant, who commenced his career in the stove business, and whom, in connection with Messrs. Cushing and Mack, of Lowell, I started on that career, has for many years contributed an average of $3,000 a year to various departments of Christian benevolence. Many of our Christian merchants in America, of larger means, the offspring of our oldest Christian civilization, do not exceed this.

What I claim to show by these facts is, that the secular occupations demanded by the most urgent wants of life, do not of necessity depress the standard of Christian living.

Now that I have passed off from the stage, I rejoice in their noble, useful lives; and, dead, live in them.

But there was, outside of the seminary, an uncertain number of the evangelical community out of employment, some of them capable men, and some of that unlucky class found everywhere, the wide world over. Providence is always against them, thwarting their best laid plans, overthrowing them at the very point of distinguished success. I have heard such affirm that they suffered not only for their own sins, but for the sins of their ancestors. "Who did sin, this man or his parents?"

I endeavored to give them work such as I could protect. One I taught to manufacture camphene, by which he supported his family a year or more, until he found better employment.

Another was a good oriental cutler, supporting himself, mother, and two sisters, in comfort. He **was driven from his shop; he was compelled to sell** his tools for bread; he would not receive charity; and, finally, he became a hypochondriac. He believed himself stone and would stand for hours without winking. Seeing him by chance in this state, and learning the facts, I offered him a day's pay in advance, to come to Bebek to work for me. It was amusing to see with what difficulty he opened his hand to receive the money, as it slowly changed from stone to life! He came; and, although very silent and melancholy, I found him a good blacksmith. He worked for a while in setting up stoves, after he had finished my work; and became cheerful and happy.

After that work had come to an end, and its gains were consumed, he fell back into his former state. I must do something to rescue him and others from misery. I had just received a *right smart* American rat-trap.

With no little difficulty, I induced him and one of his *confrères*, Hohannes, to undertake the manufacture of traps on that model. We made one together, and, finally, they tried it in the way I proposed. I hired a place for them in Galata; the division of labor was well applied, Jewish boys sold the traps, and some half-dozen persons found full employment. The hypochondriac was thoroughly cured, and made a happy and useful man, by rat-traps. But this only touched the edge of the difficulty, and showed a possibility of reaching it.

One evening, as I was going home from the city

and was conversing with Mr. Charles Ede, our English banker and friend, I remarked that there was one way to solve the whole problem, but rendered impossible for want of capital. "What way is that?" A steam flouring-mill and bakery. "That is not the difficulty," he replied. "The Millers' and Bakers' Guild is the closest in the capital; a thousand pounds would not buy your way into it, and you would have ten thousand millers and bakers against you." But I can claim it as a right, direct from the Sublime Porte, I replied. Mehmet II., when he took Constantinople, gave every foreign nationality that should locate at his capital the right to its own mill and bakery. Americans have never claimed it, and I can therefore claim it. "If that is so," said he, "I will furnish you all the capital you want, you securing me on the buildings and machinery. I would like nothing better than to have you fail, and pass it over to me, so far as the investment is concerned."

The missionary station doubted the feasibility of the thing. I knew nothing about a mill or bakery. It would secularize the missionary work. It would injure the missionary character. The Board would disapprove, and it would all end in disaster. But there were some who took a different view, especially Dr. Schauffler and Mr. Benjamin. The alternative to finding employment is a pauper Christianity, and a diseased, unnatural state of feeling. We, the missionaries, have protection, safety, and all the comforts of life. They are persecuted by their own people. Some of them have been reduced from affluence to poverty, to beggary even; and their present life will never show to the world the Gospel in its true light. Until they can live by their own labor, and not by charity, their faith will not commend itself to others. To help them out of this condition is as truly a Christian work as healing the sick or restoring sight to the blind. Instead of blotting or blearing the missionary character, it will vindicate it.

As for myself, I was ready to incur the responsibility, and abide the judgment of the future.

The station so far yielded, as to pass a vote, not to be recorded, that they would not object to my acting upon my personal responsibility. Hon. Geo. P. Marsh was then our Minister Resident. He entered heartily into the plan; and, notwithstanding the opposition of the guild, he claimed and obtained the firman, under the Capitulation Act of 1453. There was some curious experience connected with the firman, which so well illustrates "the way things go" in Constantinople, and in the East generally, that I will narrate it. The government readily promised the firman; and, had no opposition occurred, would have given it. But one of the great pashas was a very extensive owner of mills and bakeries. The mills were all horse-mills then, and he evidently feared that the small steam-mill proposed would grow. He knew what usually comes of giving foreigners an entering wedge. He had the immense guild, also, whose interests were one with his. The promise of the firman was not performed. No government on earth was ever so skilful in putting off a thing, as the Turkish.

At length, I began to build, on the faith of the promise. We had not proceeded far, before engineers from the Porte came to examine and take a plan of our works. I knew that foretold an interdict, and counselled all to shut the gate, if they saw an officer approaching. By treaty right, no one could thus enter without an officer accompanying him from our embassy; and I was sure they would not even apply for one, but hope to carry the point irregularly, and to arrest and imprison all the men found working.

One day, at noon recess, the officer came, and Demetri, whom he wished first of all to arrest, was standing in the street, eating bread and olives. "Where is Demetri Calfa?" said he to Demetri himself. "I just saw him at the wine-shop," was the cool reply. "Turn round the corner to your right, at the foot of the street."

The officer soon returned; the workmen were all in the attic, the students and I were below. "Who is the master-workman here?" "I am, sir." "I want the *rayah* master." "There is no such man here." "I arrest you all, young men, and make 'pydos' interdict." "Keep to work, boys! You are students, and can't be arrested in this way." "But these are workmen." "No, sir; they are all my students!" An unwary workman

Confusion of the Officer. 221

in the attic had, in the meantime, thrust out his head; and the officer saw him. "Ho! you skulker, *you* are a workman! Come down here, you will go with me!" "I am one of Mr. Hamlin's scholars!" was the cool reply. "*You* a scholar! Let me hear you read!" The man, who was a good carpenter and a great wag, and belonged to no particular faith, turned round, found a New Testament in Armeno-Turkish, and began to read appropriate passages. The officer was confounded. I then put my hand upon his shoulder, told him he was violating treaty rights, that he could reign on the other side of the wall, but I, within, until he should come in a legal manner; and so I led him out, and shut the gate. He sat down upon a stone, and began to soliloquize. "Such an *interdict* never saw I! The master-workman is a foreign hodja; the workmen are all his students! I am breaking the treaty! My soul! what reply shall I carry back?" I went out and comforted him, and told him to say, that if the Porte should violate the treaty again I should accuse it to the embassy and the American government. And, as the right was included in the "Capitulations," I should inform other embassies of the act. It can enter this establishment again only through our embassy.

The Turkish government had placed itself in a false position. It must now apply to the embassy and ignore its oft-repeated promise; or it must give the firman. It wisely chose the latter; and the interdict became the amusement of the village, and the chagrin of the pasha and bakers who had instigated it.

A small steam engine came from England, and it required more than all my knowledge of steam to set it up. The steam-pipe, by some unpardonable error, was six inches too short. I found some sufficiently adhesive sand on the hills, made a mould, and using my largest assay furnace, I essayed to cast it. The sand was too damp, the iron too hot, the gas-escapes too small—the result —an astounding explosion! The burning metal went whizzing everywhere, setting the place on fire, and making things lively generally. The fire was soon extinguished; nobody was hurt, and the next trial was a perfect success; illustrating, what I have before confessed, a capacity for blundering and getting out of it. The piece cast is still faithfully performing its duty.

At length, the parts were together, and the steam was to be let in. I had some doubts about the adjustment of the eccentric, and I wished the eager crowd away. If it should fail of working well, the report would not stop short of the Seven Towers. It was, however, all that could be desired, and it required no after adjustment. No one knew the inward exultation I felt. It was like the first attempt at Bowdoin.

I had solicited the mill from the American Board. It consisted of simply one run of French bühr millstones with all the accompaniments, costing six hundred dollars. I promised to repay principal

BREAD FOR DONKEYS. 223

and interest. The Board refused the request; but John Tappan, Esq., one of the Prudential Committee, sent the articles required; and, though some smiled at his confidence, he lost nothing by it; and he afterwards expressed his high gratification in having thus saved me from disappointment and delay. The reasons of the Board were perfectly satisfactory, and I should not have made the request.

We employed a skilful man to manage the heating of the oven and the baking; otherwise there was neither miller nor baker in the whole establishment. Our first efforts were not entirely successful. The bread came out sour, and *flat as a pancake!* Donkeys alone were able to eat it.

It is almost always so, when one first applies mere book-knowledge to actual work. Let him expect a failure, and he will not be disappointed. Let him determine to succeed, and he will not be disappointed in that.

What baffled me more than any mechanical work I ever undertook, was the *dressing* of the bühr millstones. No blacksmith could temper the picks so that they would hold. I was compelled to experiment upon this attempering process, until I hit it exactly. After that, there was no trouble on that score; but it was a long time before the stones were properly dressed.

Whatever blunders we made—and they were not few—and whatever losses we incurred—which can not be avoided under such circumstances, and which seem necessary to all tentative progress—the result of the first year was beyond our expectations. When I closed the accounts, I had repaid to Mr. Ede one half the capital invested, with interest; and had given employment to all whom I proposed thus to aid.

I had reduced the work to such system, that it occupied but little of my own time. I found the men, for the most part, intelligent, active, and faithful. They evinced good mechanical ability; and it may be said that we learned the business, and triumphed over difficulties, together.

With the same steam power I also established a factory of lasts. But it resulted in failure, and involved the establishment in a trifling loss.

During this first year, I received some letters of reproof, of great severity. They were written by excellent, conscientious, Christian men, who were jealous of the honor of the missionary work. They either did not know the facts of the case, or they had erroneous views. To one only I replied with full explanation, and I fear, with considerable severity. But he showed the nobility of his nature by enclosing with his reply five hundred dollars to aid the work.

A very slight matter had secured a large patronage to the bakery. Our bread was made a little over weight, instead of following the example of the bakers, who always make it a little under weight. As often as the examiners tried our bread, they said "Mashallah!" and passed on.

The people soon learned the fact; and the amount of time that they would spend to obtain this bread would exceed in value fourfold the difference of weight they would thus gain. The truth is, all men like to be treated well in a bargain, and do not so much mind the amount.

We had introduced another improvement. Attempts had been made to bring into market yeast bread, but had failed. The bread of the country is universally leavened bread; and no one but foreigners knew any thing about making bread with hop yeast.

Having first mastered the art of making good hop yeast, the bread we produced became known as "Protestant bread," and commanded a good sale at an advanced price. In a short time I hoped to pay off the whole debt, and to hand the work over to the employés. It was not so to be.

CHAPTER XV.

CRIMEAN WAR.

During the second year of our industrial operations, the Crimean war began to mutter its thunders. So much has been written upon it in a partisan spirit, that I shall pass it by. It was then never supposed that England entered into that contest for any other purpose than to drive Russia back. Both France and England then considered Russia at Constantinople a menace to the Mediterranean.

It is only the distorted vision of party spirit that can see in that any wish to support the Crescent against the Cross, except as incident to political views. Governments are too selfish to either build up or pull down, except in reference to their own interests; and England is no exception to this rule. She fought that war in her own interests; not in the interests of Turkey.

One can hardly claim more benevolence for Russia than for England. She wants to protect "the Christians" * of the Turkish empire.

* The word "Christian," in Russian use, applies only to members of the Greek church. She speaks of others as Protestants,

While she would do this, she would probably exterminate the Protestants and other infidels, so far as in her power. Mr. Layard declared, in his place in Parliament, that one reason why Russia hastened the Crimean war was to arrest Protestant influence. The first auxiliary Bible Society was holding its first anniversary in a hall adjoining the very room where M. De Boutineff declared, "the emperor of Russia will never allow Protestantism to set its foot in Turkey;" while the English fleet was entering the harbor, and the place was shaken by its heavy salutes. A splendid Christian officer, Hedley Vicars, was present at the meeting, and made an earnest appeal for the salvation of the land by Bible truth and grace.

That fearful war resulted in certain compensatory changes, but they were not such as either party sought; and it may turn out the same with the present conflict.

The fluctuating prices occasioned by the approach of war, compelled the bakery to work with caution; until it became certain that a great conflict was to disturb the peace of Europe.

The English hospital was established at Scutari, near the camp of six or eight thousand, more or

---

Catholics, Heretics, and other confessions; but never as *Christians*. When the emperor speaks of "Christians of all kinds," he refers to the different divisions of his own church. The Russian looks upon Europe as wholly infidel, and Russia alone as Christian. This should always be borne in mind when reading any thing Russian.

less, as they landed, and after a few days' rest, proceeded to the destination.

Dr. Mapleton, Lord Raglan's chief physician, was sent by him to inspect and organize the hospital arrangements. Happening to see some of our· "Protestant bread," he sent a messenger to ask me to call upon him. The interview was rather comical, as he "wanted a baker, and not a missionary!" It terminated in a contract to furnish the hospital with bread to any amount required. The commencement was one hundred and fifty loaves, of one pound each. It continued to increase as the war advanced. We had to construct another oven, hire a third, and build a fourth. The increase of the work did not very much increase the time demanded to oversee it. I had trained and faithful men. In one thing they failed. No one of them could purchase flour without being cheated in price, weight, or quality, especially the latter. Our little mill could work but half the time, for want of water, except in winter; and as the flour went at the rate of sixty to seventy barrels per day to produce eight and one half tons of bread, and there must always be two weeks' supply in store, it was a matter of prime importance to make good purchases. The Greek flour merchants of Galata generally treated me with fairness and perfect confidence. One firm, to whom I had frankly stated that I had no property whatever of my own, sold me flour to the value of $30,000, upon my simple word that I would pay him by the tenth of the next month. When I carried him the bills of exchange, he waved them, with a smile, to a gentleman whom I recollected as present at our bargain. After he had gone, I asked Mr. M. what that meant? "That gentleman," he said, "told me I was a fool to sell in that way, and that he would like to see the money paid! Now he has seen it!" "How did you justify yourself to him?" I inquired. "I told him I knew the American missionaries by reputation, and I knew that no one of them would sell his character for money." It was testimony all the more pleasing, as he was no friend to the evangelic movement in Turkey.

I am sorry to say that there were three efforts at fraud, but each of them ignominiously failed, and subjected their authors to ridicule. Failure in deception does not annoy the deceiver so much as exposure.

The Crimean war brought out the noblest and the basest attributes of human character. Hedley Vicars among the officers, Rev. Dr. Blackwood among the chaplains, his noble wife, Lady Alicia Blackwood, in all works of benevolence among the soldiers' families, Florence Nightingale in the hospitals, are specimen characters, of whom there were many, less known to fame, who are the glory, not of England only, but of our common faith and our common origin.

But while the Crimean war exalted my ideas of humanity, it also debased them.

When the great hospital at Scutari became crowded, and the doctors and servants were overworked, the men, whom I visited, told me their greatest sufferings were in the night. At ten o'clock, every light was extinguished, and no one came near them till morning. Often the cries for water, or the groans of the dying, or the ravings of the delirious, made night horrible. I went to Dr. Menzies, the chief physician, and proposed to come, with a dozen or fifteen of my most trusty students, as night-watchers. I could not understand the asperity with which he rejected this. I then wrote a note to Commissary-Gen. Potgeiter, proposing to organize a force of volunteer night-watchers from among the American and English residents, and I pledged myself that we would strictly adhere to all the rules which Dr. M. should propose, and said that my only design was to alleviate the immense amount of human suffering which seemed to be so needless. Gen. P. forwarded my note, with his own, and received the brief and curt reply, "We can not admit any outside interference." So thousands of brave men must suffer darkness, torture, and death!

To one going in from the pure fresh air, the smell of the hospital was nauseous in the extreme, and indicated not only carelessness, but great incompetency.

My refusal to enter into any *relations* with Dr. Menzies and a Mr. Rogers, with respect to the bread, may have produced this asperity, and it certainly condemned the bread. It was shut up in an atmosphere and heat which made it ferment. It was then condemned and thrown back upon me; and other bread bought, at my expense, and at a higher price. Counterfeit bread, of the vilest character, was introduced as mine, reported upon, and condemned. As soon as I found there was a combination that I could not resist, I went to Commissary-Gen. Smith, threw up my contract, and told him I should pay the penalty of two hundred pounds, under protest. Gen. S. was fully convinced of the combination, but had no power over it. He forwarded my protest to Lord Raglan, to whom I appealed the case. I also wrote to Dr. Mapleton, and insisted that I be exonerated from the penalty of non-fulfilment of contract. I said nothing about the two hundred pounds, or more, of loss on condemned bread, further than to state the fact. A speedy reply came from the commander-in-chief, not only remitting the penalty, but requiring the hospital to pay for all it had condemned! The officer who read to me the despatch, added, "It is the most remarkable despatch of its kind I ever read! You have more than you asked, and there is Dr. M's death-knell in it, besides!" There is no doubt but many accusations, far weightier than my own, had been forwarded against him.

The triumphing of the wicked was short. They had a new contract at fifty per cent. advance in price; but, at the same time, there was a panic in the flour market, and flour rose fifty per cent.! The gains were small, but they had saved me from ruin. The hospital at Kulelie would not receive their bread, and I continued to supply it *at their price*, fifty per cent. in advance of the old. And, finally, the whole work reverted to me at the advanced price, and the ovens, thanks to their enemies, went on their way rejoicing. I resolved to take for my motto in future, "Fret not thyself because of evil-doers, because of the man that bringeth wicked devices to pass."

Dr. M. was finally removed in disgrace.

When Miss Nightingale came, with her nurses, all was changed. She had many coadjutors; and improvements followed one another in rapid succession, till it became a model hospital. But no one thing in the change was spoken of with such gratitude, by the men, as the night-watching. Their long, hopeless, tedious nights were now enlightened by wise, gentle, and tender care. In the high attributes of Miss Nightingale's character, I think there was no one that surpassed her soundness of judgment, her excellent common sense.

In connection with the Kulelie hospital, I had another *Crimean episode*, which was attended with some good results. The battle of Inkerman was fought on the 5th of November, 1855. A week or so after, I saw, lying at Kulelie, on the Asiatic side, a huge English steamer, and recognized it as the Himalaya, the largest iron merchant steamer then afloat. I crossed over at once, and found two hundred and fifty of the wounded in the cavalry barracks. Some Russian wounded were lying on the float wharf, and I helped place them upon stretchers, to be carried in. The day was cold and stormy for the season, and the men were suffering.

"Look well to yourself, sir," said the English soldier. "All these *fellers'* blankets are chock full of lice, and our'n as well."

I picked off eleven of the most atrocious beasts I ever saw, from my woollen gloves. I then went to see the poor English wounded. They were in a pitiable state. There was no adequate preparation for them. They said they had had no washing for five months—for want of wood and water. "Have you no under-flannels?" I said. "Yes, but they are so full of vermin, we prefer to suffer from the cold. There's lots of clothing, but it can't be worn."

I went to the chief physician, Dr. O'Connor, to ask him if he found any difficulty about the washing. He replied, surlily, that it couldn't be done. The Greeks washed some in sea-water, and brought them back wet, and that killed the men. I suggested to him what could be done. He damned me as an intruder, with an old dirty meerschaum hanging in the corner of his mouth. I made a few remarks to him, and left him. Passing in front of the barrack, I met a soldier. "Can you tell me where I can find the 'sargent' of the clothing?" "I am the sergeant of the clothing." "Then you are the man I want. Let me see all you have." He opened a great hall, with clothing piled up, I should think for a thousand men.

"But why don't you ventilate this place? You'll have the plague!" "There is a great window, sir, taken out." It was even so. There were beds and bedding, and clothes of every kind, taken from the wounded and the dead, with all possible abominations, and incredibly full of vermin! If any thing could make war utterly accursed, it would be the Crimean lice! They are large, fat, disgusting, overgrown, *hellish* looking creatures! I have tried their bite, personally, and found it irritating, maddening in the extreme. Each puncture is surrounded by an intensely red inflammation, with an intolerable burning itch, which nothing but ammonia, as strong as can be safely used, will allay. I have no doubt they killed more English soldiers than all the Russian bullets. The effect of their ravages upon those who survived, was interesting and peculiar. Nature threw up her defences in the best way she could, the skin, after a while, becoming thickened, dead and corky in appearance. The tissue having thus lost its sensitiveness, the suffering would be diminished.

The sergeant told me that, despairing of washing the clothing, they had built a place for burning it; and he showed me the furnace, with a tall, rude chimney, at the back of the grounds. How much they consumed, I know not. He said the authorities at Scutari could neither provide the men with new, nor secure the washing of the old clothing. I went immediately to Scutari, and made known the state of things, the conduct of

O'Connor, and the perfect ease with which the want could be supplied; there being thousands of women, Armenian, Greek, Turkish, in the Bosphorus villages, who would be glad of the work. Mr. Parker, the chief purveyor of the great hospital, said he found it next to impossible to get the washing well done for the five thousand under his direct care; and if I could do any thing for Kulelie it would be the greatest possible favor. I asked for no contract and no price. I was determined to do the work, and change the aspect of things in Kulelie. My doing it in spite of Dr. O'Connor, may have added to the zest of rescuing the sufferers.

On returning to Bebek, I met the Armenian kehyah (head man) and told him what I wanted. "I have just the place for you, a tumbled-down house, but with a large garden excellent for drying purposes, a huge kitchen, and an unfailing supply of water, right in the kitchen itself." I examined, and hired it at a reasonable price, monthly, so long as I should want it. I never undertook to do any thing that went so glibly. Usually the obstacles to a work require more time than the work itself.

In a very few days, two large copper kettles were set in masonry, so as to deliver the hot water through twenty-two faucets, into twenty-two washing places. A large pump delivered the water into the kettles or cold-water tubs, lines were stretched in the garden, to the amount of nearly half a mile, a small sloop-load of wood was most fortunately obtained, and two capable men employed to oversee the whole: one the work at the laundry, the other the transportation from and to the Asiatic side of the Bosphorus. Twenty women, Greek and Armenian, were engaged, and eager for the work. I made satisfactory arrangements with them all, intending to charge every expense to the British government, and let it go at that; every body assuring me that *red-tape* would make the payment impracticable.

While I was hearing a class, the overseer burst into the recitation room, in great excitement, saying, "Oh, sir! come quickly! the mob will tear down the whole establishment, and the women have all fled!" The truth was, the clothes were so filthy, disgusting, and loaded with vermin, that the women feared to touch them; and declared they would never enter the place again. About three thousand articles had been brought over, in large bundles, and opened in the court; and the offensive odor had gone up into the windows of the houses on that side. The people, naturally excited, were assembling in angry haste. Here was trouble all around! I told the people their complaints were reasonable, and the clothes should be immediately removed to the magazine on the other side; but if they made trouble, I should immediately send for a guard of English soldiers, and they would have the pleasure of dealing with them. The people became quiet, and departed. What was

I to do? I was certainly *in a fix*. I could not blame the women or the people.

A thought struck me. It came of itself. A complete idea of one of the empty oak beer-casks lying at Kulelie, changed into a washing machine. I sent for my best workman, Pandazee, to come, with another man, to work all night, if need be. The malicious O'Connor would not let me have a cask, without an order from Scutari, which cost me three hours' time to get. But the next morning, about nine o'clock, the machine was ready, and on the ground. A few women sullenly came, after much persuasion, to see it tried. I must produce a surprising effect on the first trial; and a large quantity of melted soap had been put, unnoticed, into the barrel. I took up the articles with tongs, and put them in, let on the water, and told the man to work the brake twenty minutes. Five or six minutes were found to be quite enough. The water ran off with a filthy, muddy color. Pure water was let in, till, after rinsing, it came away pure. The articles were taken out, transformed. The women had no objections to the finishing work. The twenty-two women returned, more machines were made, and the work went on merrily, without further care. The bodies of the vermin lined the channel through which the waste water flowed, and yet so many were entangled in the furze of woollen articles, that they all had to be brushed with stiff brushes. But what surprised me most was, that the boiling water did not destroy the vitality of the eggs deposited by the million on the flannels. There were patches of these, sometimes as large as the hand; and we had to employ brushes made of fine brass wire. I found these by accident in Galata, and the owner himself did not know what they were made for. He- had them by accident. They did our work effectively.

As soon as a complete set of all articles for two hundred and fifty men could be prepared, they were sent over, and produced both joy and comfort.

Dr. O'Connor was removed. I think he was a brutal, unfeeling wretch, and cared nothing for the sick and wounded. Dr. Tice, a gentleman, came in his place, and he ordered the men to change twice a week.

In good weather for drying, with a force of thirty persons and six washing machines, three thousand articles were sometimes *put through* in one day. In rainy weather, packages of one hundred each were given out to many houses in Bebek and neighborhood, and thus, although the sick and wounded, with the hospital force, amounted finally to eight hundred, the laundry always kept ahead of the demand; so as to work off and save all the stuff that had been brought down from the Crimea. It was a long time before the whole hospital could be cleansed of every sign of vermin. Every bed had to be turned out and worked over, and, in the end, the Crimean enemy was utterly subdued.

Comfort in Poor Homes. 239

The women in the laundry, working by the piece, and aided by the washing-machines, earned from thirty dollars to forty-five dollars per month, a sum never dreamed of as possible by them; and the comfort it diffused in their poor homes was one of the richest rewards of the work. There was not a house I had not visited in sickness, and they were as ready to acknowledge, as I to notice, the change.

In due time, I went to Mr. Parker with the accounts. What had been expended for getting up the works was paid without any questions or examination of particulars. The washed articles had all to be separated into three categories, and paid at the rate of seventy-five cents per doz. for the larger articles, fifty cents for medium, and thirty-seven and one half for small articles.

I am glad to testify that, in all my relations with the British army, I never personally encountered, what was so much decried,—*Red-Tape*. I do not question its existence; but I think my services were looked upon as rather exceptional, and treated accordingly. With the two exceptions of Menzies and O'Connor, all the gentlemen of the British army whom I had any relations with were, to use an English phrase, "the soul of honor," and by this I mean just, kind, and prompt.

At the rate of pay above mentioned, there would evidently result a profit. What should be done with it? The poor little church at Bardezag was in great need of a church building. I proposed *to wash them out one.* As the great bread business demanded some of my leisure time, and I was rebuilding a church destroyed by earthquake at Brusa, Mr. Minasian, always ready for every good work, kindly offered to look after the laundry, in my absence, and the building of this church; and without such partnership, I could not have accomplished it. It cost nearly $3,000, and yet I built it, entirely, out of an English beer barrel!

During this work, a stolid-looking, strong, poorly-clad young man came to beg employment. I did not think he had intelligence enough to make a useful workman, and presumed he would be a nuisance. I soon found that he was not only strong, but that he did carefully and faithfully whatever I gave him to do. Quiet, unassuming, retiring, indefatigable, competent to every duty with which he was intrusted, his value forced itself upon me in spite of his looks. There was nothing mechanical which, after seeing me do once, he could not do better. He has been the very useful steward of the college, from the beginning, was my right-hand-man in erecting the buildings, and has never been known to be faithless to a trust, or to flinch from the most arduous duties, day or night.

Mr. Williams, whom I have referred to in Chapter VI, had, in the meantime, returned to Constantinople from Malta. He had a large family, and was in absolute destitution. I gave over to him the laundry, to make what he could out of it; and

Storm and Cholera. 241

it soon placed him, for the time, in circumstances of comfort.

I am told that my dear college friend, Dr. Bartol. has humorously assigned to me sixteen professions. I have never seen the list which his brilliant imagination has produced; but I presume he did *not* include what I am most proud of—the profession of a washerwoman!

One stormy day, in the winter of 1855, a messenger came with the terrible news that the cholera, which had been sporadic, rather than epidemic at Scutari, had reached our men. Two were dead, five were sick, all had stopped work in panic; and the ten thousand pounds of bread required from those two ovens could not be delivered on the following morning!

I took a carpet-bag of medicines, and started immediately for Scutari, sending the man to the bakers' market-place, to engage half-a-dozen men, at any price, and get them carried over in the English messenger steamer. He could get them there for night work. I must go direct and speedily, for cholera doesn't wait nor lag in doing its work! No caique could be persuaded to set me across the Bosphorus to the Asiatic side. A fierce south wind was fretting the waters into foamy waves, and the light caiques would not venture out. No entreaties, no offers of reward, had any effect upon men who had never refused before. Just then, a Scutari boat, manned with two powerful men, put in to escape the storm. For ninety piastres, nearly twenty times the legal price, they engaged to put me over. The Scutari boatmen are famed for skill and boldness in these southern storms. I have never seen a finer contest of human strength and skill with the forces of nature. We had to go in the trough of the sea, but the light caique would turn quickly its sharp bows into every toppling wave, and its foam would go hissing by, as we rode over it or through it, and so we gained the Asiatc shore in safety.

Our courage comes from circumstances. I am naturally timid, and nothing but stern necessity would have forced me to the encounter, but imperious duty called me, and I felt no fear. I found the men at the bakery utterly *demoralized*. I called them together, assured them of safety if they would go quietly to work, and that every one of the sick would recover. They rallied at once. I made every possible preparation for uniform warmth and good diet, and pledged them my word that not one of them would be attacked, except he should transgress. Those attacked brightened up into hope, and one even insisted upon getting up and going to work. I promised to stay with them through the afternoon and night. The relay came over from the city, and the work went bravely on. The bread would all be ready three or four hours before the time of delivery. The sick all recovered, and there were no more attacks.

The Orientals have an admirable kind of coolness and courage. Give them a leader in whom they have confidence, and they will follow him to the death. They had now recovered their balance, and, towards evening, insisted that I should go home, because my family would be distressed about me. I attempted it, but could find no boat. I went up the Asiatic shore to Candili, opposite Bebek, but every boat was drawn up, and no one would put out at that hour. Darkness was coming on; but, just as I was turning to go up to Mr. Hanson's house for the night I discerned a boat putting out, and hailed it. Will you take me across to Bebek? "If you will go." What do you ask? "Six piastres!" If he had said sixty or seventy, I should have given it! When I was fairly seated, in the bottom, he began to say, "How glad I am to have you for a passenger? I must go across, and I had nothing for ballast? I know you will keep the trim of the boat. The night is bad, but we shall go nicely. Ha, ha, cheliby! I said, six piastres, I know you won't grudge me that, such a night as this; but I would have taken you for nothing!"

Never were two parties better satisfied with a bargain! We crossed nicely. Wife and children had anxiously given up hope of my return that night, and rushed upon me like bashi-bozooks. I slept soundly, and found all in good cheer at the ovens, next morning.

CHAPTER XVI.

CHURCH-BUILDING.

The subject of church-building was now pressing forward for consideration, over all the field of the Board in Turkey. The little Protestant churches had, as yet, not one church edifice. They met in such halls as could be obtained in private houses, or by throwing two or three rooms into one. These were often Turkish houses, because such use of a house in any Armenian or Christian quarter would not then be tolerated, while the Turks, in certain cases, would allow it. The wants of these feeble churches in this respect was pressed upon the attention of the board; but Dr. Anderson replied, that we must not attempt to compete with the Jesuits in building costly churches! Our real demand was for an uncostly church.

At this juncture, the little Protestant community at Rodosto, European Turkey, sent a messenger to say that the Turkish house and garden, which had served them both as place of worship and pastor's residence, were to be sold, and the Turkish owner would give them the refusal till such a date, and at a price which was regarded as very moderate. If this place should be lost, they knew of no place which they could obtain for use as a chapel; their own houses were very small, the pastor would have to leave, and the flock would be scattered. Every one felt a sympathy for them; but nothing could be done.

I had then paid off every debt, principal and interest, and had enough in hand to buy the place, and save the church from distress. It was no less a joy to me than to them, and to the mission generally.

But, previous to this, another work had occasioned us all a common anxiety.

In Brusa, the house long occupied as pastor's residence and chapel perished in a conflagration which swept the quarter. The pasha, governor of the province of Bithynia, called the chief man of the Protestants, and told him, "Now is your chance to erect a regular church-building, I can not authorize the building of a church, but I can the *rebuilding* of one. The house destroyed was known as the Protestant Church. While I am here, you may rebuild as you please. Another governor may come, by and by, who will be your enemy."

The importance of seizing this chance for erecting the first church edifice in our mission was such, that we resolved not to lose it.

Dr. Dwight and I agreed to superintend the work, and collect the money from England and America, by correspondence; and the mission authorized its treasurer to indorse us while doing it. Our appeals brought little money; but we built a very solid brick church. The native architect drew upon Dr. Dwight for payment of a very heavy bill for oak timber for the roof. Dr. Dwight came and begged me to go up and see to it. I sold off his oak, at a good advance, and built a roof of less than one fourth the weight, and four times the strength, of the one he had planned. The building was not quite finished within, when it was injured by an earthquake. Brusa was terribly shaken. A mass of tufa weighing hundreds of tons, broke off from the brow of old Brusa, the Brusa of Hannibal, fell upon a *filature* (silk-winding establishment), and crushed about thirty operatives within it. Many buildings were cracked, but few were seriously injured. The city was thrown into great consternation. I went up to see to the repairing of the church, which was not very seriously injured. The roof was singularly displaced, but it was brought back without great difficulty. I worked upon the church till sundown, and then had a ride of twenty-four miles to Ghemlik, the latter half in darkness, mud, and mist that made the getting through at all a matter of doubt. We had been told that some loaded horses, the day before, had sunk down in the mud and died.

Before we reached the port, we had a good instance of the sagacity of the horse. Our animals stopped; and when we urged them forward, they turned to the left, into the bushes. "Let them go," said the guide; "they see what we can't." After a while they made a plunge safely into a new road.

The old road had been intersected by a cut full ten feet in depth, as I afterwards saw it; and we had attempted, in the darkness, to drive them down. Not the slightest parapet had been put up to guard it.

The day had been occupied with hard labor, running up and down ladders, and replacing the roof; the ride of twenty-four miles, to one who hates the saddle, fatiguing; the weather (February) black and chilly, paralyzing all vital power. The steamer gained, I thought only of rest. An infernal growl, from the very centre of the earth, arrested every ear; and then the steamer, at anchor, seemed to be struck by Titanic hammers from beneath. There was a cry, "The boiler's burst?" Steam not up! I replied, for I had just noticed them lighting the fires. Then there burst, in half-a-dozen languages, from the multitude on deck, the word earthquake! seizmos! Zerzelé! yergrisharjootiune! tremblement de terre! etc., in English, Greek, Turkish, Armenian, and French! Woe to the church of so much labor and anxious care, our first church-building in Turkey, rocked by earthquakes, like the spiritual work that had preceded it!

I had hardly laid down upon the sofa again, before another came, still more violent. The captain had never experienced an earthquake at sea, and was considerably agitated. He said, however, there was ten feet of water under the keel, and the steamer could not be injured.

At Brusa, the church-building was destroyed; the house from which I started and where they had earnestly pressed me to stay for the night, also went down. All the solid stone and brick buildings were either ruined or injured. The twenty-four domes of Ooloo Djami fell in. Every minaret but one was decapitated, and that the one highest up the side of Mt. Olympus; the bazars were destroyed and burned. Well-built wooden houses of course escaped, but the *adobes* were wrecked. It was reported that six thousand persons perished. The whole population spent a fearful night in the cold open air.

The last time I was at Brusa, I heard the amazing fact asserted, that I returned to the city in the morning following this night, instead of going home, and began, that day, to rebuild the church, declaring that I would make it earthquake-proof, and defy the earthquakes! Even when I positively denied this, some asserted their personal remembrance of the fact! In times of great excitement, fact and imagination lose themselves in each other. It was two weeks before I could return. Brusa, at first sight, seemed to be in ruins. Its "six hundred minarets," which gave such life and brightness to the distant view, were gone. All the people who could not flee were under canvass. Dismay and woe were on every countenance.

The earthquakes were still frequent, but mild. I enjoyed three one night; and every twenty-four hours there would be one or two; but the force was spent. I slept in a wooden house, which had, as most of the Eastern houses have, wooden ceilings. I persuaded others to do the same. The plastering of the walls was generally ruined, and the house had slightly *lurched* to the east, but the doors had plenty of leeway for other lurches still, before they would bind at any point.

Some of our evangelical friends thought it impious to build a church, as I proposed, with an internal skeleton of oak and iron, so combined as to resist an earthquake. Nobody would enter it. It would be defying "the anger of the Lord." It would be a weak mortal's challenge to Omnipotence to a trial of strength. I asked them how they would build a ship, for fair weather only, or for storms? We had stormy weather in Brusa, and I should build the ship accordingly. It was finished, and dedicated on the same day that the Turks, with solemn religious services, *commenced* the repairing of their great mosque. The Turk is strong when he moves, but is always behind the time.

I soon began to see in the course of my ten visits, that while the destruction of property was immense, the loss of life must have been small. The great solid structures, the churches, the mosques, the baths, the bazars, were all unoccupied at the time. The first shock sent people out of their houses. It was the next which spread destruction. The houses were empty. Those that fell, the *adobes*, mainly in the Jewish quarter, fell every way, leaning against each other, presenting a scene of wild confusion, and yet few fell so as to bury their owners if within.

Lord Napier came up from the English embassy to distribute aid to the sufferers. I helped him in the distribution; and we found surprisingly few widows and orphans, made such by the earthquake. No one of my acquaintances could say that he knew personally a man who had been killed. Some began to put the number down to five thousand and even to four thousand. I came finally to the conviction that *two hundred* would be near the truth. And yet there was a way in which the large number could be justified. Had the earthquake occurred when people were in the mosques, baths, bazars, and khans, six thousand *might have perished!* This is oriental. So of the "Bulgarian Horrors"; the numbers were sixty thousand at first, then thirty thousand, then fifteen thousand, twelve thousand, four thousand, and if it should be finally reduced to two thousand, it would be horror enough to satisfy any but a depraved mind, and would be in accord with all I have known of numbers, in a land where feeling and imagination rule the facts.

On returning from Brusa with Lord Napier, Consul Sandison, who was of the party, raised the question of the proper keeping of the Sabbath. After we had debated it at some length, he appealed to Lord Napier if a poor operative would be guilty of Sabbath-breaking in cultivating, on that day, a patch of flowers, those most touching and beautiful witnesses to the divine goodness? The Scottish nobleman dryly replied, that he would not undertake to decide the question, but he did not doubt that the man who began with his flower patch, would end with his potato field!

The consul dropped the question.

The rebuilding of the church excited not a little the disgust of the Armenian bishop and his clergy, who hoped the destruction of what was an eyesore would be final. The position was a very prominent and beautiful one, and this made it the more annoying. It was necessary, from the beginning, to rebuild the wall separating the church lot from our neighbor A———. As soon as I began this work, there came an interdict from A———, who claimed the wall and the ground as his own, compelling me to begin a new foundation, six inches inside of the old. This would bring the wall too near one corner of the church. The wall ran on three different lines, and towards the street, it turned inconveniently towards the church; and we could not submit to the injustice. We had incontestible proof that the whole wall, ground and all, belonged to the church, not to its neighbor. Eight times the case was tried, and eight times decided against us. There is one excellence of Turkish courts. You are not compelled to employ lawyers, and you can make the expenses very light. There is another, if it be an excellence; if the case goes against you, you can always find some way of opening it again. The ninth trial was a notorious one. I had found, in studying up the question of boundaries, that although the personal testimony of "the oldest neighbors" will usually decide a case, yet, where a wall exists, recesses half-way through prove the wall to belong to that party which has the recesses.

Again, a water-pipe carried through the centre of a wall, proves the wall to belong to the party owning the water. Now the remains of the wall showed recesses about one third of the way; there was a central water-pipe, still bringing us water, for the rest of the way. I had three venerable master-builders, an Armenian, a Turk, and a Greek, to testify that this had always been the law and the custom (*adet*) in Brusa. The other party had twenty-one witnesses. The trial was a farce. The judge, with all his attendants in grand array, had the twenty-one witnesses sworn in line, and all testified, with one voice, against the church. They were vile fellows, whom the bishop had sent, and their very looks were quite enough to discredit their testimony. The judge would neither look at the wall, nor listen to the law. He coolly told me, that if I could bring forward twenty-*two* witnesses, he would give the case to me!

I denounced him, to his face, as an unjust judge, and one who disregarded Moslem law. I despised him and his decision, and would report him at Constantinople. So I left, in simulated wrath, and real; and besides, had I remained, there might have been a row.

In the evening, this same judge, evidently fearing that I might injure him, sent an old, venerable gentleman to say, that if I would give him fifteen hundred piastres (sixty dollars) he would reverse his sentence, and gladly, because all the world knew that justice was on my side! This was almost equal to some of our city governments! The poor judge would like well enough to be just, but he must live. The bishop had doubtless promised him as much. Thus, where there is money, two parties will bid against each other, and if one gets justice, he has to pay all it is worth. I have known instances of just and upright judgment in favor of the poor and against the rich, and in favor of rayahs against Moslems; but it is to be feared that the example of the Brusa judge has a large following in the Turkish courts.

I declined the offer, and sent my respects with the message. that I had not decided what to do.

It had become a perplexing contest. We dared not put in the windows while the wall was down, for our neighbor, with whom, in appearance, we had the contest, had his walls destroyed; and thus we were exposed to the rabble.

In the morning, I called upon S—— Agha, the chief Armenian banker of the city. His life had been saved by Dr. Grant in Mosul. The banker presented the doctor a fine horse, in gratitude for his skilful treatment; and I knew he felt kindly ever afterwards towards all Americans.

I said to him, I have come to ask of you a favor. "You can ask nothing which I shall not with all my heart perform." You know our boundary case? "Ah, sir, there's a bishop there. I am powerless to help you against him." But I wish to leave bishop and judge entirely out of the contest. I want you to represent to A—— that his interests and mine are one. He wants to sell his lot, but no one will buy it until this litigation ceases. The bishop is using him to his injury. I propose to buy a part of A——'s lot; such that, commencing from the lower cut of the old wall, I shall draw a line parallel to the church, putting both his lot and ours into regular shape, and increasing our space on that side, where we need it. I will give him five thousand piastres (two hundred dollars), for the land thus taken. "That is a good plan; and if A—— is not a fool, he will agree to it. I will see him immediately." He returned, saying A—— would sell the part proposed, but demanded ten thousand piastres (four hundred dollars). This I positively refused to give, as being twice the price of land in that quarter. The banker replied that, although that might be true, it was worth all that, and much more, to the church. A compromise was finally arranged by the banker at three hundred dollars, the money paid at the recorder of deeds; and the banker insisted upon the deed being made out and delivered

THE BISHOP AND THE JUDGE. 255

over. By his influence, and a little extra pay to the clerks, the work was all done, the copies made, and red tape fully satisfied, in the space of a couple of hours, instead of a couple of weeks. I put on all the men I could command in order to finish the work at once, and remove all possibility of further annoyance. The second day, the police came, in great indignation, to arrest the workmen for building on ground in litigation. They were too late. I showed them the deed; they read it, and silently departed. I saw no more of them.

The bishop and the judge both remained out in the cold. How they settled their affairs, I never knew. The judge doubtless claimed his reward, and the bishop would be sure to refuse payment. But the bishops and Turkish officials never have long quarrels. They are mutually useful and needful. Neither could accomplish his designs without the other.

The rebuilding of the church with a spacious and excellent school-room in the basement, cost six hundred liras (about two thousand seven hundred dollars) and the profits of the bakery had become sufficient to meet all the bills. The old debt of eight hundred liras for the church destroyed remained, an ugly burden.

Twenty-two years have elapsed since the building of this church; and we can now fairly estimate its value to the community.

The station at Constantinople was mildly rebuked by the senior secretary of the Board, as wishing to ape the Jesuits in their anxiety for showy schools and expensive churches. The charge, repeated and published in his lectures on Foreign Missions* (pages 292, 293), is true, if by "costly churches" a plain and simple brick building, costing three thousand dollars, and furnishing the school as well as the church, can be so called. It is all the missionaries ever demanded. There is not one sign of "costliness" about it; and all its subsequent history has convinced us that it was a good investment.

It contributed to call back the scattered and terrified members of the little evangelical community. The congregation, at first, was so very small that the building seemed unreasonably large. When I last visited Brusa, in 1873, the building was crowded every Sabbath, and they were talking of galleries or enlargement. The church began, at first, to pay one fourth of the pastor's salary, then half, three fourths, and finally the whole. They also assumed the care and expense of their school; after a time, they established a girls' high school, and, more lately, a high school for boys. The little, feeble community has become an independent one, managing, developing, paying for, all its institutions of education and religion. It has long ceased to draw any thing from the American Board. It is a missionary church only in the sense of prosecuting a missionary work. It is an

---

*Foreign Missions, by R. Anderson, D.D., LL.D., Boston, 1874.

example, to all the churches in the world, of devoted giving to Christian work, and of rising out of great poverty, and manifold discouragements, to a full and noble manhood. I am sure that every missionary will say, the having a comfortable, well situated church-building has been an aid rather than a hindrance to its progress. The same will hold true of other places; Nicomedia, Adabazar, Bardezag. Neither a good school-house nor a good simple church-building, if paid for, can be other than a blessing in any mission rightly conducted. The people of the little evangelical communities were then in such poverty, just emerging from a long and exhausting persecution, that they could do but little for themselves. They were aided on the principle commended by St. Paul to the Ephesian Church, that they "ought to support the weak, and to remember the words of the Lord Jesus how he said (or how he used to say) it is more blessed to give than to receive." The venerable secretary was in error with regard to church-buildings, and especially in applying the words "costly" and "splendid" to the most simple structures ever erected for divine worship. If that is "competing" with the Jesuits, to what sort of buildings ought evangelical worship to be consigned?

The Crimean war came to a close, and peace was declared in April, 1856. There was no reason why I should hold farther connection with the industries which, for the past four or five years, had demanded so much attention. Their legitimate end had been fully gained. The persecuted had become comparatively free. The obstacles which they could not surmount had disappeared, and they had become fully able to take care of themselves. To throw them now entirely upon their own resources would be best for them in the end.

It had been no object of mine to have any balance in hand. But in such extended operations, if there be enough balance to secure safety, it may, as it did, become unexpectedly large. It amounted, with what had already been expended for the churches mentioned, to twenty-five thousand dollars.

The question then arose, what should I do with it? It was plain that I ought not, as a missionary, to claim any part of it for myself. Besides, I had passed safely through years of hard service, involving an amount of night labor not often borne with impunity; that result was the price of blood, and should be consecrated. It was finally determined to make a church building fund of it, to aid the feeble nascent churches in erecting their first buildings. It paid off the onerous debt of the Brusa church which was destroyed. The other churches aided were eleven; thirteen in all. As the buildings erected secured both church and school-house, they were timely and cheering helps. I obtained permission to sell off the material remaining at the ovens, and bring my two eldest daughters to America to place them at school, and to go and come by steam. All missionary voyages were then by sail.

I sold every thing connected with the industries, except a pair of scales which I purchased for weighing gold coins. The proceeds were more than the expenses of travel. When I returned to Constantinople, I had forty dollars in pocket, which I gave to a church-building committee; and of all those works I have retained nothing, absolutely nothing, but memories and a pair of scales. I am firm in the conviction that under the circumstances it was all good missionary work, and no desecration of the missionary name.

The history of these industrial operations would not be complete, without mentioning a few incidents.

The flourishing missionary station at Kharpoot was occupying by rent for its schools and theological seminary, a noble situation, unrivalled, unequalled in all the region. Its Turkish owner was compelled to sell it, and offered it to the station first of all. The station had no power to purchase, and was distressed at the thought of being driven from that position. This fund came just in time to save them from disaster. The money was forwarded to be repaid, without interest, by the rent. It was so repaid and used for church-building, having contributed to save the "College Hill" where Armenia College now stands. To have lost that choice position, would have been a sad drawback to that educational work on the Euphrates.

Another item turned to the advantage of the American Board, in a different way. The buildings for the mill and bakery were on land belonging to the seminary. When the work closed, and the machinery was sold off, the buildings remained quite useless. Some friends in America contributed the funds to change these buildings into a dwelling-house, which should be the property of the American Board on my ceasing to use it. I turned it over to the mission in 1871—equivalent to a donation of at least three thousand dollars.

I hoped, in building that house, that I had given the finishing touch to all secular employments, and that the remainder of my life would be devoted exclusively to the training of young men for the native pastorate, and for other departments of Christian work; but "it is not in man that walketh to direct his steps!"

CHAPTER XVII.

THE BULGARIANS.

Previous to the Crimean war, the Bulgarians had begun to attract the attention of the missionaries at Constantinople. Dr. Riggs, who has only to look at a language to take possession of it, had edited for them a translation of the New Testament, and it had sold with wonderful rapidity. This was all the more singular, as the universal impression had been that the Bulgarians were in the lowest state of ignorance, except such as had become Hellenized, and had adopted the Greek language. Every spring, there was an *advent* of Bulgarian shepherds and ostlers in the streets of the capital,—strong, rude men in sheepskin clothing, with their shrieking bagpipes and rude country dances, dashing their sheepskin caps upon the pavement to every passer-by for *bakshish*. They seemed but little above savage life.

A much higher class were the Bulgarian gardeners, quiet, industrious men, skilful in their work, with a natural eye for the picturesque and the beautiful. My Turkish neighbor, the Hekim Bashi, had six of them to cultivate his garden; and there was no garden on the Bosphorus to compare with it. As our knowledge of this people increased, our interest in them became stronger. Dr. Riggs visited Varna and neighborhood, and found much encouragement for the distribution of the Scriptures.

When I visited the United States, in 1856, I was commissioned by the Constantinople station to press upon the secretaries of the Board the necessity of a mission to the Bulgarians. The secretaries felt the full force of the argument, but the resources of the Board were not such as to allow them to act.

It was then agreed that I should present their claims to the Methodist Episcopal Board. I had an excellent opportunity to do so, at the great conference in Palmyra, N. Y., in the summer of 1856. This led to the formation of their mission to the Bulgarians on the Danube, and to my becoming a Life Director of their Board,—a recognition of brotherhood which I highly esteem. If this mission has seemed to be somewhat slow of development, it has not been more so than the missions of the American Board, and, unless the Russian war should efface it, it must lead to great results. For the first time in history, a pure Gospel is taught on the lower Danube.

As the American Board already had commenced a work in Roumelia, Rodosto and Adrianople being occupied, it was agreed that, south of the Balkans, the territory should be considered as the missionary sphere of the Board.

In May, 1857, I went as an explorer into this

field. The Rev. Henry Jones, an English traveller, and afterwards secretary of the Turkish Mission Aid Society, accompanied me.

The authorities at Rodosto, whither we went by steamer, found our travelling permits not in order, and threatened to send us back. While they were discussing the question, we found an opportunity quietly to depart, and we heard no more from them.

We went directly to the house of Pastor Muggerdich, the story of whose "bed" has already been told, and were received with oriental hospitality. It was impossible to obtain a man who could speak English and Bulgarian; and Mr. J. knowing nothing but English, was excluded from a great share of the enjoyments of the tour, since I could only occasionally act as his dragoman.

I inquired of Pastor M. if a Bulgarian of good repute could be found, who could speak Greek and Turkish, as well as his own language. "Gabriel is just the man for you, serious, intelligent, amiable, and always interested in evangelical truth." I made an arrangement with the said Gabriel to accompany us as dragoman and servant. Neither of us could forecast the results. One result to him has been, his permanent entrance into the evangelic work; and he is now an ordained preacher of the Gospel in the mission on the Danube.

We found, to our surprise, a large Bulgarian population in the region of Adrianople, where we stopped and spent the Sabbath. A small Armenian community was here formed, and through them we ascertained many interesting facts with regard to the Bulgarians. They were rapidly increasing south of the Balkans, and were manifesting a great desire for education. A Bulgarian teacher had been to our book-store, and bought a large number of tracts and Testaments as reading-books in his school. He had put out the Greek language, and welcomed any book he could find in Bulgarian. I first learned from him of the depth of the national feeling, everywhere springing up, with regard to the restoration of the national language.

I called upon the pasha, in order to present my travelling firman, and ask for an order for post-horses to Philippopolis. I found the Greek bishop in deep, earnest, low conversation with the pasha, and I could only make known my request, which was readily granted, and depart.

I easily found out the cause of the bishop's earnestness with the pasha. A Bulgarian sheep merchant had established in his village a school for Bulgarians, and had excluded Greek; whereas the policy of the church was to Hellenize the Bulgarians, and allow nothing but the Greek. The bishop, about a week before, had visited the school, and demanded that a Greek teacher should have charge of it. The founder of the school told the bishop not to trouble himself about the language, since he did not pay any thing for the school. The bishop was the stronger man. From words

THE GREEK BISHOP. 265

he proceeded to blows, threw the merchant down, and, in his righteous anger, might have beaten him to death, but that his own men interfered. The bloody Bulgarian had to keep his house a few days, until he could appear before the pasha. The bishop had already prepared the case by proving that the merchant assaulted the bishop, and he only defended himself. He hadn't touched him himself, his attendants had beaten him for his impiety. So the Bulgarian was thrown into prison, and was lying there at the time. I afterwards learned that he got free by paying twenty thousand piastres to the bishop. The case excited such indignation among the Bulgarians, that I heard many say with suppressed breath, "No more Greek bishops for us!" After all, it was the bishop's head that was broken.

In a few days, the Bulgarian recovered, and the honor in which he was held by the people was the measure of their detestation of the bishop. It was only one of many instances in which the worst oppressors of the Christians were their own clergy.

On our way to Philippopolis, we overtook a man who was riding by himself, and who saluted us in Greek. I soon perceived, by his physiognomy, that he was not Greek, but rather Bulgarian, and I asked him to what race he belonged. I was quite astonished to hear him reply, "Εγώ ειμί Παυλικανος" (I am a Paulician)! I did not suppose that any remnant of that old and very interesting sect was in existence. He knew but little of their history,

He knew only that once they were very numerous. that Philippopolis was their chief city, and that persecution had destroyed them. Five villages were all that remained. They were in the church of Rome, and had an Italian priest to look after them. He was a pleasant, intelligent man. His representations of the ignorance of the Bulgarian peasantry was painful in the extreme, and may have been colored by his prejudices as a Romanist.

In Philippopolis, we found a great excitement about the termination of serfdom, and the freedom of the serfs. Serfage existed before the Mohammedan conquest. At the conquest, all who became Moslems retained their lands, serfs, and whatever possessions they had. I found here, to my surprise, *Turks* who did not speak Turkish, or who spoke it very imperfectly, their common language being Bulgarian. On inquiry I found they were no Turks at all. They were Moslems, not Turks. By race, they were Slavs, like the Christian Bulgarians. I fell in with an officer of the Turkish army, who spoke English. He declared himself to be a Slav. Most of the Moslems there were Slavs. and some of them retained secretly certain Christian rites. He believed the time would come when there would be a great return of these Moslem Slavs to Christianity. He would rather be a Christian than a Moslem, but being in the army, it was impossible. "But," said he, "the day is coming!" Thousands of this cast of thinking lost their hopes when Sir Henry Bulwer, as English ambassador,

HATTI HUMAYŪN. 267

betrayed the cause of freedom of conscience in Turkey.

We met, at the pasha's konak, commissioners sent by the Porte to inquire into the serfdom, and the degree in which it came to an end.

It appeared that, upon the promulgation of the Hatti Humayūn, the people had been incited by their leaders, and perhaps by Lord Stratford de Redcliffe's influence, to claim their freedom. The Porte also had declared that serfage, like the slave-trade, must come to an end. This was firmly resisted by the land-owners. The people sent a deputation to the Porte. The deputies were all imprisoned. A larger number was sent with the same result. Then the people rose insisting that they would all go to prison. They knew they could rely upon the English ambassador as their friend. The Porte was in straits, fearing an insurrection of the land-owners, and also fearing England, who then had a power which she has since sacrificed.

I asked one of the commissioners how the thing would end. He made up faces, which probably meant "nothing will come of it"; and then added, "little by little!" He became more communicative, at length. I found he was a Greek Moslem, and spoke the Greek perfectly. "If the people hold out, they will get free." They did hold out, and serfage came to an end.. In Bosnia, it required however the strong arm of Omer Pasha to bring the Moslem land-owners to submission.

At the same time with serfage, the whole Bulgarian people arose to two other questions: their language and their church government. The Greek church, with the sanction of the Turkish government, had introduced the Greek liturgy into all the Bulgarian churches, and Greek bishops ruled the flock, and very carefully fleeced it three times a year. To throw off the Greek language and the Greek bishops, was the vow of every Bulgarian heart. To have schools, newspapers, a literature of their own, were among their strongest aspirations. Ten years before, when I inquired about the Bulgarians in Macedonia, they were spoken of as "animals." Now, they were roused to a sudden life. And this is one of the incidental results of the Hatti Humayūn. Most of its provisions were never carried out. But it gave the people a knowledge of their rights. It was to them a political education. It wrought a revolution in their ideas, and that has led to a revolution in their condition.

On returning we spent the Sabbath at the large village or city of Orta-keuy, composed of Moslems and Christians. It was a special feast-day in the church, and about forty pilgrims, to some shrine at Tatar-Bazajik, were to return. We went out to see them come; the population, arranged on two sides of a very broad street, awaited them. There was no noise, no rude conduct. The children were well-behaved. We had never seen, in any land, among any people of any faith, so large an assembly, of such a promiscuous character, so well-behaved. There was no soldiery, and we saw no police; and we said, this Bulgarian people is entirely different from other peoples.

At length the cavalcade appeared, forty horsemen in Indian file. As they entered among the people, each one took a child on before him, and forty men and forty children passed on quietly to the church. Seeing that we were strangers, the *ephoroi*, or chief men of the church, with true politeness, conducted us to a place where we could see the ceremony of reception of the pilgrims. Each one was blessed in turn, and soon all quietly dispersed to their homes.

The ephoroi took us next to their school, which they had good reason to show with pride. They lamented the want of Bulgarian books; they had the Bulgarian Testament edited by Dr. Riggs. I found that many peasants had purchased that Testament who knew not a letter of the alphabet; but they believed that, some time or other, their children would learn to read! Such faith always removes mountains.

The ephoroi complained of the double taxation of the government and of the bishop. After all that, they had their priests and schools to support. The bishop came round to every house three times a year, with his train of followers, gathering up rice, wheat, barley, butter, cheese, fowls, eggs, sheep, swine, money. No house escaped, no man escaped, every house must be blessed, and the blessing paid for; the rich must entertain him with a grand feast, with wine and music, and dancing, and things which often accompany them; and besides all this every member of his train expects a present. If one is poor, he can't escape, and if one is rich, the bishop knows better than the pasha what he is worth; and if he should be disposed to hold back at all, the bishop goes to the pasha and *the two grind him together.*

"But," I said, "if you had Bulgarian bishops, they would do just the same, after getting the power." "Never, never, we Bulgarians love each other. We are one family. Our bishops would all be good men!"

Athanase, the Greek teacher, probably did not relish the conversation. He came to our room at the khan. He had something on his mind. He wanted to tell me about the Turkish oppressions. I listened to him with eagerness. It was my object to learn all the facts I could. He then told me a harrowing story of the governor's seizing a beautiful maiden and taking her to his harem, and the awful cruelties he perpetrated upon friends of the poor girl who tried to rescue her. I took down the chief points. I was determined that atrocity should be made public at Constantinople, and in England, and America, and that Lord Stratford de Redcliffe should know every particular. I thought of even going to the old monster, and telling him that, by his own law, he could not escape Gehenna. And then, it occurred to me that Greeks sometimes exaggerate; and that the story was a little too complete, rounded out into a fulness of iniquity, a little suspicious! On inquiry, I found that the whole thing was a fabrication; and when I threatened Athanase with exposure, he begged with such abject terror, that I let him go. How many he had actually deceived with this well-told story, who can tell? I have met this same story, in all its chief points, so often, that it is evidently the stock in trade of a certain class of story-tellers, who love to practise upon the credulity of foreigners. That outrages of this nature have occurred in Turkey, is undoubtedly true. That every Greek dragoman manufactures them for every traveller who falls into his hands, is equally true. It is not absolutely necessary for one to put unlimited faith in all that he hears from people of that class. And yet, it is very hard for a traveller to disbelieve any thing, especially if it is wonderful. There is a place on the Bosphorus, called Jason's Wharf. A distinguished and eloquent divine asked what that meant? His attendant coolly told him "it was where Jason and his Argonauts landed, when they were in quest of the Golden Fleece!" "What a conservator of historic truth tradition is!" exclaimed the learned traveller! He doubtless put it in his note-book, and has charmed his people with it. I was just behind him, and heard it all. I did not wish to break his pleasing delusion, by telling him that I had often seen the English steamer "Jason" coaling there, in the times of the Crimean war, and perhaps *that* might explain the name!

Our return to Constantinople was by land; and the impressions we received of a people waking out of sleep were only deepened.

A report of this tour was made to the annual meeting of the Turkish missions. A fuller report, upon the whole subject of a mission to the Bulgarians, was drawn up by Dr. Schauffler and myself, adopted, and sent to the American Board, and to the Turkish Missions' Aid Society, London; and the Bulgarian mission south of the Balkans was thus inaugurated.

Since then, the progress of this interesting people has been most hopeful. They attained what then seemed so difficult, the exclusive management of their own schools, language, liturgy and church government. They have their own bishops, and instead of the Greek patriarch, they have as their civil and ecclesiastical head a Bulgarian *Exarch*. They were making unexampled progress, when the benevolent interference of Russia involved them in the horrors of the Eastern conflict. Those who shall survive the sword, the famine, and the pestilence, the two latter invariable attendants of these Eastern wars, will have to begin anew, in the deepest poverty, their interrupted course. May it be under such circumstances as shall involve no future upheavals! Oppressive government, frequent attempts at insurrection incited by foreign agents, and bloody wars, have been the constant obstacles to any regular progress. The Bulgarians are naturally peaceable, industrious, social, quiet; but instead of being allowed to choose their own way, and work out the problem of national life and progress, they have been ground between the Russian upper and the Turkish nether millstone, to their ruin.

They will again rally. They have a strong, invincible national life and character, and I rejoice to bequeath to my heirs the memory of what I have attempted to do for their deliverance.

CHAPTER XVIII.

EDUCATION.

About the middle of this century, the methods of prosecuting Christian work in unevangelized lands began to receive a new and earnest attention among the responsible conductors of foreign operations. In some lines of effort, very great good has resulted. The native church and the native pastor were brought into their true position. The absolute importance of *self-support and self-development* were urged upon the native churches, with admirable results, and they have become watchwords of the work through Asia and Africa, and the islands of the ocean.

Among the topics of discussion, no subject received so much attention as that of education; and no one caused such wide divergence of opinion.

Up to the time of this discussion, the educators in the work had been carrying forward their institutions to higher efficiency, and introducing an enlarged curriculum of study.

In 1854, the American Baptist Board of Missions sent the Rev. Drs. Peck and Grainger to India, and the year following, the American Board sent the Rev. Drs. Anderson and Thompson to India and

Turkey. The result of these delegations was, that the character of the education of nearly all the missionary institutions of the highest grade was wholly changed. The English language was proscribed, and the curriculum of studies reduced to a vernacular basis. Many schools were closed, some missionaries came home, and considerable friction was occasioned, but the new system was rigidly enforced.

There have been three systems advocated, with reference to education in unevangelized lands. The first is the vernacular. No foreign languages should be taught. Teachers and native pastors require nothing but their own language. By acquiring foreign languages they are tempted to enter other employments, or are puffed up with a sense of their superiority, and their spiritual earnestness is injured.

The second is that of no education at all. The Gospel should be preached, and education should be left to take care of itself. This is one step beyond the position taken by Dr. Anderson, in revolutionizing the system then existing. The Baptist mission at Burrisal, India, has been an advocate and example of this system. President Seelye, of Amherst College, seems to advocate it in his "Lectures on Missions." I quote from his fifth lecture.

"It is admitted, on all hands, that the apostolic method was that of direct evangelization. The apostles did not plant schools. They preached the Gospel and planted churches, and, so far as we can learn, they left all questions of education to adjust themselves, as the new spirit which followed their labors would direct" (p. 146).

"If we should go to the heathen as Paul did, determined to know nothing among them save Jesus Christ and him crucified; attempting no schools for the unconverted, but establishing these only to train those who have become Christ's disciples, for the new work, in the new relations of life, into which they are called, speaking wisdom among them that are perfect, I can not but believe that the number would be immeasurably increased of those whose faith should stand, not in the wisdom of men, but in the power of God" (p. 149).

He sums up the subject in the following concluding sentence of the lecture: "In Christian or unchristian lands, therefore, the teaching of schools *is alone valuable* when applied to cultivate the understanding of *those whose wills are already converted*, or when penetrated through and through with the preaching of Christ, and him crucified, to those who are dead in sin" (p. 154).

On page 144 he maintains that the moral nature is not reached through the intellect, and he would therefore, on philosophical grounds, condemn education as barren of good results, although he admits (page 147), that it may have very debasing influences.

The third system which has been advocated is that of giving the soundest Christian education possible to youth of both sexes, on our mission fields. It would give to unconverted children—contrary to Dr. Seelye's principles—and even to adults, the knowledge of letters; hoping to reach their moral natures through their understandings.

The above theories have all been tried, under circumstances favorable to testing their merits.

The Baptist mission at Burrisal, India, was prosecuted mainly without education. That was left to take care of itself. The preaching of the Gospel, pure and simple, was to do the whole work. Such undivided attention to one line of action is, for a time very effective; and in this case great results seemed to follow. In 1861, there were three thousand one hundred native Christian, and four hundred and forty-seven communicants (Mullen's Ten Years in India, p. 56).

But what was the state of education? Mrs. Martin had had a girls' boarding-school, with twenty-five scholars, and two or three adult classes, with a few women in them. But, at the above date, the girls' school was reduced to eight, and no adults were reported. There were three small boys' schools, with an average of twenty-one each; but there is nothing said about their being converted children. In this Christian community, there were five hundred and ninety-two boys, of whom five hundred and twenty-nine were growing up without being able to read one sentence in the word of God, and having no claim, indeed, while unconverted, to any intellectual light. There were four hundred and nine girls, of whom four hundred and one were growing up in equally hopeless ignorance, to be suitable helpmeets to their future stolid consorts. The intellect was as completely ignored as President Seelye could wish.

But the mission saw, by bitter experience, that the results were bad; and felt compelled to establish a system of education.

There is no abler or more impartial observer of the results of different systems and methods, than Dr. Mullen; and, in another place, he remarks (p. 151): "Are our native converts getting the sound broad Christian education which they need? For instance, in the missions in the suburbs of Calcutta, three missions, containing three hundred and sixty converts, have eight hundred and sixty-two boys at school, but two others, with two thousand three hundred and forty-five converts, have only two hundred and seventeen boys at school, and two missions with four hundred and fifty-seven converts, have no schools at all!

"In all these missions there are six thousand six hundred native Christians, and the number of girls receiving education in them all is *ninety!*

"In Chota Nagpore, with two thousand four hundred converts, the boarding-schools contain fifty-eight boys and thirty-three girls. When the year 1861 ended, there were no other schools in the mission!

"In the Decca missions, with two hundred and five converts, twelve boys and six girls! In Jessore, with five hundred converts, one hundred and fifty-four boys (a good proportion) but only seven girls."

The above statements are sufficient to show that President Seelye's plan has been fully tried and found wanting. It has been tried too, by able, devoted, enthusiastic men, and given up as destructive to the interests of evangelization. One fact only is wanting. It is not stated how many of the few scholars were converted. Dr. Seelye maintains that none but the converted should be educated. From the fewness of the scholars it may be inferred that most of them were regarded as converts, and if so, his system has had the fullest possible trial, that is, a trial to the point of becoming intolerable, and has been laid aside.

What, then, shall we do with the example of Paul? These excellent men believed they were following his example. Were they mistaken? I reply Paul could not establish Christian schools and colleges, if he would. There was no Christian literature, no system of Christian public instruction, no teachers, no freedom for Christians to act in that direction, and no patrons to meet the heavy expense. Neither did he build churches; and his example in either case does not apply to us. But, further, was not the Apostolic Church very soon corrupted?

In a little more than two centuries after the death of the Apostle John, Constantine almost paganized the church. Peoples rushed in with all their heathen festivals, changing only the names.

Most of the heathen festivals and observances of Italy and Asia Minor are found in the Roman and Greek churches, to this day. Little will be gained by the labors of modern missions, if they are to result in nothing purer, nothing more abiding than the past. At all events, the experience of missions during this century, so far as can now be seen, tends towards a great development of education. No society, no body of men, no theorists, have been able to resist it.

But while some have fully agreed to the necessity of common school education, they have been willing to do nothing beyond that, except a limited vernacular training for a native ministry. This is the position that was taken by the senior secretary of the American Board, in 1855. Not only in India, but in Turkey also, the study of the English language must be abandoned, and no studies pursued for which the vernacular languages did not furnish the means. With the very limited amount of science, philosophy, and history, which they possess, education was cut down, at once, to a meagre form. So late as 1874, Dr. Anderson states his views as follows:

"I now offer some practical suggestions, though with diffidence, as to the best manner of working Protestant missions among the heathen, in presence of missions from the Romish Church.

"1st. Not by using their weapons. If we do, we shall be beaten in the use of them. A good while since, missionaries from Constantinople wrote that the Jesuits had attractive schools, teaching the modern languages, and the fine arts, and the accomplishments; and that they would be likely to draw away the best youth, if the Protestant missionaries had no such schools. The reply was, that Protestants can not go into that line of operations. Such schools are the forte of the Jesuits, and do what we may, they would out-do us in that direction" (Lectures on Missions, p. 292).

No one worthy to be a missionary, or an educator, ever proposed the Jesuit schools as a pattern to follow. Nor are the Jesuits formidable competitors in the matter of education. I have worked by their side all my life, and seen their great French College go to ruin. Give the two systems a fair trial, the Protestant and the Jesuit, in education; and if the Jesuit survives, let him survive. It is the "survival of the fittest." I object to the admission made by the venerable secretary.

If, however, you have no schools, or very inferior schools, the Jesuits will undoubtedly take the advantage offered them. It was so in this case, at Constantinople. The Bebek Seminary was allowed to exist for a while, and also the female boarding school. Ultimately, both were closed, and in their stead, vernacular institutions were opened elsewhere. The worst results anticipated followed, and the whole theory has been finally abandoned. It was tried by its warmest advocates, and, if success had been possible, it would have succeeded in their hands.

It has failed as signally in India as in Turkey. On this point, we have the eloquent testimony of Dr. Mullen, of the Allahabad Conference of Missionaries, of the veterans Dr. Wilson and Dr. Duff, and, finally, of the American missionaries of the Mahratta Mission, who now, after twenty years of experience, and of observation of the two systems, are earnestly calling for institutions of a higher education. The use of English, so much insisted upon, results from various circumstances.

There must be some linguistic study in a course of education. The nature of the human mind demands it. Every system of education without it, has been barren of good results. And the native pastor, especially, must have resources beyond the poverty of his own language, or he will never maintain himself as an acceptable teacher of truth. If there are any exceptions to this, they are so rare as to prove the rule.

As so large a proportion of foreign missionaries and educators are Anglo-Saxons, the English has been naturally chosen. Its wide diffusion by commerce and colonization favor it. Its rich stores of Christian thought, science, and philosophy make it the most useful for this purpose, and it seems destined to form a band of sympathy and intercourse among the nations, beyond any other language. Dr. Wilson says of it, "The English language is the grand store-house of knowledge in literature, science, and religion; and if missionaries are to have any thing to do with the mind of India, as

IMPORTANCE OF ENGLISH. 283

it appears developed in the most active and advancing classes of society, they can not slur the English language, in their efforts to advance the cause of Christianity, either by education, by the press, by prelection, or by public preaching. With this conviction the mission has been deeply impressed, ever since its first establishment. Year by year, this conviction has been strengthened by the experience and observation of all its members, and that, without the disparagement or neglect of any of the vernacular instrumentalities, which can be made to bear on the advancement of our holy faith, and the grand triumph of grace and truth in India."

The venerable Dr. Duff is still more eloquent in the same line of defence, but his remarks are too extended to be here quoted.

The conviction of the necessity of abandoning the purely vernacular system, in higher education, does not belong to any one mission or society. It is so nearly universal that it may be said, generally, the system has utterly failed, and the English language has returned to its rightful place as an instrument of education. But few of those who were dispossessed of their positions by refusal to join in the new experiment survive, in old age, to enjoy the vindication of their course, and "the revenges of time."

It had evidently been decided to close both the seminaries at Constantinople, and open them in the interior, on an entirely different basis. Fully convinced that this new system was erroneous in principle, and must be disastrous in effect, I should have retired to some other department of labor, leaving that plan of working to those who believed in it. I was providentially spared the necessity of further opposing it, by being unexpectedly invited to continue my life's work under other circumstances.

Christopher R. Robert, Esq., of New York, had visited Constantinople, in 1856, just at the close of the Crimean war. Seeing, along the shores of the Bosphorus, a boat laden with bread, the appearance and grateful aroma of which drew his attention, he inquired where it was made, and this led to our acquaintance, out of which has grown Robert College. But for that incident, secluded as I was in the village of Bebek, five miles from the city, we should never have met. The lost screw and steam engine before spoken of, the steam mill and bakery, the work provided for the persecuted, the laundry, the churches, the college, are all links in that chain which seems to be chance, but is strong and sure as the will of God.

The idea of the college did not originate with me. The sons of my esteemed and beloved associate Dr. Dwight, the father of the mission, first proposed it.

The correspondence which Mr. Robert commenced with me, in 1858, resulted in the experiment of establishing a Christian college in Turkey.

It was, then, a doubtful, an untried experiment.

CHRISTIAN COLLEGE PROPOSED. 285

The probabilities of failure consisted in the division of Eastern populations. Religion has divided them into the Greek Church, the Armenian Church, the Roman Catholic Church, the Protestant Church; and among all these there are subdivisions, `not tending to unity. There are Moslems and Jews. The Bulgarians were breaking loose from the Greek Church, and the religious aspects of the East were unquiet.

The spirit of race was also strong. The different nationalities composing the population of Turkey have preserved their separate existence, organization, and national spirit with wonderful tenacity, under all governments, religions, and systems, in pagan, Christian, and Moslem times. These it was said will never unite in one institution of learning. To suppose it possible is absurd.

But, on the other hand, it was urged, the East has made great progress in enlightenment. The old system of things is broken up. There is more freedom of thought. There is a large element in Eastern society that rightly apprehends and esteems freedom of conscience, without being infidel. A Christian college, that shall offer the best intellectual training, and as broad a culture as our best New England colleges, will meet the wants of this class, of whatever race or faith.

The Scriptures would be the authoritative source of religious and moral instruction. The Gospel would be clearly and faithfully preached, the Bible read, and prayer offered morning and evening, but the rights of conscience would be held sacred. It would be a Christian college, preparing young men to enter upon professional study, or into any of the active pursuits of life.

In full harmony with this plan, the connection of twenty-two years with the American Board came to an end, but the work in which I had been engaged only assumed another form; and, on entering upon it, I considered myself more a missionary to Turkey than before. I was to labor, so far as possible, for all its peoples, without distinction of race, language, color, or faith.

CHAPTER XIX.

ROBERT COLLEGE.

The experiment of a college having been decided upon, in 1859, the first step was to purchase a site. I had fixed upon one which seemed unequalled by any other on the Bosphorus. It was impossible to obtain it. The twenty-fourth site examined was purchased, near the close of the year; not what we wanted, but the best that could be obtained.

Mr. Robert had proposed, originally, to give thirty thousand dollars towards the enterprise. The attempt made, in 1860–61, to raise a fund sufficient to carry out the design was abandoned, in consequence of our pro-slavery insurrection and war. Mr. R. was not a man, having put his hand to the plough, to look back; and I returned to Constantinople, to erect the building. Before that could be done, it was thought this Southern storm would pass over!

Sultan Abdul Medjid died soon after my arrival. Abdul Aziz ascended the throne and a new set of ministers came into power. His favorite, Mehmet Ali, was a man of splendid appearance, fearless character, and desperate morals. His kiosk overlooked the site upon which we began work, by digging a well. The new sultan often held his nightly revels there, and the pasha declared his determination to allow nothing to be built there. A Turkish gentleman of great intelligence, who had shown me repeated proofs of friendly regard, strongly advised me to drop all thoughts of building there. "If you do so quietly, you will make him your friend to help you elsewhere. If you persist, and try to carry your case by foreign influence, he has that revengeful character, that he will make your enterprise impossible." I found, on inquiry, that his character was even worse than this friend had represented; and after due consultation with our advisory committee, the work there was given up.

Just then was offered the first site I had selected; and it was purchased, with the proviso of paying over the money when I should first have leave from government to erect the college. This was obtained, after some months of delay, and the money was accordingly paid. All the friends of the enterprise rejoiced in this purchase, and wondered at its successful issue. The Turkish government had guarded these glorious banks of the Bosphorus for four hundred years from being occupied at any prominent point by any Christian institution. The Jesuits, with all their craft, their intrigues, and their political power and push, had always been baffled by this Moslem jealousy.

The permit for the college was not easily obtained. The minister of public instruction, a certain Sami Pasha, declared that the Christian communities of the empire already had more schools, more books, more education and intelligence, than the Moslem inhabitants, and his business was to bring the Moslem schools up to a level with the Christian schools. This frank admission of an undeniable fact was refreshing in a Turkish official; but, until he was displaced, there was no progress toward the attainment of our object.

His successor, Kemal Effendi, was an intelligent and reasonable man. He demanded a full programme of the college studies, and a declaration that I would conform to the laws of the department of public instruction; which, as no laws existed, I was ready to do. The leave so long sought was thus obtained. Every thing had been kept as quiet as possible, but our friends the Jesuits had taken the alarm. The influence of the French and Russian embassies were sufficient to arrest the work. My neighbor, the Abbé Boré, director of the French College of Bebek, was specially busy. His private secretary told a friend that he had written thirteen notes that day with regard to the American College, and he wondered at the Abbé's excitement about it. Every Turk belonging to the Russian party, or having any affiliations with the Russian embassy, opposed it. A'ali Pasha, the celebrated diplomat in all the foreign relations of the Porte, drew back. He had made a false step. He had not dreamed of such opposition from such sources.

No positive withdrawal, however, was made; but only the intimation that I must wait a little. Certain *formalities* between the departments of public works and public instruction were to be finished, and in a few days, I should have leave to go on. Those few days extended to *seven years*. The Sublime Porte did not care a fig about the question, but it did not wish to offend its great enemies, the Russians, nor its great friends, the French. This has always been the character of Turkish diplomacy, to *trim* between parties on questions not vital to the Turks themselves, and to play off one party against another.

It was very difficult, to use a military phrase, to develop the enemy, to ascertain the relative forces that would be employed in the contest. Mr. J. P. Brown, our interpreter and secretary of legation, believed the government would ere long yield the point. He had been long in diplomatic service, and had carried many measures which required long and patient following up. The active prosecution of the question, under Mr. Morris, fell to him. When at length it became evident that there was a settled determination not to allow the college to be erected on that site, I proposed to hire the empty premises of the Bebek Seminary, and commence the college itself without asking leave.

Adet (custom, precedent), is a grand source and fountain of law, of legal decision, in the Turkish

NAME FOR THE COLLEGE. 291

administration. I had conducted an institution of learning, in that building, for twenty years, and no Turkish authority could possibly interfere with me. Mr. Robert advanced the money very readily for the thorough repairing, painting, and papering of the establishment, the purchase of a geological cabinet, and all the apparatus for a laboratory and a course of study in physical science.

In order to send forth our programmes, it was needful to fix upon a name. This was found unexpectedly difficult. No name could be proposed that did not find warm opponents. American College, Anglo-American, Washington, the College of the Bosphorus, Oxford (which is the translation of Bosphorus), and many other terms, were proposed and rejected. It seemed easier to establish the reality, than to get the name. I finally said, "What shall we do, gentlemen? I propose that we call it Robert College!" supposing that this proposition would, in like manner, find warm opponents and sharp critics, as every other name had. On the contrary, it was received with universal approbation. They said, first of all, it means nothing, here. It touches nobody's sensibilities, and nobody's prejudices. It sounds well, is a name both French and English. It was run through six or eight languages, with their terminals, and found to fit them all. If any one asks the meaning, there is a good and satisfactory reply to give. No suggestions of a further consideration were listened to, and thus the name was irrevocably fixed at a blow.

When communicated to Mr. Robert, he positively rejected it; but the committee said, "It is our business to fix upon the name for this country, and no other has any concern in it."

The growth of the college, the first two years, was slow, yet encouraging, and after that, was rapid. The government took no notice of it whatever. The Abbé Boré witnessed its growth, while his own college was declining; and he was at length recalled to Rome. His successor wound up the concern. The Abbé was a man of great attainments, but he was too great a politician, and too fond of intrigue. He had so many irons in the fire, that some of them burned in the furious heat, and burned his fingers when he tried to pull them out. I met him once, at Sir Philip Francis'. He had been attentively examining a superb edition of "Reynard" (the Fox). He closed it with the words, "A sarcasm, I believe!" and retired with a great deal of formal dignity. No book could more fitly represent his own character and life.

Neither Mr. Robert nor myself had any intention of giving up the claim to build the college on the chosen site. The American legation not being able to bring the question to any conclusion, I endeavored to act by direct appeal to the grand vizir and minister of foreign affairs. It was kindly received, and, had we been disposed to trust to appearances, there was every prospect of success. But A'ali Pasha, who had doubtless given his word to our great enemies that the college should never be built, found means to thwart what measures the grand vizir had ordered.

The case was at length laid before Sir Henry Bulwer. He was a man, we knew, of no principle; but he knew that to carry the measure would get him credit in England. He took hold of it with the intention of carrying it through. After a long time, and wearisome delays, he wrote me a note, saying that the question was decided, and that, within three days, I should have leave to go on.

I next received a note from him, telling me that I had made an unwise and inconsiderate bargain, in purchasing that place, and the consequences should justly fall on my own head. He saw no reason why the English embassy should have any further trouble with regard to it!

It was a treachery so base that I made no reply to it, and had nothing more to do with Sir Henry Bulwer. I felt curious, however, to know the reason for such a sudden facing about. Nor was it at all difficult to find.

He had received a magnificent "gift" from the Pasha of Egypt, with a request that he would arrange some important and pressing affairs with the Porte. Another was sent to the Countess G——, one of Sir Henry's mistresses; and, of course, he undertook the pasha's business. Among the conditions made by A'ali Pasha, in return, was, that he should throw that college question overboard; which he accordingly did, as not worth a moment's consideration. It is a good specimen of Sir Henry's character. In similar circumstances, he would have thrown overboard any English interest, with equal coolness.

Lord Lyons succeeded Sir Henry Bulwer, and would have secured all we asked, had he remained a little longer. A'ali Pasha had, at length, promised it, and would not have dared to play false with him. The last note which Lord Lyons wrote, on leaving Constantinople for Paris, was to thank A'ali for his promise. But, before Lord Lyons had time to reach Paris, His Highness A'ali Pasha sent for me, wishing to have a personal interview at a designated hour. He then proposed to "swap" lots. The one he offered was worthless. I told him so, and he laughed quite heartily. As there was neither wit nor stupidity in my reply, the diplomatic meaning of his laughter is not apparent. He made one more attempt at "swapping," and gave it up. But he was angry, although naturally a man of a very amiable disposition, as every diplomat should be and is. He said in the hearing of one who reported it, "Will this Mr. Hamlin never die, and let me alone about this college!" What could he hope to gain by my dying? I had told him that the question did not depend upon my life, or any other man's life. The college was in the hands of an organized corporation, which was self-perpetuating, and would never give up one of its rights.

Seven years this contest had lasted, and, in the

meantime, the building we had would not contain our students. About thirty applicants had been rejected, each of the last two years, which was a sure indication that many more would have applied, but for the known fact of rejection.

One day, when I was thinking what step I should next take, and was at my "wit's end," Mr. Morris' messenger entered, with a note.

It was a note of congratulation that the long contest was ended. It contained, also, a copy of His Highness A'ali Pasha's brief note to him, very nearly as follows: "Please inform Mr. Hamlin that he may begin the building of the college when he pleases. No one will interfere with him, and in a few days an Imperial Iradé will be given him!"

It was a mystery of good news! It was an almost incredible gift of God, coming when least expected, when most needed!

The "Imperial Iradé" is a tenure of property most highly valued, the safest, the most sacred, that can be given. We had never dared to ask for it. It was now bestowed without our asking!

The building was erected, and the college transferred to it, before we understood in full, if we ever did, the motives which led the Turkish government to so unexpected a measure.

A number of persons enter into it, but the time to write the full history is not yet. Mr. Morris of Philadelphia, our minister resident, Mr. Seward, Mr. G. D. Morgan of New York, Dr. Seropyan, Admiral Farragut, all had an active share in it;

but there can be no doubt that singular misapprehension, on the part of the Turkish government, contributed to the efficacy of other motives, than those we urged.

During all this contest, the severest things said about the Turkish government were said directly to its highest officers and not to the public papers. When A'ali Pasha finally yielded, he recognized this, I think, in the uniform kindness of his treatment. His younger sons came often and pleasantly to visit the college. When I asked him to have the goodness to order all the material I should import to pass free of duty, he replied, "I will speak with Kiani Pasha, chief of customs, with regard to it, and you can arrange with him." I feared it meant a negative. But when I went to Kiani I found it all arranged; and I never had the slightest difficulty in passing all the iron, nearly two hundred tons, the cement and bricks from Marseilles, the planks from Roumania, with nails, locks, glass, and whatever else was required from various ports without any delay, and without one cent for duties.

The Turks will better bear very vigorous treatment directly *to them*, than *about them*. Vituperation, though eagerly read, does very little good, and besides it stirs up evil passions and all mischief.

The corner-stone of the building was laid, July 4, 1869, with appropriate ceremonies. Hon. E. Joy Morris made the first address, and laid the stone. A mass of documents had been put into a copper box, and subjected for some hours to oven heat, so

THE GREEK ORATOR. 297

as thoroughly to desiccate them, and then it was carefully soldered up. This, having been placed in a cavity in the corner-stone, was cemented in with boiling asphalt, and, during the operation, persons from the assembly threw in coins, copper and silver, American, Turkish, German, English, Greek, French, Italian. Addresses were made in English, French, Turkish, Greek, Armenian, and Bulgarian. Sir Philip Francis, and the Rev. Canon Gribble, took part in the exercises. The Greek orator very eloquently compared the building, the corner-stone of which had just been laid, with the neighboring fortress, built by Mehmet II. for the taking of Constantinople, and the destruction of the Byzantine empire. "It stands on higher ground than those towers. It dominates them. Its forces are spiritual and eternal. It shall see them pass away."

The building is one hundred and thirteen feet by one hundred and three, external measurement, with a court in the centre for light, ventilation, and access by galleries. The stone is the same as that of the fortress built in 1452–53. Four and a quarter centuries having had no apparent effect upon it, the material may be regarded as good. It is fireproof, the floors being of iron beams with brick arches, and the division walls of brick. It is constructed with great solidity, and is one of the most prominent buildings upon the Bosphorus.

If time shall affect any part, it will be the quoins, horizontal lines, and cornice of light-colored sandstone, introduced to relieve the sombre color of the limestone. But when all these perish, there will be nearly two feet of very solid wall behind them; and marble should be used in replacing them. Motives of economy prevented its use originally. When the working plans were completed, an estimate of the cost was asked from practical building architects. The lowest estimate was £14,000. It actually cost but £12,000.

The building was occupied by the college May, 15, 1871; but the formal opening was reserved to the visit of the Hon. William H. Seward, our late distinguished secretary of state, and occurred on the Fourth of July. There is a kindly notice of the college, and of the ceremonial opening, in the volume which records his journey round the world.

This college, reduced in numbers by the derangements of the present war, has been regarded as a great success in gathering students from eighteen nationalities, from twelve languages, and from all the religions of the East.

Its site, unsurpassed for the varied charms and magnificence of scenery, affords ample scope for future development. There have been but two instances of fatal sickness, in the fourteen years of the existence of the college, although the students come often from malarious districts, with constitutions saturated with the poison. Its successful planting has been followed by that of other similar institutions at Beirut, at Cairo, at Aintab, and Harpoot. This fact proves conclusively that the time for the establishment of the Christian college in the East had come. Such education supplies a felt, an acknowledged want. To a certain extent, other institutions among the other nationalities have copied from it, and been incited by it to a higher and better course of study. Although it has encountered opposition from certain quarters, it has quietly pursued its course, turning neither to the right hand nor the left. Its diploma is now acknowledged by all the institutions of France as equivalent to their own. Its sphere of influence and usefulness is constantly widening. When these troubles of war shall have passed, I question not it will start on a new course.

Just before the opening of the college, in May, Mr. Robert visited Constantinople. His visit was noticed in the newspapers, and came to the knowledge of his highness, A'ali Pasha, the grand vizir, who for seven years, either as minister of foreign affairs, or as prime minister, had opposed the building of the college. On this occasion, as on others, he exhibited that trait, for which the Osmanlee is famed, of *giving in wholly and frankly*, if at all.

Through our secretary of legation, J. P. Brown, Esq., he invited Mr. Robert and myself to a personal interview at his palace, and received us with the greatest cordiality possible. He told Mr. Robert that his imperial majesty, the sultan, had ordered him (the grand vizir) to bestow upon Mr. R. a decoration as a sign of his majesty's high approbation. Mr. Robert, in courtly and courteous language, begged the grand vizir to ask his majesty's leave to decline the honor and to express the great pleasure he had in the assurance of his majesty's approbation. The pasha was both astonished and amused. He had probably never heard of a man's declining a *"decoration in brilliants"!!* The impression upon the public was excellent—that Mr. Robert was a gentleman, of antique republican wisdom, simplicity, and prudence, who wished to do good, but did not fancy honors out of the sphere of his own citizenship.

One of the early and sinister prophecies against the college had so much of probability, that its entire failure was hardly to be looked for. I refer to the race hatred that was supposed to exist. On the contrary, a more harmonious college does not exist in any land. Not only are the students of many nationalities, but the faculty of instruction, as well. The preponderating element is American, but it has also the Greek, Armenian, Bulgarian, German, Italian, French, and Turkish professors.

After the faculty meeting on Monday evening, an hour is spent socially with the families, refreshments are partaken of, a short portion is read from the word of God, and all kneel together to commend the college to his almighty care and love.

Mr. Robert has stood by the college in all its difficulties, with unfaltering resolution, and has expended more than two hundred thousand dollars upon its founding and development. All that remains to insure the prosecution of its great work is, the endowment of four professorships. We have labored together for almost twenty years with unbroken harmony. When we have differed in opinion, each has recognized the right to differ. We have grown old in the service. We shall soon hear the *recall* from Him under whose banner we have served in this warfare. Anticipating this, we earnestly commend the college to the Christian hearts to whom God has given power to aid it, and to perfect the work which he has signally blessed.

CHAPTER XX.

PLAGUE, CHOLERA, MALARIA.

When I entered my own hired house in Pera, in the spring of 1839, a friend gave me a bottle of medicine for the plague. In 1837 it had raged in Constantinople, and among its victims were Mrs. Dwight and child, of the American Mission. It was taken for granted that every few years its ravages would be repeated and every head of a family must have his plan of defence. This bottle *contained the plague*, and must not be opened until the disease should actually appear. Its contents had been prepared in the following manner. A drop from a plague pustule, in a moribund patient, had been taken and carefully mixed by violent agitation with a gallon of pure water. Then *one drop* of that mixture was taken and in like manner mixed with another gallon of pure water. As a gallon is estimated at seventy-six thousand eight hundred minims, or drops, there would be mingled in the second gallon the seventy-seven thousandth part of one drop of plague matter very nearly. In the third gallon there would be less than the five hundred and eighty-nine millionth of a drop. This process had been carried on with most laborious

The Plague Drop.

fidelity to the thirty-sixth gallon, where it was believed to have arrived at a degree of potency that would triumphantly meet the plague. This thirty-sixth "potentiality" would require one hundred and seventy-six figures in the denominator to express the fraction of a plague drop found in the ultimate gallon. When it was announced as "bottled-up plague" I looked upon it with awe and reverence; but when I found *how* it had been bottled up, I threw it into the Bosphorus. There seemed to be little agreement as to any mode of treatment. The greatest safety was in seclusion. Its greatest ravages were among the Mussulmans whose fatalism and trust in Allah prevented their taking any precautions. Like the cholera it begins in low filthy places and there gathers strength to invade the highest and healthiest.

Sultan Mahmûd had recently established a strict quarantine against it. This was such an outrage upon Moslem piety that he accompanied his firman with a skilful argument reconciling the measure with Islam. During the first few years of my residence there were repeated cases, and at one time fifteen deaths were reported in quarantine, all in ships from Egypt, but there were no cases outside the grounds. It would seem that quarantine laws have been of some use with regard to this disease. It has never invaded Constantinople since the quarantine was established; and that great enemy of human life, the plague, I have never seen. It is apt to follow the campaigns of Eastern armies, and the Russians may bring a more formidable foe than themselves. The poor inhabitants, however, will be the chief sufferers. They can not flee, while armies can burn their infected material, change their quarters and diet, and find immediate relief.

No quarantine has been found effectual to stop the progress of cholera. It comes irregularly every five to ten years, seeks out its victims, does its work ruthlessly, and departs.

Its most terrible ravages were in the onset of 1865. During the last days of August of that year, business ceased and the great capital attended to nothing but the burial of the dead. By the actual count of an English friend, more bodies were carried out of one gate than the whole number of deaths reported by government; the latter hoping to diminish the panic by false reports. On one of those days I went to three pharmacies in search of a new supply of laudanum, and I met but fourteen persons, although I passed through streets where one is always jostled by the crowd. I met near the bridge that crosses the Golden Horn, on the Constantinople side, an Armenian friend who said, "Don't come this way, I have been trying to dodge the dead and can't do it."

On the first day of September there was an evident diminution in the number of new cases, and in the virulence of the attacks. Its force was spent. Every day lifted up the gloom from the city and had not a terrible conflagration made many thousands homeless, there would have been a burst of joy. The fire swept from the Golden Horn to the Sea of Marmora, chiefly through Mussulman quarters, and nothing could withstand the fury of its course.

At the close of these calamities I wrote the following letter home. It was widely published at the time, and as it contains the results of much experience, it may be worth preserving.

"The cholera, which has just left us after committing fearful ravages, is making its way into Europe, and will probably cross the Atlantic before another summer has passed.

"Having been providentially compelled to have a good degree of practical acquaintance with it, and to see it in all its forms and stages during each of its invasions of Constantinople, I wish to make my friends in America some suggestions which may relieve anxiety, or be of practical use.

"1st. On the approach of the cholera, every family should be prepared to treat it without waiting for a physician. It does its work so expeditiously, that while you are waiting for the doctor, it is done.

"2d. If you prepare for it, it will not come. I think there is no disease which may be avoided with so much certainty as the cholera. But providential circumstances, or the thoughtless indiscretions of some member of a household, may invite the attack, and the challenge will never be refused. It will probably be made in the night, your physician has been called in another direction, and you must treat the case yourself or it will be fatal.

"3d. *Causes of Attack.*—I have personally investigated at least a hundred cases, and not less than three fourths could be traced directly to improper diet, or to intoxicating drinks, or to both united. Of the remainder, suppressed perspiration would comprise a large number. A strong, healthy, temperate, laboring man had a severe attack of cholera, and after the danger had passed, I was curious to ascertain the cause. He had been cautious and prudent in his diet. He used nothing intoxicating. His residence was in a good locality. But after some hours of hard labor and very profuse perspiration, he had lain down to take his customary nap *right against an open window through which a very refreshing breeze was blowing.* Another cause is drinking largely of cold water when hot and thirsty. Great fatigue, great anxiety, fright, fear, all figure among inciting causes. If one can avoid all these he is as safe from the cholera as from being swept away by a comet.

"4th. *Symptoms of an Attack.*—While cholera is prevalent in a place, almost every one experiences more or less disturbance of digestion. It is doubtless in part imaginary. Every one notices the slightest variation of feeling, and this gives an importance to mere trifles. There is often a slight nausea, or transient pains, or rumbling sounds when no attack follows. No one is entirely free from these. But when diarrhœa commences, though painless and slight, it is in reality the skirmishing party of the advancing column. It will have at first no single characteristic of Asiatic cholera. But do not be deceived. It is the cholera, nevertheless. Wait a little, give it time to get hold, say to yourself, 'I feel perfectly well, it will soon pass off,' and in a short time you will repent of your folly in vain. I have seen many a one commit suicide in this way.

"Sometimes, though rarely, the attack commences with vomiting. But in whatever way it commences it is sure to hold on. In a very few hours the patient may sink into the collapse. The hands and feet become cold and purplish, the countenance at first nervous and anxious, becomes gloomy and apathetic, although a mortal restlessness and raging thirst torment the sufferer while the powers of life are ebbing. The intellect remains clear, but all the social and moral feelings seem wonderfully to collapse with the physical powers. The patient knows he is to die, but cares not a snap about it.

"In some cases, though rarely, the diarrhœa continues for a day or two, and the foolish person keeps about, then suddenly sinks, sends for a physician, and before he arrives, 'dies as the fool dieth.'

"COURSE OF TREATMENT.

"1. *For Stopping the Incipient Diarrhœa.*—The mixture which I used in 1848 with great success, and again in 1855, has during this epidemic been used by thousands, and although the attacks have been more sudden and violent, it has fully established its reputation for efficiency and perfect safety. It consists of

> 1 part of Laudanum,
> 1 part of Spirits of Camphor,
> 1 part of Tincture of Rhubarb.

Thirty drops for an adult on a lump of sugar, will often check the diarrhœa. But to prevent its return, care should always be taken to continue the medicine every four hours in diminishing doses— twenty-five, twenty, fifteen, ten, nine—when careful diet is all that will be needed. (This is labelled Mixture No. 1.)

"In case the first dose does not stay the diarrhœa, continue to give in increasing doses thirty-five, forty, forty-five, sixty, at every movement of the bowels. Large doses will produce no injury while the diarrhœa lasts. When that is checked, then is the time for caution. I have never seen a case of diarrhœa taken in season which was not thus controlled, but some cases of advanced diarrhœa, and especially of relapse, paid no heed to it whatever. As soon as this becomes apparent, I have always resorted to this course. Prepare a teacup of starch boiled as for use in starching linen, and stir into it a full teaspoonful of laudanum for an injection. Give one third at each movement of the bowels. In one desperate case abandoned as hopeless by a physician, I could not stop the diarrhœa

Perfect Rest Enjoined.

il the seventh injection, which contained a teaspoonful of laudanum. The patient recovered and is in perfect health. At the same time I used pre— chalk in ten-grain doses with a few drops of ⬛ to each. But whate⬛
⬛
diarrh⬛

"2. *Mustard Poultices.*—⬛ to the pit of the stomach, and kept on till the face is well reddened.

"3. The patient, however well he may feel, should rigidly observe perfect rest. To lie quietly on the back is one half the battle. In that position the enemy fires over you, but the moment you rise you are hit.

"When the attack comes in the form of diarrhœa, these directions will enable every one to meet it successfully.

"4. But when the attack is more violent, and there is vomiting, or vomiting and purging, perhaps also cramp and colic pain, the following mixture, which we label Mixture No. 2 for convenience of reference, is far more effective and should always be resorted to. The missionaries, Messrs. Long, Trowbridge and Washburn, have used it in very many cases, and with wonderful success. It consists of

> 1 part of Laudanum,
> 1 part of Tincture of Capsicum,
> 1 part of Tincture of Ginger,
> 1 part of Tincture of Cardamom seeds.

(If more convenient, camphorated spirit may be substituted for the latter). Dose, thirty to forty drops, or half a teaspoonful in a little water, and be increased according to the urg[...] In case the first do[...]
[illegible due to obscuration] has ceased. [...] siege no one of us failed of [contr]olling the vomiting, and also the purging, by, at most, the third dose. We have, however, invariably made use of large mustard poultices, strong and pure, applied to the stomach, bowels, calves of the legs, feet, etc., as the case seemed to require.

"*Collapse.*—This is simply a more advanced stage of the disease. It indicates the gradual failing of all the powers of life. It is difficult to say when a case has become hopeless. At a certain point the body of the patient begins to emit a peculiar odor, which I call the death odor, for when that has become decided and unmistakable, I have never known the patient to recover. I have repeatedly worked upon such cases for hours with no permanent result. But the blue color, the cold extremities, the deeply sunken eye, the vanishing pulse, are no signs that the case is hopeless. Scores of such cases in the recent epidemic have recovered. In addition to the second mixture, brandy (a tablespoonful every half hour), bottles of hot water surrounding the patient, especially the extremities, sinapisms and friction, will often, in an hour or two, work wonders.

"In case of *sinking*, brandy at intervals is all-important. I undoubtedly saved one valuable life by continuing its use with the other means during the whole night. At seven o'clock in the morning the patient fell into a quiet slumber and was saved.

"*Thirst.*—In these and in all advanced cases, thirst creates intense suffering. The sufferer craves water, and as sure as he gratifies the craving, the worst symptoms return, and he falls a victim to the transient gratification. The only safe way is to have a faithful friend or attendant who will not heed his entreaties. The suffering may be, however, safely alleviated and rendered endurable. Frequently gargling the throat and washing out the mouth will bring some relief. A spoonful of gum-arabic water, or of chamomile tea, may frequently be given to wet the throat. "Sydenham's white decoction," an English preparation, may also be given both as a beverage and nourishment, in small quantities, frequently. In a day or two the suffering from thirst will cease. In a large majority it has not been intense for more than twenty-four hours.

"*Diet.*—Rice water, arrowroot, Sydenham's white decoction, crust water, chamomile tea, are the best articles for a day or two after the attack is controlled. Chamomile is very valuable in restoring the tone of the stomach.

"*The Typhoid Fever.*—A typhoid state for a few days will follow all severe cases; there is nothing alarming in this. It has very rarely proved fatal.

Patience and careful nursing will bring it all right. The greatest danger is from drinking too freely. When a patient seemed to be sinking, a little brandy and water or arrowroot and brandy have revived him. In this terrible visitation of the cholera, we have considered ourselves perfectly armed and equipped, with a hand-bag containing Mixture No. 1, Mixture No. 2 (for vomiting, etc.), a few pounds of pounded mustard, a bottle of brandy, and a paper of chamomile flowers, and a paper of gum arabic.

"I lay no claim to originality in recommending this course of treatment. I have adopted it from suggestions of able and experienced physicians. Having been the only doctor of many poor families living near me, I have tried various remedies recommended by physicians, but I have found none to be at all compared with the above. During the recent cholera, I can not find that any treatment has been so successful as this." (Written at Constantinople, Sept., 1865.)

The Mixture No. 1 was given me by Hon. A. D. F. Foster of Worcester, in 1838, from his family physician, Dr. Green. No. 2 was recommended by an English physician of long practice in India. The above letter was widely circulated in this country and I received many notes of thanks for it, and many have attributed to it their rescue from the destroyer. These testimonials, verbal and written, have come from places far apart, from

Florida, Alabama, Brazil, the Mississippi, the Danube, and the Nile.

As to the contagiousness of the cholera, we have always acted upon the belief of its not being contagious. The Rev. Dr. Washburn, now President of Robert College; the Rev. Dr. Long, also of Robert College, then missionary to the Bulgarians; the Rev. Mr. Trowbridge of Aintab College, and the late Rev. Dr. Pratt, all went into this work with unrestrained freedom. They visited the filthiest abodes of sickness and death every day, worked over the sick and dying, and often breathed an atmosphere dank and disgusting with the smell of death, and they all came through the long campaign of six weeks unharmed. They used every possible precaution, watched their own symptoms, and repelled the first advance.

There is one fact however to be carefully observed. In no instance known to us did those who washed the clothing and bedding of a deceased patient escape a severe and generally a fatal attack. All such articles should first be boiled, the steam not inhaled, then rinsed in pure water and hung up to dry without trituration by the hand. In this hand-washing there is some absorption that is very peculiar.

As in the plague, so in the cholera the Moslems and Jews were the greatest sufferers; the latter for their filth, the former for their fatalism. Filth and fatalism are grand aids-de-camp of the enemy. I had a pleasant old Turkish neighbor. In the height of the cholera season, he was placidly preparing some long cucumbers for his evening meal. "Osman Effendi," said his Greek neighbor, "dont you know that food is forbidden, and the government has ordered all the cucumber vines to be destroyed?" "What do I care," he replied. "What is written is written (*i. e.*, on the preserved tablet). My appetite demands these and I shall eat them." He died serenely during the night, and the Greek told me of the warning and response.

Another enemy to life in Turkey is malaria. All its valleys are malarious and especially to foreigners. All its rivers and streams and lakes send up the destructive effluvia. Foreigners often discredit the danger until experience gives them a lesson. It has cut down many a young missionary at the commencement of his course. A Scotch missionary, the Rev. Dr. K——, came a few years since to search out a good place for a Scotch missionary colony near some Circassian emigrant colony. He had a certain place in view against which I warned him on account of the malaria. He thought I was unfriendly to his project. He persisted in visiting the place. Within two or three weeks he returned to Constantinople to die of congestive chills.

But while the native inhabitants are less affected they suffer not a little. Many of our students coming from the interior have the power of the poison developed on reaching a different climate and mode of living. Some are old cases and difficult to manage. The liver becomes enlarged and

GREEK PRESCRIPTION. 315

torpid. Quinine in many such cases has only a temporary effect.

I inquired of a Greek physician over a hospital where thousands of such cases had been treated by him during the past ten years, and he gave me the following directions. I think I have applied it to some hundreds of cases during the past twenty years, and with such success that I will here give it.

1. Take two grains of tartar emetic and dissolve in a glass of water. Take one third of this each morning on waking. It will act as an emetic the first morning, if not the dose is too small and one grain may be tried. The second and third mornings the effect will be less.

2. Prepare twelve pills of quinine, three grains each. Take four of them each morning on waking, for three mornings, observing to give fifteen minutes to each pill before another is taken.

3. For one week take the quinine in diminishing doses each morning, ten, nine, eight, seven, six, five, four grains, after which stop the quinine, and for a fortnight take five to ten grains of carbonate of iron before each meal. Diet light, but nourishing, soups, boiled mutton, etc.

Whatever may be the philosophy of this course of treatment, it is one which has for many years been pursued with great success in the hospital of Balukli.

Joshua Jones, Esq., resident on Fifth Avenue, New York, can testify both to the power of oriental malaria and to the efficacy of this mode of treatment.

In the malarial season, travellers should be very careful not to expose themselves to the evening air however pleasant and tempting. They should eat but little fruit, if any, and should take a grain pill of quinine before each meal. Any great fatigue, exposure, or taking cold, gives the poison an opportunity to effect a lodgement. Every year many youthful travellers learn too late the necessity of these precautions.

CHAPTER XXI.

MOHAMMEDAN LAW.

It has been often affirmed, in periodicals of the highest, as well as of the lowest authority, that the Ottoman empire has no law but "the Koran." One writer asserts, with great authority, that "the Koran administered by a priest" is all the law the empire has! Assertions of this character, more or less extended, are so numerous as to form a large part of the literature of the subject in the English language, exposing us to the wonder and contempt of all oriental readers.

That, twelve and a half centuries ago, Mohammed's word was received as the only law of the faithful, does not prove that the Koran is the only law of the Turks. Any one who will carefully read it, will see that only a small part of it is adapted to be law, at all, and that the wants of great and powerful empires like the empires of the Saracens, Moors, and Turks, could never be satisfied from the brief suras of the prophet.

Mohammedan law has grown up by gradual accretions, both losing and gaining, as time and circumstances have demanded.

The first caliphs, successors of Mohammed, leaning on the prestige of the holy prophet, added to the scant resources of the Koran the "*oral laws*"* of the prophet. As the empire grew, innumerable cases presented themselves for which nothing was found in the Koran: but the oral laws of the prophets were very conveniently drawn upon for all occasions, and thus the body of Mohammedan law was growing from age to age.

After a time, these traditions were separated into three classes. First, all that came directly from the mouth of the prophet, his sayings, remarks, counsels, and oral laws. Second, his acts, works, habits, practices. Third, *his silence.*

The skilful and learned Saracens had little reason to regret the poverty of the Koran, when they had such boundless resources at command.

But tradition, once resorted to, proved an unmanageable authority. Writers multiplied. Every one had a tradition of some kind, taken from some word, act, or silence. Every generation added to the stores of the preceding; and it finally became necessary to distinguish between the relative authority of conflicting traditions. The Saracenic mind was never much troubled with contradictions, of which the Koran itself is an eminent example. But when traditions, claiming the force of law, directly contradicted each other, some theory must be introduced, to relieve the mind of the conscientious judge, who might find it difficult to decide a

---

* In a similar manner the Jewish Talmud has grown up.

SIX REVERED BOOKS. 319

case both ways. This confused and immense mass of tradition was therefore divided by the Mohammedan jurists into four categories, on a descending scale. 1st. Those of public notoriety and credibility in the first three ages of Islam. 2d. Oral laws, less known in the first century but taught in the two following. 3d. Private laws, little known in the first, and less still in the two following ages. 4th. Laws of feeble tradition.

Among those who have labored upon this vast mass of tradition, there are six authors of such authority that their works are called "The Six Revered Books." They are received as containing the soundest commentaries and decisions of cases, and the most sacred portion of tradition. If the Koran is the first, this is the second source of Mohammedan law.

The third is also from tradition, but it is composed of the traditions derived from the first four caliphs and chief disciples of Islam. The Mohammedan jurist, who goes back to original sources, has a wide field for research in this third division.

The fourth is the collection of decisions made by the celebrated imams, interpreters of the law in the first ages. The student must wade through scores of volumes in Arabic, to get at the sources of Mohammedan law.

There is a fifth source, always increasing, which resembles the decisions of our supreme court. It is the "fetvas," the formal decisions of questions proposed to the Sheikh-ul-Islam. There are five collections of these fetvas, which are of received authority, made in 1631, 1686, 1687, 1703, 1730. They are regarded as commentaries upon the law, and no Mohammedan judge would dare to give a decision in direct contradiction to a fetva; unless he could find another fetva to support him. The Eastern judges, it must be admitted, are as skilful as the Western in *managing* such matters, and they seldom stop for, or are appalled by, difficulties.

It has always been a very convenient principle of Mohammedan law as administered by the Ottomans that *adet* (custom) is equal in authority to positive law; and generally it is supreme. Even local customs in a city or province are respected, and many a decree of the imperial government, or of the governor of a department, has been set aside by the judge, because conflicting with established custom. Many instances are given, in which the highest officers of government have completely failed in their efforts to go counter to some mere local *adet*. The oriental mind and heart hold *adet* in sacred honor. "It is not our custom," or, "This is our custom," as the case may be, ends all controversy in law and in logic.

The Ottoman sultans inheriting this huge mass of Arabic law from the Saracens, were much perplexed by it. Mehmet the Conqueror, after taking Constantinople, committed to Khosrev Mollah, his most learned priest, the work of forming a code for the empire out of all these Saracenic treasures. His work was called the "Pearl," as containing the most precious portions of Mohammedan law condensed.

Under Solyman the Magnificent, whose reign was from 1520 to 1566, the work was undertaken anew by Ibrahim Haleby, and so achieved as to satisfy the Mohammedan world from that time to the present. He gave his code the ambitious name of Multeka-ul-ubhurr, the "Confluence of the Seas," as indicating the vastness of the sources from whence he had made flow together all that was needful for the great empire of his master. This immediately became the code of law for the empire. It was translated into Turkish, and thousands of transcribers were employed in multiplying copies of it. Kadis and higher judges, who could have no access to the original sources, and who, often, would be so deficient in the Arabic as to be unable to derive much advantage from them, were now able to study the whole code of the empire in their own tongue. Having the sanction of the Caliph, the most distinguished of the sultans, this code was everywhere received in all Mohammedan lands.

It consisted of fifty-five books, subdivided into many chapters.

D'Ohsson, to whom the European world is chiefly indebted for its knowledge of this code, in his great work, "Le Tableau L'Empire Othoman," has arranged the whole in five divisions, omitting, so far as possible, the parts that are repeated, but giving the substance complete. He remarks that "this code is almost the only book of jurisprudence observed in the empire. It embraces, together with all the practices of external worship, the laws—civil, criminal, moral, political, military, judiciary, fiscal, sumptuary, and agrarian."

The first division of the universal code given by D'Ohsson, is the religious code. We shall attempt to indicate only a few leading facts with regard to it. It has three general divisions: dogmatic, ritual, and moral.

The first part contains the fifty-seven articles, with some of the comments of Osman Nessify, universally received as the expression, par excellence, of Mohammedan orthodoxy, and taught in all Moslem theological schools.

The first article asserts the fundamental principles and sources of knowledge, and the creation of the world; and the second, that the creator of the world is God, Allah; that "He is one and eternal, that he lives, is all powerful, knows all things, fills all space, sees all things, is endowed with will, and action; that he has in himself neither form, nor figure, nor bounds, nor limits, nor number, nor parts, nor multiplications, nor divisions, since he is neither body nor matter; that he exists of himself, without generation, dwelling-place, or habitation; outside of the empire of time; incomparable in his nature as in his attributes, which, without being exterior to his essence, do not constitute it. Thus God is endowed with wisdom, power, life, force, understanding, regard, will, action, creation, and the gift of speech. This speech, eternal in its essence, is without letters, without characters, without sounds, and its nature is opposed to silence."

The third article asserts that the "Koran is the uncreated word of God. It is indeed written in our books, engraven on our hearts, spoken by our tongues, heard by our ears, but this is only the sound of the word, and not the word itself, which is uncreated and *self-existent!*"

In these two articles, we have two very strong points in the Mohammedan faith—the belief in one God, and in the Koran as his eternal word. It is also called The Book, The Book of God, the Supreme Law, The Sacred Word, The Distinction of Good and Evil. The Moslems generally believe that it was taken from "the preserved tablet," the great book of the divine decrees, and given to the prophet in small portions, as he needed. It contains one hundred and fourteen suras, six thousand six hundred and sixty-six verses. As to the question of its being self-existent, there have been fierce disputes among the learned.

Under the 22d article, both free-will and predestination are strongly asserted. Predestination is disposed of as having reference solely to our spiritual state, and no relation whatever to our moral, civil, and political condition, in which all men are free. Notwithstanding such efforts to save human freedom, nothing is plainer than the universal reign of *Kismet* (fate) over the Moslem mind.

Articles 23d–25th, upon the prophets, make Mohammed the last and most excellent, and Jesus supreme over all who had preceded him, and call him "Ruahh-ullah," the Spirit of God, miraculously conceived, without taint of sin, of the holy virgin Miriam, who is frequently confounded with the sister of Moses. The immaculate birth of the virgin is also believed by Moslems, and this doctrine was first asserted by them.

Articles 33d-37th respect the caliph, or sovereign of Moslems. He must be an imam, and perform the public prayer on Friday, and he must be of the tribe of the Koreish. In defiance of this law, which has become obsolete, the sultan of Turkey, of the Tartar race, is universally received as caliph.

The 52d article is another pre-eminent instance of the universal disregard of a religious law. It is as follows: "To believe in the predictions of diviners with regard to events occult and future is an act of infidelity." Notwithstanding this most positive prohibition of divination and all occult arts and signs, the whole Moslem world, and, to a sad extent, the Eastern Christian world, have remained full of all superstitions of this nature, to this day. D'Ohsson, in commenting upon this article devotes twenty-eight folio pages to an *exposé* of the magic arts, superstitions, and foolish beliefs of Moslems distinguished in history, or sovereigns of the realm.

The 53d article is, that nonentity, or the thing non-existent, is nothing; the 54th, that prayers and alms avail the dead; 55th, that God hears prayer; 56th, announces the signs of the end of the world, among which is the descent of Jesus Christ, the son of Mary, upon the earth, and the rising of the sun in the west; 57th, that doctors of divinity are not infallible!

The second part of the religious code contains the ritual of the faith. In this part, we see its Jewish character most clearly. The Pharisees were never more exact with regard to legal purity of food, drink, and person. Every legal defilement must be purified by ablution, before prayer can be offered. One can hardly keep himself pure from one prayer to another, and the cheapest way is not to try, but wash before every prayer. The mode of ablution is described with great exactness, and if any mistake is made in the process, it must be begun anew. The ritual of prayer is still more onerous than the laws of purification.

There are many kinds of prayer, all to be executed with the minutest exactness, and with the attention undistracted. There is the common prayer, to be offered five times a day. In its general mode of performance, it demands twenty-six postures, but the devout use many courses of eight postures each. Nine times eight is an excellent number which, with the two concluding postures, make seventy-four. There are also special prayers for Ramazan, for the seven holy nights, for drought, famine, pestilence; the funeral prayer, the battle prayer, the marriage prayer, and many others, each of which must be executed in its own way with the utmost particularity; and the slightest deviation or mistake destroys the merit of the whole. The performer must begin anew. The following are the words of the common prayer, without any of its wearisome repetitions, which protract it to great length. Some portions are repeated three, six, and even nine times at each course.

"O God Most High, there is no God but God. Praises belong unto God. Let thy name be exalted, O great God. I sanctify thy name, O my God. I praise thee, thy name is blessed, thy grandeur is exalted, there is no other God but thee. I flee to thee against the stoned demon,* in the name of God clement and merciful. Praise belongs to God most clement and merciful. He is sovereign of the day of judgment. We adore thee, Lord, and we implore thy assistance. Direct us in the path of salvation, in the path of those whom thou loadest with thy favors, of those who have not deserved thine anger, and who are not of those who go astray. O God, hear him who praises thee. O God, praises wait for thee. O God, bestow thy salutation of peace upon Mohammed and the race of Mohammed, as thou didst upon Ibrahim and the race of Ibrahim, and bless Mohammed and the race

---

* Satan—so called according to some because every prayer is a missile hurled at Satan; according to others, because at certain sacred places, every pilgrim hurls a stone at the Evil Spirit.

of Mohammed, as thou didst bless Ibrahim and the race of Ibrahim. Praise, grandeur and exaltation are in thee and to thee."

Each of the eight separate postures has a portion of this prayer assigned to it, and the shorter parts are repeated three, six, or nine times to each posture. At the close of two, four, or six *courses*, when the prayer must at length end, the postulant repeats the confession of faith, and salutes his guardian angels on the right and on the left, with "Peace be unto thee, and the mercy of God." This must all be done five times a day.

The Moslem regards this prayer as an offering of praise and worship, and no request for temporal blessings is allowed in it. There are special prayers for success in the affairs of life.

In this ritual law are included also the rules for the mode of sepulture of the dead, for tithes upon luxuries and articles of commerce in order to the relief and support of the poor, and also for the management of the *vacufs*, or estates consecrated to religious and philanthropic purposes, chiefly, for the support of the mosques.

There are four chapters upon *fasts*, and spiritual retreats for prayer and contemplation. There are seven chapters upon *pilgrimages*, giving minute directions upon the mode of performing them, and upon the offerings, sacrifices, and expiatory observances accompanying them. A pilgrimage to Mecca is one of the most meritorious acts of piety which a Mussulman can perform, and it is therefore surrounded by an exact and onerous ritual, every item of which must be observed, or the merit is lost.

The third part of the religious code is styled *Morals*. It treats with exactness upon the kinds of food, pure and impure, upon drinks lawful and forbidden, launching its thunderbolts at wine and opium. It once included tobacco, which is now of universal use, as also coffee. It treats of dress, colors to be worn, of ornaments, furniture, equipage, in all which the law demands great simplicity. It treats also of various employments suited to the interests of man—of charity, probity, modesty, duties to society, duties of propriety, cleanliness; interdiction of gambling, of music, of all images, whether of man or beast, and of using the name of God profanely. It enjoins upon all Mussulmans the sanctity of oaths, the practice of virtue, and the fleeing from vice.

Finally, it treats upon the character and duties of magistrates. They must all be learned in the law, and must have passed through all the studies required for the different orders of magistracy, from the Sheikh-ul-Islam, or Grand Mufty, to the lowest rank. Theoretically, every officer of government must be a learned man, skilled in all the learning of the East. The grand and fatal fault of the system is, that it ignores the *West*. There is no provision for the study of foreign languages, no recognition of other systems of government, or of the existence of other powers. The Ottoman government and people have, for ages, surrounded themselves with darkness as to foreign affairs of every kind. A few able men have generally been found, who could perfectly appreciate the situation of the empire in all its foreign relations, and who had even a profound knowledge of European affairs. But the deep darkness in which both sovereign and people dwelt prevented their seeking any thorough remedy, and forced them to that policy, in which they have shown surpassing skill, of playing off one foreign power against another. This has now come to an end, and a better system may possibly follow.

The political code is divided into four parts. The first treats of the sovereign and his rights, adding some particulars to what is contained in the religious code. The sovereign of Moslems must be a male, adult, a believer. He, as the vicar of the prophet, the supreme imam, must conduct public worship on Friday and on the two Bairams; his authority, absolute, can never be questioned, except in case of public transgression of the laws of Islam. He must conserve the law. "Every new law is an innovation, every innovation is a going astray, every going astray conducts to eternal fire."

But in civil affairs, in the administration of the empire, he can make such changes as *the exigencies of the times may demand.*

This has opened a wide door for the caliphs and sultans to set aside the law at pleasure.

The inviolability of the person of the sovereign is stated in the strongest manner possible; but of seventy-two caliphs, seven were assassinated, five were poisoned, twelve killed by mobs, and many others had their eyes dug out, and perished in prison!

Of the Ottoman sultans, thirty-four in number, including the sultan regnant, nine have been deposed, the two last without bloodshed. Of the seventy caliphs, one in three met a violent death; of the Ottoman sultans, one in four has been deposed. Mohammedan law is very imperious in form, but is very precarious as to execution.

The second part of the political code relates to finance, but later administrations have so modified its laws that it may be regarded as abolished.

The third relates to strangers in Mussulman lands. It is a mixture of hospitality and exclusiveness. Anciently, the foreigner could reside in Turkey only for a number of months, less than twelve, the number to be specified in his permit. If he remained longer he lost the rights of hospitality, and must be taxed as a rayah, and in all respects be treated as a rayah. But when European nations began to form treaties with the Porte, they gained many immunities and privileges, which have been pushed to such an extent as to set aside entirely this part of the code. Foreigners have many rights which Moslems themselves do not enjoy. These rights have been collected and arranged in chapters, and hence called the "Capitulations." They have been the pivot upon which a great deal of oriental diplomacy has turned, for the last century.

The fourth part of the political code relates to Moslems in foreign lands. It gives them rules for living so as to honor their faith. They are to be very exact in performing their religious duties; they are to be temperate, just, chaste, prayerful, and not consort more than is necessary with unbelievers. If they transgress these laws, they will be treated as infidels. Those who take a milder view of the exclusiveness of the law as regards foreign intercourse, support it from the declaration of the prophet that "The faithful, also Jews, Sabæans, and Christians, who believe in God and the day of judgment, are exempt from the torments of the other life." The Koran has been much misunderstood, from not remembering that most of it was aimed at the Arabian pagans, and that Mohammed had but little contact with Christians.

Some general features of the political code have survived in the Ottoman government, but otherwise it is now of no value.

The third division of the Multeka-ul-ubhurr, "Confluence of the Seas," is the military code. It is divided into six parts, which treat of: I. War. II. Legal Booty. III. Captives. IV. Conquered Countries. V. Rebels. VI. Tributary Subjects.

"I. Art. 1st. War is surely a great evil, a true scourge of humanity, but this evil is necessary, and often unavoidable.

"(Commentary). Every thing which afflicts the human race, every thing which destroys the work of God, is a great evil, and, as our holy prophet said, 'Man is the work of God,' cursed be he who destroys it. But with us war has for its object to exalt the word of God, glorify the faith, and dissipate political evils."

Every male Moslem, sound, and of age, must bear arms. The rich even must give, not only their money, but their lives. Before commencing war, the enemy must be exhorted to avoid it by turning to Islam. This religious summons being rejected, the caliph must summon the enemy to become tributary, and pay the exemption tax. No hostile act can be allowed until after due notice, and a formal declaration of war. All who die in war, are martyrs for their faith, and pass directly into paradise.

The Ottoman sultans do not observe the prescribed formula preceding war, but follow the customs of Christian powers. The laws of booty are such as characterized the middle ages. Every thing that could be seized, property, persons, lands, were lawful booty. The sultan could claim one fifth, and the rest went to the soldiers, those not in battle sharing equally.

As to captives in war, all were reduced to slavery, except orthodox Mussulmans, who were free before their captivity. The principle that no true Moslem can ever be rightfully deprived of his freedom is universal. But in the bloody wars of past ages with the Persians, who are of the Shiite sect, the Turks have often sold their prisoners at the rate of two for a sheep. And the Persians, when they got hold of Janizaries, would sell them at the rate of one for a drink of buttermilk, making them the basest of circulating mediums.

The law strictly forbids allowing captives to return to their country, even if ransomed. The Ottoman sultans have paid no regard to this law, although apparently sanctioned by the prophet. Captives have been freely ransomed, have also been exchanged, and have been released by treaty. There is no law so sacred as to resist "the exigencies of the times."

Eastern wars having been generally religious wars, as well as political, have always been exceptionally savage and cruel. Islam itself was originally a religion of war.

The chapter on conquered territories, gives great latitude, either to possess them, or only make them tributary. They may be secured to their ancient proprietors, by voluntary submission, or by capitulation. In a reconquered country, the ancient proprietors recover their rights.

The fifth part makes quick work of rebels. They are to be summoned to surrender, the cause of their rebellion is to be listened to, and if there is justice in their complaint, the cause must be removed. But the sovereign must attack them with all his force if they remain under arms, and crush them at once; but, if they are Moslems, spare them when they throw down their arms and submit.

The sixth part treats of the condition of the people of subject lands. If they become Moslems, they retain all their property, and enter into the full enjoyment of the superior rights and dignities of the faithful. Otherwise, they are to pay a capitation tax, being Christians or Jews, are to be protected by the laws, may dwell where they please, buy and sell lands, and houses, or other property, not only among themselves, but with Moslems. They may have their churches or synagogues, may repair or rebuild them, but no new churches or synagogues shall be built. The rayahs shall have also their own costume, and shall not wear the turban of the Mussulman, shall not ride on horseback or, at least, not in the presence of a Moslem; and thus their subject state was always made apparent, and it bore heavily upon them.

The wearing of a different costume has passed away from most of the cities; so far indeed as the modern costume has been introduced, it has passed away everywhere. Forty years ago, both Christian and Jew were compelled, when they wore the fez, to wear a piece of black ribbon, or cloth, sewed on in such a manner as not to be covered by the tassel. After the promulgation of the Hatti Scheriff of Gûl Hané, these began to disappear, and no effort was made to restore them. The law with regard to dismounting when meeting a Moslem has become obsolete in most places. If the Moslem is a pasha, or dignitary of high order, it will be observed in some places, in others, not.

Rayahs, by changing their religion, can rise to

THE CIVIL CODE. 335

the highest offices of state. Some of the most distinguished Mussulman families have been of this origin. But it should be remembered, to their honor, that for a whole century and more, such cases have been very rare. Among mere nominal Christians, there is still a light, by the side of which the Koran is darkness.

The tendency of the last half century has been to soften the intolerable severity of the distinctions against the subject races.

The civil code is the most extended, after the religious, and contains more of what is still in force. ₄ I will only name the chief subjects, so far as to show how utterly inadequate the Koran would be, as any source of law, with regard to them. Tradition, rather than the Koran, has formed both law and religion for the Moslems. One is astonished at the temerity, or shall we say ignorance, of J. Bosworth Smith, in taking the Koran as containing the whole of Islam. He might as well take the four Gospels as containing the whole Roman Catholic system, Jesuits and all.

The first book of the civil code has twelve chapters on marriage. It minutely defines the duties and privileges of husbands, wives, children, parents, nurses. It gives the laws with regard to slaves and rayahs. The marriage of the latter is legal according to their own religious rites. A Moslem may have a Jewish or Christian wife without constraint to her religion. The children must be Moslem.

The second book has fourteen chapters on repudiation or divorce. The husband must pay back the dowry; the divorced woman is marriageable after three months; in ordinary cases. The legitimate causes of divorce are given, but every thing is in the power of the husband. The widow and the divorced must not wear red or yellow colors or ornaments, until remarried.

The third book has eight chapters upon children, legitimacy of children, rights of mothers, duties of parents, duties of children, parental power, power of tutors, of majority, of foundlings. The age of majority is fixed at fifteen. This is the suitable age for marriage.

The fourth and fifth books have eight chapters on inheritance, wills, legacies, etc. The different tenures of real estate make wills of little value. No man can will away more than one third of his property. The remaining property is divided so that the sons shall have twice as much as daughters. The owners of slaves can manumit them by will. The rayahs can also will away one third of their estates, but in no case to foreigners.

The sixth book has ten chapters upon slaves and slavery. The Mohammedan law and the Koran both alike sanction slavery. It has never failed to exist wherever the faith has borne sway. The law modifies and restrains, but does not abolish it. It is a principle of law, that no free Mussulman can be reduced to slavery, and also that he can not beget a slave. However many slave concubines he may have, his children by them must all be free. It is a principle of morals, rather than of law, that the mother should also be made free. It is also regarded as a work of peculiar merit, expiatory of many sins, to manumit a slave, and the dying Mussulman who sets all his slaves free, is sure of going straight to paradise. The slaves are chiefly house servants, and are not, in general, badly treated. There being no industry to develop slavery, it does not increase. Under English pressure, the slave-trade and slave-market have been abolished, and so far as the traffic exists, it is secret.

The seventh book has fifteen chapters upon commerce. Among the things interdicted to all believers, whether in buying or selling, are wine, swine, blood, dead bodies of men or beasts, woman's milk, human hair, bristles and fat of swine, skins untanned, and of any two objects of which one is illicit. These laws are almost entirely null and void, for many of the above articles are everywhere freely entered at the custom-houses; they pay a regular duty, and are as much articles of commerce as grain or rice.

The eighth book has seventeen chapters containing various laws regarding persons and property. A proselyte to the faith is clothed at once with all its graces and felicities. His children, if minors, go with him into the centre of felicity, his wife may conserve her faith, and the husband can divorce her or not, as he pleases. There are some good laws defending "squatters" upon unclaimed lands. The rights of artisans to be paid at the end of a job, or of the day's work, and of servants at the end of each month, are strongly guarded. But sports, farces, music, dancing, funeral mourners, and all the acts of public worship, and even the teaching of the Koran, are, for various and differing reasons, classed with unpaid employments; but, in point of fact, they are all paid. It legalizes all commercial acts by procuration, and the procurators may be either Moslems, rayahs, or foreigners. The power of the procurator must be specified, and his appointment officially legalized and witnessed by two witnesses.

There has been so much conflict with foreigners on commercial affairs, that a mixed court, called the Tidjaret, has been established, presided over by a Moslem judge, with associate judges from rayahs and foreigners. Commerce breaks in upon the exclusiveness of Mohammedan law. Egypt has already introduced the Napoleon Code and set entirely aside the old Mohammedan law. The Ottoman empire is more slowly following on the same track. (See Baker's Turkey, p. 445, and onward.)

The ninth book, as designed by M. D'Ohsson, is printed as the Judicial Code, in his work which was issued after his death. It contains fifteen chapters. The judge must be a Moslem, pious, virtuous, learned, uncorrupt, and given to the study of jurisprudence. He who gains the cause, must pay the cost of court. The declarations against bribery,

THE PENAL CODE. 339

and venality of every kind, are very strong, and very much disregarded.

The worst feature of the law is its rejecting non-Mussulman witnesses in a case against a Mussulman. The commentary allows that rayahs may testify in all cases in which no religious question is involved.

The law prescribes the form of oath to be used by the Moslem, the Christian, and the Jew. It wisely advises litigants to settle their disputes by choosing a referee, and failing in that, to refer the case to a commission. This latter is a favorite way of disposing of a case; but whether the commission will ever come to a final action, depends very much upon the *push* of the parties concerned. This book is framed in a spirit of wisdom and justice, from the Moslem point of view, but most of the Turkish courts have a bad repute for delays, neglect, or corruption. It is an antiquated system, ready to pass away.

The penal code is composed of three books upon penalties affixed to certain crimes, upon reproofs and corrections assigned to others, and upon restitutions. The first alone contains subjects for notice.

We have referred, in a previous chapter, to blasphemy and apostasy, the first to be punished with immediate death, the second to be dealt with in hope of restoration to the faith, failing which, death must be inflicted.

Sedition is a capital crime. Murder in the first

degree is capital, but to almost every kind of homicide, the price of blood, and imprisonment, are allowed. A man may murder his wife, his children, and his slaves, at a cheap rate. But the full price in ordinary cases, when one of the faithful kills another, is the payment of one hundred camels, or their value, and the manumission of a female Mussulman slave. In all cases of involuntary, accidental killing, the price of blood, for a man, is about $1,500; half that for accidentally killing a woman, and for slaves, according to their value, about one fifth or one sixth of the penalty for a woman! Always some *expiatory* gift for the shedding of blood must accompany it.

Much of the law of homicide, and that of wounds and mutilations, is apparently taken from the Jewish law.

Those guilty of adultery, are to be beaten with one hundred blows, for the free, and fifty for slaves. If the guilty are Moslems, married, and of sound mind, they are to be stoned to death; the man bound to a stake, and the woman buried in the earth to her waist.

All injurious language addressed by one to another, is punishable to the amount of twenty-four blows. The Turkish language, however, is so rich in depreciatory terms, that the law makes a wise distinction. If you only call a man, "a beast, an ass, a dog, a monkey, a pig, a calf, a snake, a miser, a buffoon, an ignoramus, a demon," these are not worthy of personal chastisement. But if you call a man an "infidel, a heathen, a thief, a drunkard, a bastard, a usurer," you will receive from the hand of exact justice a fustigation of twenty-four blows.

If two persons are together guilty, the two shall receive each the full penalty; but if they be husband and wife, the wife alone shall be punished!

The eighth chapter is against false witness. The perjurer, in criminal cases, shall suffer eighty blows; and if his testimony has caused death, he shall pay the price of blood. In other cases, his penalty shall be the infamy of riding on an ass through the city, faced about, holding the animal's tail in his hand, the public crier going before and crying, *Yalan shahidin hali bou dur*—" This is the fate of false witnesses!" False witnesses are abundant, but the penalties are very rare.

The law against drunkenness assigns the penalty of eighty blows. But to drink wine publicly in Ramazan shall be punished with death. The high officials, and the inhabitants of seaports are more or less guilty of intemperance, but, taken as a whole, the Osmanlees are probably the most temperate people in the world.

The laws against theft and robbery are severe. There are many misdemeanors which may be punished by public reproof, or by fine, or by imprisonment, at the discretion of the judge. Many which ought to receive severe punishments pass unnoticed.

Enough has been presented of the nature and

history of Mohammedan law, to show that it has been a vast and changeable body, growing up out of the necessities of the times, under the form of traditions, many of which are held as sacred as the Koran. It is based upon the Koran, and the traditions of the prophet, and of the four caliphs, and of the first learned imams, and upon other *feeble* traditions. Much of it has been set aside. Moslems hold it in superstitious reverence, and when the Sublime Porte takes any new measure, however directly opposed to many principles of this code, it always throws a sop to Cerberus by professing the profoundest veneration for it.

Its entire disappearance, its complete abrogation, would only indirectly affect the authority of the Koran.

CHAPTER XXII.

ISLAM.

No religion has been more misunderstood than that of Islam. The fear and hate which the fall of Constantinople and the dangers of Europe, four centuries ago, introduced into the European mind and literature, have had an abiding influence upon modern thought and feeling. The oriental Moslems never come among us, and few go from the West to make an impartial study of their system.

The Koran is within every one's reach, in a translation, and this book is generally misunderstood, or not understood at all, by us. The testimony is perfectly satisfactory that its power over the oriental mind is partly from its incomparable style. Besides this, it is all cast in an oriental mould which is as far from all our modes of thought, imagination, and reasoning, as the East is from the West. I have toiled through it three times, from beginning to end, with some advantages perhaps for comprehending it, but I could only slightly feel its oriental charm of thought, fancy, and assertion. It is generally read without keeping in mind that it is aimed at paganism. Its fierce and bloody wrath against the enemies of the faith, its exterminating fury, is against the idolatrous enemies with which it had its early contests. It always assumes a milder tone towards the "Kitablees"—the religions founded upon a revelation, as Judaism and Christianity. There is much that is every way excellent in the Koran, taken plainly from Old Testament sources. There is much that is puerile and absurd, and its sensualism can not be denied. But whatever it is, *it does not contain the religion of the Moslems* except in germ. For that religion, we must go to the "Sonnah"—to tradition. But, before remarking upon this point, let the four leading characteristics of this singular faith be noticed —its Theism, Fatalism, Ritualism, and Sensualism.

Koran, tradition, and law are alike theistic. There is but one only living and true God, is the corner-stone of the faith. This single declaration is pronounced by Moslem doctors as equivalent in value to one third of the Koran. The doctrine was a protest against the idolatry and polytheism in the midst of which it rose. It was so developed as to exclude the fanciful deities, numberless and monstrous, to which all around the prophet were abjectly enslaved. In announcing it, the prophet declared that he proclaimed nothing new, but only restored the religion of Adam, Noah, Abraham, Moses, and Jesus, and indeed of all the prophets. This assertion, so often made, and in so many forms, of the power, presence, agency, and universal government of God, was the purest and noblest part of the faith. It left nothing for any inferior order of deities to do. Every event of life, every change in the physical world, and the condition of the weakest and mightiest, were alike expressions of his will, and subject to his supreme control.

It was not only a protest against the idolatry of the Arabs, but against the polytheism of a debased Christianity which worshipped the images and the bones of saints, holy places, and holy fountains, more than God. It was a bold and mighty reaction against the debasement that had nearly annihilated Christianity, and yet had left enough of truth in the world to form a rallying point. This theism being the fundamental truth of all true religion, contained in itself nothing to excite the opposition of human depravity, but much to secure the approval of human reason. No divine honors are ever given to Mohammed. He declared himself a sinner, and, as we have seen, he is prayed for in the daily prayer as on the same level with Abraham. All worship is offered to God, as to a spiritual and everywhere present being to whom praise belongs, and before whom all creatures are nothing. His wrath is deprecated, his aid invoked against Satan and all his hosts. He is the sovereign of the day of judgment, before whom all must appear, and neither in this world nor the world to come, can they be blessed who do not entirely resign themselves to his will. This grand truth gave Islam a great advantage among the ignorant nations around its birthplace. It drew to the standard of the prophet and the early caliphs men of the most enlightened and clearest reason. In every age, it has been the bulwark of the faith. Reason and conscience approve it. Other things may be doubtful, but here is one truth for the human reason to rest upon, to stand by, and to maintain against the world. The worship offered to God is simple and profoundly reverent. It levels all human distinctions, and the highest and lowest bow together, without regard to station, birth, or wealth. There are souls so absorbed in this truth that they retire into it, and take no part in the empty superstitions of the faith; just as, among Romanists, there are occasionally men of devout and holy character.

The second leading attribute of Islam is *Fatalism*. The word Islam, submission, implies fatalism. It grows out of its theism. The Moslems are not only Unitarians but high Calvinists. The predestination of all events, good and evil, is a part of their briefest confession of faith. They take no pains, generally, to reconcile predestination and freedom. They believe in the former fully, and in the latter partially. Mohammed, in the sixth chapter of the Koran, refers to the book of decrees from which nothing is omitted. This is usually called by Mohammedan writers, "The preserved tablet." Upon it is written, from all eternity, whatever shall come to pass. It is called, "preserved" because it is guarded by God Himself from all intrusion of finite beings. It is the unchangeable law of all things, but God is the executive of that law.

Mohammedan writers have many strong and beautiful expressions about the reign of law as expressing every possible event, minute or great, from eternity to eternity. Dr. Draper, with very culpable carelessness, has represented this as coinciding with the materialistic view of law, and excluding the Creator from the universe. He professes to quote from Al Ghazzali as though he believed in the material origin of the soul by law, and its reabsorption,—whatever that is.

His quotation is a *hash* made up of sentences brought together from distant pages, and, like some other hashes, it contains ingredients which can not be identified with any honest and honorable origin. Ghazzali accepts fully the doctrine of the "preserved tablet," and as fully, of God as the executive of this eternal law of all events, and as the Creator of all things, and of all beings.

The effect of this doctrine of fatalism upon Moslem character is very marked. It leaves the course of things to Kismet and Allah. It induces resignation, quietude, and apathy. To speak of the Turkish race as stupid is very unjust. That which we call stupidity, and which does wear the aspect of stupidity, is the *apathy* induced by fatalism. When strong passion breaks this up, and the Osmanlee mind and soul are fully roused, it has always showed itself capable of surmounting the most formidable difficulties.

The influence of this doctrine, though terrible in war, is directly opposed to any hopeful progress towards a high civilization. The history of twelve and a half centuries proves this. It hangs like a heavy weight upon the national character and life. The Moslem writers, who know this, and who contend earnestly for human freedom, can make no impression upon the mass. This attribute provokes the worst oppression; for a Moslem people will endure quietly oppression from their rulers which would drive any other people to revolution. And yet, though so bad in some aspects, this belief gives a quiet strength to the Moslem character and faith, which is rare to find. The man who believes himself backed up by Allah and Kismet, stands firm. The ills of life are endured with patience. Danger is encountered with unflinching courage, death is met without fear or regret. The sympathies of life are blunted by it. In famine, pestilence, and war, it sustains the selfish and hard-hearted side of humanity, and shows the element of mercy, compassion, self-sacrifice for the good of others, to be wholly wanting.

Another very peculiar and striking attribute of Islam is its *Ritualism*. Its worship is so simple, and so regardless of place and surroundings, that the general impression has been often made that Islam is destitute of rites and ceremonies. But the truth is, the Moslems are pharisees of the pharisees in the performance of all the externals of worship and religious duty. The ceremonial defilements and purifications, clean and unclean food, the ablutions for prayer, with all the postures, divisions, and repetitions accompanying the daily prayer and many other kinds of prayer abundantly prove this.

This severe ritualism, ingrained from early childhood, infuses into the Moslem character the attributes accompanying all ritualism—a self-righteousness, a spiritual pride, an I-am-holier-than-thou spirit. Reason often rebels against this onerous observance of so many cautions. Many of the more enlightened, or of those accustomed to moral reflection, neglect the ritual almost entirely. It is persons of this character who are prepared for a higher and better system. It is they who, like Ghazzali, fall back upon theism, and ignore the rest. "Our refuge is in God," is their oft-repeated motto.

The fourth and worst attribute of Islam is its sensualism. J. Bosworth Smith has tried to palliate or explain away the proofs which are usually brought from the Koran. Were the Koran the only authority, no one could read the 52d, 55th, and 56th suras, and have any honest doubts as to their meaning. But the Mohammedan religion is found in the *traditions* more than in the Koran. The multitude know little of the Koran, except through tradition. This is sensualistic to the extreme. It is untranslatably vile. One may just as well argue that there is no theism in Islam, as that its paradise is not a sensual abode. The fundamental doctrine of that state shows it to be so. It is, that the enjoyments of this life may be pursued to any extent *without satiety or disease.* The prophet forbade wine, because it intoxicates. But, in paradise, the true believers shall quaff the most delicious wines from flowing bowls, with no possibility of intoxication or of even a headache.

Polygamy is an institution which has little direct influence upon the common people. Not one in one thousand of the common classes is able to have more than one wife. If he has two, he must keep up two establishments. I once asked a servant of a Turkish dignitary, how the two wives of his master got along together. "Oh," said he, "they make *gehenna* for the master. If one of them should die, he never would take another." "But what do they do?" "Why, the other day, the son of one wife, a bright little roguish fellow, set fire to the apartments of the other, and only a hair remained that the house had been destroyed." Do Constantinople fires sometimes originate in the harems? It is polygamy in the ruling class, in the high officers of government, among those who lead the destinies of the people, that curses the land. Whatever debases them afflicts the whole country, in all its interests. A few among them know this, and there is a tendency in the party of progress to abandon this old Eastern vice, which has come down from prehistoric times. The most disgraceful record of the Prophet is his course and example with reference to it.

This sensualism is doubtless attractive to the

heathen mind, and may explain in part the progress of Islam among the heathen tribes of Africa; but no form of Christianity has fallen so low as to accept it. Since it laid down the sword, this faith has gained very few converts, even from the most corrupt Christianity.

Tradition has introduced an immense mass of error and superstition into the Moslem world, of which the Prophet was not guilty, and of which very little can be found in the Koran. As Mohammedan law is made up chiefly from tradition, so is the Mohammedan religion, and if you can have but one, you will learn more from tradition than from the Koran. Writers who, like Mr. Bosworth Smith, undertake to enlighten the world out of the Koran, only multiply and diffuse their own ignorance.

The above attributes are admirably adapted to make a strong religion, strong in its truth, and strong in its errors. It has lost less by conversion to other religions than any other faith, ancient or modern.

But this has doubtless been owing in part to its environment. It has always confronted heathenism, or a false Christianity. Both it could heartily reject, with all the sanctions of reason and conscience. As to worship and dogma, it saw nothing which it could not despise. It read the four Gospels, and then looked at the Christian church, and saw image, saint, and relic worship, and turned away in disgust.

The political relations of the Ottomans with the Christian nations of Europe, have not been such as to make favorable impressions upon the Moslem mind with regard to Christianity.

Its relation to Russia, when not at war, has been that of an armed neutrality. She has always had innumerable political agents in every part of European Turkey, to stir up all the bad feelings possible, and to prepare insurrections and atrocities. It would be impossible for a conscientious Mussulman to regard such Christianity but with abhorrence.

England once occupied an enviable position with regard to moral influence upon Turkey.

After the close of the Crimean war, which was a war quite as much in English interests as in Turkish, this influence, under Sir Henry Bulwer, was entirely changed. No man ever worked so effectively for Russian interests, and for the ruin of Turkey, as Sir Henry Bulwer. His treachery to the cause of religious freedom has been referred to. He thought it a master-stroke of policy to show the Turks that England watched over Moslem interests. It displeased English Christians, but they were a class he cared little for. His great measure, however, was to introduce the Circassians into Bulgaria. The great Circassian chief, Schamyl, had been subdued, after a contest of thirty years, by Russia; and the Circassians had been driven from their mountains, with unparalleled sufferings. Cherishing an undying hate to all Russian or Greek

SAVAGE CIRCASSIANS. 353

Christians, they were a fine element to throw into Bulgaria. The Bulgarians besought, protested, plead, to be delivered from the coming scourge, but Bulwer sustained the Porte with all his influence in pushing them in. Quite as savage and blood-thirsty as the Montenegrins in their character and habits, they have proved the scourge which, by their very nature and antecedents, they were destined to be. In all the horrors of the present war, they have borne a distinguished part. They have been turbulent and predatory, and have done more to discredit the Turkish government than any other class of marauders.

Sir Henry Bulwer's other great achievement was introducing the Sublime Porte to the loaning mania. Hence the lavish expenditures, the overwhelming debt, the loss of credit, and the financial embarrassments of the Ottoman Empire. The conditions on which the loans were made were ruinous to the empire, the capitalists acquired millions for their share of the spoils, and the loss finally fell upon the public, and excited the rage and vengeance of suffering Englishmen.

In all these affairs, Turkey has been the victim. Following blindly her leaders, with the apathy which is a part of her nature, she finds herself bereft of resources, and surrounded by hostile and indignant nations. It is impossible, then, that any favorable moral influence should be felt by the Moslems from their intercourse with Christian nations.

But that Islam, from various other causes, is losing its power, there can be no doubt whatever. The Koran and tradition are losing their power. Laws once held sacred, have passed away. The spirit of conquest and military supremacy have disappeared.

The Moslem treats Christians with a respect he never did before. There is a toning down of his fanaticism. You can, anywhere, converse with Mohammedans on religious subjects, with a freedom impossible thirty years ago. I once overheard, in a steamer on the Bosphorus, some Turks discussing this point; and, to my amazement, they attributed the change to the influence of American missions, wholly unaware that an American was sitting behind them. By their books, schools, newspapers, translations of the Scriptures into all languages, missions have had their influence, a very wide and extended one, outside of their direct labors; but many other things coincide with it. The general progress of civilization, the railroad, the steamboat, the telegraph, the expansion of commerce, the increase of travel, have all united in softening the prejudices of the Moslem mind.

The boasted revival of Islam in Wahabeism may cause some political troubles, but otherwise is of no value. It is a natural reaction against liberalizing tendencies. It is a revival of ignorance, darkness, and fanaticism. It is a going back twelve centuries. It is proscribing all progress, all change, all modern arts, notions, habits, and thoughts.

It is a revival of weakness, and a sign that Islam is to pass away.

I have written about twenty pages on the errors and unscriptural practices of the oriental churches. The great contest in the East makes the times excitable; and I withhold what might be misunderstood. Some of my highly valued personal friends are among the Greek, Armenian, and Bulgarian communities, and I would not seem to be regardless of their feelings. I firmly believe those churches are coming back to the pure and simple Gospel, but whether they shall ever assume any other names than those they now bear, is a matter of small importance. Provided they are *evangelical*, all will be satisfied who labor for the redemption of the Ottoman empire. The Christian element of the empire is steadily gaining power and influence, and even if bloody revolutions do not hasten the day of freedom, it is sure to come by moral forces.

CHAPTER XXIII.

SIGNS OF PROGRESS.

This is a subject which I approach with unfeigned diffidence. On many accounts, it is the most difficult subject that one can undertake. The witnesses that testify in the case are all on one side. The Ottoman Turks never, or very rarely, study foreign languages. They pay too little regard to foreign opinions. When they hear of some monstrous injustice done them in foreign journals, one class of them will say, "That is the way with the Ghiaours," and the more pious will say, "Our refuge is in God," and smoke away; but neither will ever attempt any refutation. The present war has aroused the government to make efforts never before made to correct false impressions.

The condition of Turkey is reported, first, by travellers. They intend, generally, to report the exact truth, and, with some few exceptions of persons, who, like Macfarlane, go there with malign intentions, in the interest of some political party, they do report, unquestionably, what they have seen and heard. They do not understand the language. They get, from the hotel, a nice, intelligent, active dragoman. The dragoman knows

The Levantines. 357

every thing and every body, and has most excellent recommendations from previous travellers. He is a *Levantine*. No particular race owns him. He will perhaps tell you he is a Greek. If there is a class of men on earth utterly destitute of the truth, to whom falsehood is sweeter than truth, and who are sagacious to know in a given case how much a man can be made to *swallow* without arousing suspicions, it is these Levantines. They have a list of classic horrors about the "unspeakable Turk," to palm off upon all unsuspecting travellers. Our knowledge of Turkey really comes from them. I once said to a person of this class, who was volunteering some surprising information, "I have lived in Turkey so many years, have been in such places, and know such persons." I said nothing more, and made no reference to what he had been saying; but he did not resume his story, and departed crestfallen. The traveller who is just passing through, must be a man of rare sagacity, who can sift the truth from the falsehood, while he is in Levantine hands.

We all have a natural and noble tendency to believe what we read and hear, but when I take up Eastern news, I always pray inwardly, "O Lord, endow me with a suitable spirit of unbelief!"

Another point to be remembered is, that this whole class of Levantines are the enemies of Turkey. They never report any thing good, and their stores of bad are as inexhaustible as their imagination.

Another source of our knowledge of Turkey is to be found in the newspaper correspondent and the telegraph. As opposite parties use the telegraph, one has to take things as they come, and then judge as well as he can of probabilities, or believe and disbelieve according to his own tendencies and likings.

Another source still, is to be found in political pamphlets. A great association has been formed in England for the purpose of exposing all the faults of Turkey. The testimony is mainly from travellers. It is not necessary to impugn the honesty or integrity of the writers, or the purity of their motives. But it may be permitted to inquire whether any government could stand such an ordeal unharmed.

Suppose a great association should be formed in the United States, and money freely poured into its treasury, with the object of searching out all the atrocious murders and cases of poisoning, in England, and all the stories of selling wives and of beating them, all the mobs in Ireland and the colonies, all the insurrections and bloody suppression of the same, the hanging of ministers of the Gospel (like the Rev. Mr. Gordon), the blowing of rebellious subjects (rayahs) from the cannon's mouth, because, in the culprit's belief, it sent him to an eternal hell; suppose the state of Ireland should be depicted, when a landlord could not walk abroad upon his own property without danger of assassination, and, when assassinated, no conviction could follow, on account of combined and universal perjury; and all this should be presented as a fair specimen of the English government and people, and nothing whatever presented on the other side; would such an association be regarded as engaged in a wise or pre-eminently Christian work? If its publications were spread all over the world, would the result be a good, elevating, refining moral impression upon the people of Great Britain? Or, suppose such an association in England should expose all our Indian massacres, and our treatment of the Indians, our negro slavery of the past with all its atrocious laws, our great rebellion, our Fort Pillow massacre, Andersonville and Libby prisons, our New York mobs and massacres, our Ku-klux achievements, our Tweed rings, our many defalcations, and gather every thing of this kind together, without a hint of any thing as possibly existing on the other side; would it promote good feeling? Especially if, by any circumstances, we were incapacitated to make any reply? Should we probably consider those who engage in such a work as animated by a peculiarly Christian spirit? There would be some among us, doubtless, who would take that view, but would it be the national view? Would it work a grand reformation?

Turkey has more and worse tribes than our Indians to manage, as the Kurds, the Druzes, the Zeibeks, the Yoruks, the Gypsies, the Bosnians, the Circassians. It has mountainous regions impossible of access. It has different races, religions, and languages, that never united. A much better government than that of Turkey would find the task of government a baffling one, especially if it had a mighty and crafty enemy on its borders, always stirring up revolution.

This mine has been sufficiently worked. I could not go deeper into it without danger of suffocation.

Nor is it needful to add any thing to that side of the question. I wish to inquire if, *notwithstanding all this*, there are not some signs, under this government, of progress towards a better state? I think there are, and I do not see as any law of morals or of expediency forbids their statement. The Turkish government has never showed any hostility towards us as a nation. It defied the influence of England and France during our war, and sternly baffled every attempt at getting up a rebel cruiser in its waters. But even towards an enemy, is it immoral and unchristian to allow whatever is true?

Fully aware that what I shall say will be offensive to much of the public sentiment of the country, I would still ask a patient and candid hearing, for the truth's sake.

1st. It will hardly be denied that, under the Turkish government, there has been some progress in education during the past half century. Considering the *point from whence she started*, has not the progress been great? Fifty years ago, the Ottoman empire was in the middle ages as to education, and in some other things, remains there still. In that space of time, printed school books, in the spoken languages of the schools, have been introduced. No one can estimate the value of this step, who has not seen the old schools, either without books, or with books only in some dead language. Now, the schools of all the chief nationalities are well supplied with common school books, in their own spoken tongue.

2d. The press, as an active, living power, has been introduced into the Ottoman empire, within fifty years. The old efforts of previous ages had died away and disappeared. Occasionally, an ecclesiastical book was printed; but there were no newspapers, no current literature, and consequently but little intellectual life. For many years, the missions of the American Board were compelled to have their own printing establishments. Now they have nothing of the kind. Printing presses, and lithographic presses, are very numerous, and any thing may be printed in any language of the country. This has all grown up by permission of the government, and the government itself established, many years ago, a magnificent printing-house, at Gûl Hané. Is not this a *progressive* step? Every native race has now the beginnings, at least, of a literature. If any one wishes to print a book or a pamphlet, he will find a sharp competition of many presses for his work, whatever may be the language.

3d. Newspapers have commenced their career

in Turkey. This is another step in the right direction. The first newspaper in any of the native languages, edited by a rayah, was published in 1840. In a little more than thirty years from that time, there were fifty newspapers, in various languages, in the capital alone, about thirty of them being dailies. Doubtless, many have been closed up by the war. The censorship of the press is severe in war, but not at all so in peace. The telegraph and the press send the news of the world over the empire, and new ideas encroach upon and gradually displace the old. There is some progress in all this. It is a progress of that nature that, if you give it time, it will work out great results.

4th. The Christian Scriptures, during this half century, have been translated, printed, circulated in all the languages of the empire—in Turkish, Arabic, Greek, Armenian, Bulgarian, Albanian, Kurdish, Armeno-Turkish, Greeco-Turkish, Hebrew and Hebrew Spanish. They are sold all over the empire, wherever there is a people speaking the language.

The Bible House at Constantinople is quite as prominent a building as the Bible Houses of New York and London are for those localities. The Scriptures are publicly exposed for sale, in more than twenty languages.

Fanatical opposition has occasionally risen, but it could never make a stand. These translations awaken criticism, and bring new ideas and new life into language, literature, and religion. This is progress.

5th. A literature, Christian, educational and general, is rapidly increasing in these languages. No restraint is put upon the Christian literature of any religion or race. The fifty years have shown a wonderful progress on this line. The ignorance of some recent review writers, with regard to educational and intellectual progress in general, is very discreditable either to their honesty or intelligence.

6th. The increase in the *number of schools and various institutions of learning,* is quite as great as the advance in character. When I visited the chief Bulgarian school of Philippopolis, in 1857, I was assured that every obstacle possible had been put in their way by the Greek Church, but that the people had burst their bonds, and schools would be everywhere formed. In 1870, after a period of but thirteen years, there were reported in the province, three hundred and thirty-seven schools, some of them of a high order, sixteen thousand five hundred pupils, of whom two thousand six hundred and fifteen were girls. The end toward which all effort was directed, was that *no Bulgarian boy or girl should grow up without a good common school education.* They were then far from their ideal, but another decade of such progress would have realized it. Everywhere, among all classes and all nationalities, there has been surprising progress. It has been far less among the Moslems than the other races, but some progress has been made among them. While the schools in the mosques remain the same as in past ages, common schools, not under the power of the clergy, have been established in large numbers, and text-books have been provided for them. The most successful institutions have been the Military Academy, the Naval Academy, and the Medical College, into which the study of French has been introduced with good results.

The desire for education has extended to all classes and races. We find it the same among the Armenians, from the Bosphorus to the Euphrates, and among the inhabitants of Syria, as well as in Bulgaria.

The above are facts which have usually been considered facts in the order of progress. And their chief value consists in this, that they exhibit the life and power, and free action of the people. They are not things imposed upon the people by imperial ordinances, but the people are left in freedom to act for themselves. It is not their present condition as compared with European nations, that is to be looked at, but as compared with their former state. Progress, not perfection is all we claim for them.

Another point of inquiry is, whether the Sublime Porte has made any progress in the administration of affairs?

On this point I think there can be no doubt in any unprejudiced mind that has studied the course of things in Turkey during the last half century.

It is not to be denied that Abdul Aziz, who commenced his destructive course under the inspiration of Sir Henry Bulwer, plunged the empire into debt and brought on financial ruin. All this can be repaired. But notwithstanding this there have been great administrative changes for the better, some of which are worthy of notice.

I. Religious liberty has certainly been the gainer during the last half century. This will hardly be denied by those who have the slightest acquaintance with undeniable facts. The Protestant churches, communities, schools, and colleges that have been permitted to spring up in both European and Asiatic Turkey are proofs of it.

The great changes effected by the Bulgarians in the restoration of their language, liturgy, schools, and independent church government, are proofs of it.

Foreign missions from the Catholic and Protestant world have penetrated every part of the empire with their labors, and are protected by government. Proselytes from all Christian and Jewish sects to each other are allowed, and protected. Something has been done towards more freedom for the Moslem to embrace Christianity, as we have shown in a previous chapter. The conversion is not followed by death, as formerly, but the convert has every thing to fear from mob violence. In certain cities, as Constantinople and Smyrna, he will be safe. Freedom for the Moslem *anywhere* to profess Christianity does not yet exist, and can not, until the people themselves become more enlightened.

II. With the destruction of the Janizaries the era of confiscation and death without trial passed away. Every man accused of crime is entitled to a public trial, and the penalty of death, even when pronounced by the courts, can not be executed without the express order of the sultan. Confiscation of goods no longer follows crime. From having the bloodiest code in the world the Ottoman empire has fewer death penalties, and fewer executions, than any country where the death penalty exists. The bastinado has been abolished and the European punishment of flogging has taken its place. The recent assertions to the contrary are falsehoods. These changes are all in the direction of softening down or laying aside the brutal customs and laws of the past.

III. A fundamental change has been introduced into the whole scheme of Moslem education.

A council of public instruction has been established after the French model, and thus education is quietly passing out of the hands of the clergy and the mosques, and becoming wholly secular!

In 1864 there were twelve thousand five hundred Moslem schools with half a million of students. Their number has since greatly increased.

There is also a government university established, which is yet incomplete, but is an important step toward throwing off entirely the domination of the Mohammedan clergy. Another large institution, the Lycée, after the French Lycée, was established at great expense. All nationalities were admitted. The French language was made obligatory and a good curriculum of study adopted. It is now closed, in consequence of the war. The Moslem schools are now established on a graded system, and the pupils pass up from one grade to a higher by examination.

Imperfect as the system is, it is a great administrative revolution and proves the existence of a powerful party which the mosque can not control. Another generation will bring forward another class of men into all departments of public administration.

IV. European law, in the form substantially of the Napoleon Code, has been introduced into the courts as of equal authority with the Mohammedan Code. A litigant can have his choice of codes. He may have his case tried by the Mohammedan Code, or by the Napoleon Code. As far in the interior as Kaisereh nine tenths of the cases tried are by the Napoleon Code. Other important changes of law are coming in.

The law against building new churches was once held as sacred as any thing in the Koran. If ever a new church was built, it was always under the fiction of there once having been a church on the spot, and the permission given was to *rebuild*. There is now a definite form given by government to obtain leave for building new churches. The only difficulty that remains is in the jealousy and mutual oppositions of different sections of the populations. The Turkish government will rarely grant a permit for any building, if it is opposed by the neighborhood. The different religious communities, Armenians, Greeks, Catholics, will raise such an opposition, oftentimes, that neither can build a new church, unless they all wish to build. Aside from this, the old law has passed away. More new churches have been built, during the past half century, than in the four previous centuries. It would exhaust the reader's patience to go through with all the old severe laws that have been either relaxed, or entirely removed. In saying this, I am not commending Mohammedan law as it is, but only showing a hopeful *progress towards a better state.*

V. Material progress. The financial condition of the empire could hardly be worse than it is. It is utter bankruptcy, and with such a war on its hands there is little hope of an early recuperation. The cause of this disgraceful condition has been the foolish and wicked expenditures, and not the impoverishment of the country. It is admitted that Sultan Abdul Aziz did all a sovereign could do to make all his officers depredators upon the resources of the government, and while they had enormous loans to draw from, this could go on unchecked.

The revenue of the empire has nearly quadrupled since 1850. In 1875, it amounted to £22,552,200 or more than one hundred and twelve millions of dollars. This has not been quite all wasted. Some ten railroads, varying from fifty to two hundred miles in length, have been constructed, and they have been of immense value to the government in all its military operations.

Its greatest material progress, I regret to say, has been in the arts of war. Its iron-clad navy commands all its seas, and its great enemy can appear upon his own waters only by stealth. Its army has been well provided with the modern weapons of warfare, and has thus far shown itself capable of defending the empire against its gigantic neighbor. This is an unexpected result, and will convince men of impartial judgment that there must be some elements of life and growth in this empire, so generally misapprehended and defamed.

VI. The most vital and important question, with regard to the Mohammedan government, is its position towards its Christian subjects. That it is an oppressive government, no one will deny. That there is a great deal of misgovernment by incompetent, selfish, and unfaithful officials, no one will deny. That the lavish expenditure of the last reign increased the irregularity and oppressiveness of taxation, is sufficiently plain. It fell upon Moslem and Christian alike and prepared the whole empire for revolution.

But, notwithstanding this, the form of government is such as to place in the hands of the people a ready way of correcting abuses. The different grades of governors, as mudirs of villages, caimacams, and mutessarifs, have an administrative council, composed of Moslems and Christians. The Christian populations are represented by their spiritual chiefs and by elected members. It is a democratic assembly. It gives to villages great power over all their interests. If sufficiently united and enlightened, they can farm their own taxes, and no tax-gatherer except of their own choosing will ever appear among them. This "medjliss" or administrative council, is often a very grievous instrument of oppression. It may become a *"ring."* It will, of necessity, be what the people make it. With the progress of education and enlightenment, it will be a beneficent power in the land. The government has placed it in the hands of the people, and they can use it for good or ill.

For some fifteen or twenty years, the Ottoman government has been gradually admitting Christian subjects to a share in high offices of state. This has been so often denied, and it has been so often asserted that no rayah is ever admitted to office, that any mere assertion would be of no value.

I will therefore present, so far as I can, a list of those who have been thus raised to office. A complete list could be made out only in Constantinople. The different offices and dignities which each one has borne, will be named in their order. Those who have died are first in the list, and are marked by the letter *d*; retired, by *r*; those in

LIST OF OFFICERS. 371

waiting, that is drawing half-pay until appointed to some other office, by *i. w.*; those not marked, still bear the office which is last named.

1. Prince Etienne Vogorides, Prince of Samos, Grand Dignitary of the Empire, Capoukehaya of Moldavia, race Bulgarian, d.

Forty years ago he alone, of the rayahs, had the right to appear in a Bosphorus *equipage* of four pairs of oars, conferred as a special favor by the sultan. When the daughter of Vogorides was married to Photiades Bey, the present Turkish minister at Athens, the Sultan Abdul Medjid attended in person, a mark of personal favor from the sovereign unheard of in Ottoman history, and intended to have a political significance. It was so understood by Moslems and Christians. By some the act was abhorred, by others applauded.

Another act of the sultan attracted equal attention. He received in audience a venerable and distinguished Greek lady, Madame Sophie d'Aristarchi, and, in token of his appreciation of the services of her deceased husband and of her sons, he gave her his portrait in diamonds, together with a decoration in diamonds. It was the first *decoration* ever given by an Ottoman sovereign to a lady. When this venerable lady died, her daughter, mother of Aristarchi Bey, now at Washington, was authorized by Abdul Aziz to wear the portrait and decoration. Personally, these things are trifles. Politically, they have their meaning and value.

372 AMONG THE TURKS.

2. Djezairli Muggerditch Agha, Collector of the Port of Constantinople, Arm., *d.*

The first Christian subject that was ever appointed to that high post. This was about thirty years ago. It awakened a combined opposition, and he was finally overthrown. The office has since been repeatedly filled by Christian subjects, without remark. I can not give their names.

3. Daoud Pasha, Counsellor of Embassy (at Vienna), Governor of Lebanon, Minister of Public Works, Arm., Cath., *d.*

The first Christian subject raised to so high an office as minister of public works and member of the cabinet.

4. Aristarchi Bey (Nicholas), Secretary of Sultan Mahmûd, Grand Logothête, etc., etc., Member of the Grand Council of Justice, Greek, *d.*
5. Franco Pasha, Governor of Lebanon, Syrian, Cath., *d.*
6. Agathon Effendi, Minister of Public Works, Arm., *d.*
7. Prince Caradja, Minister at the Hague, Gr., *d.*
8. Mussurus Bey, Chargé d'Affaires at Turin, Memb. Grand Council Justice, Gr., *d.*
9. Mussurus Bey (Paul), Memb. of Grand Coun. Justice, Prince of Samos, Memb. of Coun. of State, Gr., *d.*
10. Vartan Pasha, Memb. of Admiralty, Arm., Cath., *d.*
11. Faik Pasha, Della Sudda, Director of the Military Pharmacies, Lat., Cath.
12. Aristarchi Bey (Demetrius), Director of the Press, etc., etc., Vice Governor of Crete, Gr., *r.*
13. Ohannes Effendi, Memb. of Coun. State, Arm., Cath., *d.*
14. Prince Callimachi, Minister at Paris, Ambassador at Vienna, Gr., *r.*
15. Sefer Pasha, General of Division, Cath., *r.*
16. Muhliss Pasha, Gen. of Div., Orthodox Gr., *r.*

LIST OF OFFICERS. 373

17. Sadik Pasha, Gen. of Div., Cath., r.
18. Emile Effendi, Memb. of Ministry of War, Gr., r.
19. Aristides Bey (Baltagi), Director of the Public Debt, Gr., r.
20. Prince Aristarchi Miltiades, Prince of Samos, Memb. of Coun. of State, i. w.
21. John Aristarchi Bey, Ambassador at Berlin, Gr., i. w.
22. Ibraham Pasha, Copoukehaya of the Khedive, Arm., i. w.
23. Nubar Pasha, of Egypt, Arm., i. w.

Both the above raised by the sultan to the rank of vizirs, which is above the rank of pashas.

24. Odian Effendi, Political Agent at Rustchuk, etc., Under Secretary of Min. of Foreign Affairs, Arm., i. w.
25. Diran Bey, Chargé d'Affaires at Brussels, Arm., Cath., i. w.
26. Yaver Pasha, Memb. of Min. of War, Memb. of Grand Coun., State Director General of Posts, Arm., Cath., i. w.
27. Aristarchi Bey (George), Attaché of Ministry of For. Affairs, Gr., i. w.
28. Aristarchi Bey (Alexander), Secretary of Embassy, Gr., i. w.
29. Mussurus Pasha (Constantine), Minister at Athens, at Vienna, and now Ambassador at London, Gr.
30. Prince Alexander Vogorides, now Aleko Pasha, Ambassador at Vienna; Greek, by race Bulgarian. Has borne many high offices.
31. Serpos Effendi, Overseer of the Telegraphs, Arm., Cath.
32. Artin Effendi, Dadian, Under Secretary of State of For. Aff., has borne other high offices, Arm., i. w.
33. Rustem Pasha, Minister at Turin and at Florence, Ambassador at St. Petersburg, now Governor of Lebanon, Lat., Cath.
34. Sawar Pasha, Gov. of Crete, etc., etc., now Gov. Gen. of Isles of Archipelago, Gr.
35. Ohannes Effendi Tchamitch, Director of Public Debt, Minister of Commerce and of Agriculture, Arm., Cath.
36. A. Carathéodory Effendi, Under Secretary of State in Dep. of For. Aff., has been Min. to Rome, etc., etc., Gr.
37. S. Aristarchi Bey, Grand Logothête, etc., etc., Senator, Gr.
38. Davidschon Effendi, Senator, Israelite.

39. Anthopoulos Effendi, Memb. Court Justice, Senator, Gr.
40. J. Photiades Bey, Minister at Rome, now Min. at Athens, Gr.
41. Costaki Pasha, Gov. of Mirabella, Prince of Samos, etc.. etc., Under Secretary of State to the Dep. of the Interior, Gr.
42. Reshid Pasha, Commandant of Artillery, Protestant (For. ?).
43. C. Photiades Bey, Prince of Samos, former Pres. of Galata Serai College, Gr.
44. Serkis Hamamdjian Effendi, Minister at Rome, Chief Secretary in the Ministry of For. Aff., Arm.
45. Servitschen Effendi, Senator, Arm.
46. Blum Pasha, Gen. of Div. of Engineers, Hun., Prot.
47. G. Aristarchi Bey, Director of Political Affairs in Crete, Vice Gov. of Prov. of Smyrna, Minister at Washington, Gr.
48. Etienne Carathéodory Effendi, Chargé d'Affaires at Berlin, and St. Petersburg, Min. at Brussels, Gr.
49. Conéménos Bey, Charg. d'Aff. Athens, St. Petersburg, Gov. Samos, Con. Gen. at Corfou, Gr.
50. Blaque Bey, Secretary of Em., Con. Gen. at Naples, Min. at Washington, Director of the Press, Memb. of Coun. State, Latin, Cath.
51. Bohor Effendi, Memb. Coun. State, Israelite.
52. Joseph Ikiades Effendi, Memb. of Court of Justice, Gr.
53. Yovantcho Effendi, Memb. Coun. State, Bulg.
54. John Ikiades Effendi, Memb. Coun. State, Gr.
55. Mihran Bey, Duzoglou, Memb. Coun. State, Senator, Arm., Cath.
56. Franco Pasha, Director of the Imperial Med. Col., Gr.
57. Bedros Effendi, Couyoumdjian, Commissioner of Forests, Memb. Coun. State, Arm., Cath.
58. C. Calliades Effendi, Con. Gen. Palermo, Director of the Press, Memb. Coun. State, Gr.
59. Sakissian Ohannes Effendi, Under Secretary of State of Commerce, Pres. of Municipality, Memb. Coun. State, Arm., Cath.
60. Dr. C. Carathéodory Effendi, Memb. Coun. State, Gr.
61. K. Carathéodory Effendi, Director of Railroads, Gr.
62. Constant. Pasha, Gov. Hertzgovina, Arm.
63. Faik Pasha Gabriel Effendi, Memb. of Court Justice, Bulg.
64. Mourad Bey, Minister at the Hague and at Stockholm, Arm.

List of Officers. 375

65. Vasa Effendi, Vice Gov. Bosnia, Myrdite Arm.
66. Guatili Pasha, Chief of Imp. Band, Cath.
67. Serkis Effendi, Balian, Chief Architect, Arm.
68. Dr. Mavroyeny Bey, Chief Physician of Sultan, Gr.
69. Jean Axelas Effendi, Con. Gen. at Lyra, Gr.
70. M. Axelas Effendi, Con. Gen. at Athens, Gr.
71. C. Axelas Effendi, Vice Gov. of Prov. in Crete, Gr.
72. Horasandji Ohannes Effendi, Polit. Agent in Min. of For. Aff., Arm.
73. Etienne Mussurus Bey, First Secretary of Emb, at Lond., Gr.
74. Paul Mussurus Bey, Second Secretary of Emb. at Lond., Gr.
75. Nasri Bey, First Secretary of Emb. at Paris, Syrian, Cath.
76. Falcone Effendi, First Secretary of Emb. at Vienna, Arm., Cath.
77. Xenophon Baltagi Effendi, First Secretary Legation at Washington, Gr.
78. Rustem Effendi, Second Secretary at W., Gr.
79. E. Photiades Bey, Secretary Legation at Athens, Gr.
80. Chrysides Effendi, Vice Gov. Epirus, Gr.
81. Daniche Effendi, Political Agent at Rustchuk, Con. Gen. at Ragusa, Lat., Cath.
82. Loghades Effendi, Political Agent at Salonica, Gr.
83. Dr. Parnys Effendi, Coun. of For. Aff., Prot.
84. Tarin Effendi, Memb. Coun. of For. Aff., Cath.
85. Diran Effendi, Political Agent at Smyrna, Arm.
86. Agathone Effendi, Vice Gov. of Erzeroum, Arm.
87. N. Petropoulos Effendi, Consul at Kertch, Gr.

This list might be greatly extended, but it could be done accurately nowhere except at the Sublime Porte. The above officers by their direct patronage, or by their influence, introduce many hundreds of Christian employés into positions of a lower grade, and these, by their greater capacity and activity, are sure to crowd out the Moslems, and rise into their places. The custom-houses, the public works, the navy yards, the mint, the telegraphs, the railroads, the Sublime Porte itself, are all full of Christian employés of every class. The advance in this direction, within ten years, has been very great.

How has this been accomplished? It can not be pleasing to the old Moslem party to see seventeen Christian rayahs raised to the high rank of pasha, and two of them, probably more, raised to the very highest grade of vizirs. Two forces have accomplished and are carrying forward the change. First, the intelligence and enterprise of the Christian element. This is by far the most hopeful sign. The rayahs are working up to a knowledge of their power and their rights. The Porte can no longer carry on the government without their aid, and they are pressing in on every side. The progress in education, the knowledge of foreign languages and foreign countries, the superior activity and energy of the Christians, are all in their favor; and twenty years more of accelerated progress like that of the past ten years, under the worst sovereign Turkey ever had, will change all these tens into hundreds or thousands.

Another force arises out of a division in the Moslem element. While one party adheres to the old, there is another, and a powerful party for reform. It is this party which has introduced secular education, and separated it from the mosques. It is this which has stopped confiscations and executions, which has set aside so many of the old laws, and which has so far reconstructed the machinery of government that it has little resemblance to what it was a century ago. It is the influence of this party that has made it possible for Christians to rise to some of the highest offices of state.

This party knows full well that Turkey must cease to be a pure Moslem government, or cease to exist. Two great and most difficult measures are looked forward to as absolutely necessary, and provided the present war does not change all things, are sure before long to be accomplished. One is, the limitation of the power of the sultan, for which the whole empire is ripening. I have heard Turks of the greatest intelligence speak of this as the only hope of their existence as a nation. The present parliament is a step in that direction. It will encounter the fiercest opposition of the palace, but is sure to be achieved.

The other measure is, making military service common to all. The Christians will oppose this. Whenever attempted, it is their opposition which has stopped it. For, although they cry out against the "haratch," the exemption tax, they dislike the service still more. But the empire will come to it before long. And it will contribute to some unification of the discordant materials of the empire.

The evils under which the Ottoman empire groans are great, but not remediless. War can make them greater, but can not remove them. True reforms are of slow growth. Time is an absolutely necessary element, and men are usually impatient that so much of it is required.

At the close of an excellent article in the International Review for August, the writer gives a prescription for the *sick man*—"Educate, but do not exterminate." Designating by education all the influences that accompany it, I would vary the prescription—

PEACE, TIME, AND EDUCATION!

www.ingramcontent.com/pod-product-compliance
Lightning Source LLC
Chambersburg PA
CBHW030404230426
43664CB00007BB/736